Errors of Justice

In this book, Brian Forst takes a fresh new perspective on the assessment of criminal justice policy, examining the prospect of assessing policies based on their impact on errors of justice: the error of failing to bring offenders to justice, on the one hand, and the error of imposing costs on innocent people and excessive costs on offenders, on the other. Noting that we have sophisticated systems for managing errors in statistical inference and quality control processes and no parallel system for managing errors of a more socially costly variety – on matters of guilt and innocence – the author first lays the foundation for a commonsense approach to the management of errors in the criminal justice system, from policing and prosecution to sentencing and corrections, then examines the sources of error in each sector, the harms they impose on society, and frameworks for analyzing and reducing them.

Brian Forst is Professor of Justice, Law and Society at the School of Public Affairs, American University, in Washington, DC. He is the author of several books, including *The Privatization of Policing: Two Views* with Peter Manning.

Cambridge Studies in Criminology

Edited by

Alfred Blumstein, *H. John Heinz School of Public Policy and Management, Carnegie Mellon University*
and David Farrington, *Institute of Criminology, University of Cambridge*

Other Books in the Series:

Continued on page following the Index

Errors of Justice

Nature, Sources, and Remedies

Brian Forst
American University

CAMBRIDGE
UNIVERSITY PRESS

PUBLISHED BY THE PRESS SYNDICATE OF THE UNIVERSITY OF CAMBRIDGE
The Pitt Building, Trumpington Street, Cambridge, United Kingdom

CAMBRIDGE UNIVERSITY PRESS
The Edinburgh Building, Cambridge CB2 2RU, UK
40 West 20th Street, New York, NY 10011-4211, USA
477 Williamstown Road, Port Melbourne, VIC 3207, Australia
Ruiz de Alarcón 13, 28014 Madrid, Spain
Dock House, The Waterfront, Cape Town 8001, South Africa

http://www.cambridge.org

First published 2004

Printed in the United States of America

Typeface ITC New Baskerville 10/14 pt.   *System* LATEX 2$_\varepsilon$ [TB]

A catalog record for this book is available from the British Library.

Library of Congress Cataloging in Publication Data

Forst, Brian.
Errors of justice : nature, sources, and remedies / Brian Forst.
   p.   cm. – (Cambridge studies in criminology)
Includes bibliographical references and index.
ISBN 0-521-82130-4 – ISBN 0-521-52882-8 (pbk.)
1. Criminal justice, Administration of – United States.   2. Judicial error –
United States.   I. Title.   II. Cambridge studies in criminology (Cambridge
University Press)
HV9950.F66   2004
364.973–dc21   2003046132

ISBN 0 521 82130 4 hardback
ISBN 0 521 52882 8 paperback

To Eric and Laura

Contents

      Introduction   212
      What Is Legitimacy?   213
      Operationalizing the Notion of Legitimacy   215
      Conclusion   217

      Bibliography   221
      Index   243

Preface

Requiring students of criminal justice to learn the fundamentals of statistical inference may or may not be good for them, but it surely can enlighten the instructor. In searching for a way to motivate my students to learn about Type I and II errors and the logic of statistical inference, I have asked them whether they are concerned about errors of inference made by police, prosecutors, juries, and sentencing judges. It has struck me, in discussing these metaphors, that we have a coherent, sophisticated, effective framework for managing errors in statistical inference, but no such framework for managing errors in the criminal justice system. The errors are not identical, to be sure, but they are parallel. In both domains, some procedures tend to shift errors, others either reduce or increase both sets of errors. We can examine the shifts in errors of inference in hypothesis testing that derive from changes in the alpha level, but haven't a clue as to the effect of a change in the standard of evidence on corresponding errors of justice. We haven't attempted even to ask. We know precisely how increases in sample size reduce both Type I and II errors for given parameter values, but we have no idea the extent to which DNA evidence simultaneously reduces the rate of erroneous convictions in homicide or rape cases and increases the rate at which such crimes are solved. This has to do largely with our inability to establish factual guilt, but inability to know the truth has not prevented statisticians from developing power functions and operating characteristic curves, tolerance tests, and all the other useful components of our widely accepted system for managing errors in statistical inference.

This book describes an inquiry into the prospect of developing a parallel system for error management in the criminal justice system, in a spirit akin to Walter Lippmann's observation, "The study of error is not only in the highest degree prophylactic, but it serves as a stimulating introduction to the study of truth."[1] At the very least, we should be able to catalogue more systematically the nature and sources of errors on both sides of the scale of justice and consider how they may be affected by changes in rules and laws, policies and procedures. We should be able also to examine more thoroughly than we have prospects for borrowing from systems for managing errors in other domains involving risk with often high stakes, including not only statistical inference, but quality control management, epidemiology and health care systems, and financial portfolio analysis, so that we may be able to better manage errors of justice.

Some of the more technical material in the text is likely to have the approximate effect on the reader that discussions of Type I and Type II errors have on my students. I wish to assure the reader who has difficulty with this material that it is not necessary to understand all the specifics. I have attempted to present the essentials in a manner that will leave all readers with a basic appreciation for and understanding of the nature and sources of errors of justice and approaches to minimizing their harmful effects on society. The technical material is intended for the more technically oriented reader and is included to deal with issues that are important to scholars and others who care about certain details. I have attempted to speak to both audiences in a single volume in a way that minimizes pain and suffering for all who take the journey.

Errors of justice harm us all. They undermine trust, drain our resources, create inequities, and restrict our freedom. They diminish the quality of our lives. They warrant more coherent treatment than we have given them.

---

[1] Lippmann, *Public Opinion* (1922, reissued by Touchstone Books, 1997), p. 256.

Acknowledgments

I wish to thank several people who supported the development of this work. First and foremost is my wife, Judith, who was once again the understanding and interested partner who indulged my preoccupation with yet another project of paramount importance. She made thoughtful comments on each of the dozens of drafts of material for this book that I placed before her as the work unfolded. To her I promise to make more time to play. To our wonderful children I dedicate this book.

My colleagues and friends Jim Fyfe, Jim Lynch, and Joan Petersilia gave the manuscript particularly thorough reviews and offered comments that were extremely perceptive and helpful. I am grateful also for astute readings and constructive suggestions provided by Dick Bennett, Tom Brady, Phil Cook, Heather Davies, Ron Huff, Rob Kane, Alisa Kramer, Laura Langbein, Jennifer Segal, and Peter von zur Muehlen. My research assistant, Lakera Tompkins, provided extraordinary support – accurately, comprehensively, quickly, and cheerfully – whenever I asked for it. These discerning and generous people are in no way responsible for errors of omission or commission, due process or impunity, Type I or Type II, or any other sort, random or systematic, that may be found on the pages that follow.

My publisher, Cambridge University Press, lived every bit up to the reputation that drew me to them in the first place. Acquisitions editor Mary Child, Humanities and Social Sciences editor Alia Winters, production and copy editor Laura Lawrie, project manager Anoop Chaturvedi, production controller Susanna Fry, and production contact Shari Chappell were thoroughly professional and helpful throughout in moving the project from proposal to finished product, and Cambridge Criminology Series editors Al Blumstein and David Farrington gave the levels of superior support for which they are both so renowned and respected among criminologists worldwide.

Many of the basic ideas that provide the core material for this book were set forth in the article "Toward an Understanding of the Effect of Changes in Standards of Proof on Errors of Justice," published in the Summer 2001 issue of *Jurimetrics* (Volume 41). I thank the editors of *Jurimetrics* and reviewers of the draft manuscript of that article for their thoughtful comments.

I wish, finally, to acknowledge my mentor in the quantitative aspects of justice, Hans Zeisel. He was the perfect model in so many ways. Incisive yet graceful, he understood complexity – in the law, in human behavior, and in public policy – and managed always to find a way to express it simply and elegantly in prose and say it even more clearly with figures. Hans managed always to find a way to maintain his twinkling sense of humor and goodwill even when confronted with boorish grandstanding and pettiness. He was a living testament to the idea that one's ceaseless commitment to the highest standard of scholarly integrity can faithfully serve one's passion for justice. He left an indelible impression, one that has inspired me now for some 25 years and will continue to do so for as long as I do this work.

CHAPTER ONE

The Problem

The logic now in use serves rather to fix and give stability to the errors which have their foundation in commonly received notions than to help the search after truth. So it does more harm than good.
                                                    – Francis Bacon (1620)

Introduction

Conventional assessments of the criminal justice system, its practices and policies have long been afflicted by a serious blind spot. Scholars and criminal justice practitioners typically assess justice policies in terms of their effects on crime and recidivism rates, fear of crime, equitability, costs, and levels of public satisfaction. These criteria all have considerable merit and appeal, but the recent discovery of a large number of death sentences imposed on innocent people[1] raises fundamental questions about the comprehensiveness of conventional assessments. This discovery appears to have done more to alter attitudes and policies regarding the death penalty than all other empirically based arguments against capital punishment, including the absence of systematic evidence of a deterrent effect and findings of racial disparity in its application.[2] In 2003, outgoing Governor George Ryan

---

[1] Berlow (1999) reports over 80 death row inmates released from prison since 1976, having been found innocent, 1.3% of all death row commitments. In 2001, Supreme Court Justice Sandra Day O'Connor cited 90 such releases since 1973. The number surpassed 100 by 2002 (Axtman, 2002). See also Ho (2000), Leahy (1999), and Liebman et al. (2000).

[2] The irrevocable nature of errors in the actual use of the death penalty sets those errors apart from other errors of justice. In her 2001 speech on the death penalty, Justice O'Connor emphasized this unique aspect of errors in the use of the death

1

commuted the death sentences of all 156 Illinois death row inmates on the grounds that they had been sentenced under a system that was "haunted by the demon of error."[3]

Errors of justice – both the errors of harassing and sanctioning innocent people and those of failure to sanction culpable offenders – do much more than undermine the case for capital punishment. They shake the foundation of public confidence in institutions broadly regarded not long ago as trustworthy, if not sacred, built on sworn oaths to uphold the law. In an era of considerable public cynicism of government authority generally, news of serious lapses in the workings of our formal system of justice can accelerate the drive for people to seek private remedies for protection and justice. Informal mechanisms have always been the dominant form of social control in the United States and elsewhere, but for serious crimes private alternatives to our formal system of justice can be ineffective or counterproductive, and highly unjust. Lapses in the public sector's ability to respond effectively to the crime explosion of the 1960s surely contributed to the parallel explosion in private sector alternatives to crime prevention,[4] and those alternatives have been a mixed blessing – not bound by the same standards of screening, training, and professionalism as are officials of justice, and largely unavailable to the poorest and most crime-ridden neighborhoods, those with strong claims to the highest priority need for protection.

Perhaps the most glaring shortcoming of conventional systems for assessing criminal justice policies is that they have been disassociated from the larger and more profound concept of legitimacy. Legitimacy

penalty: "the system may well be allowing some innocent defendants to be executed" (Lane, 2001). By contrast, life sentences without parole are far more pervasive than executions, and errors in the use of a sanction that condemns an innocent person to live and eventually die in prison may be viewed as equally irreversible and often no less harmful.

[3] Ryan had put a moratorium on the use of the death penalty in Illinois three years earlier, with the same essential justification: "I cannot support a system, which, in its administration, has proven to be so fraught with error and has come so close to the ultimate nightmare, the state's taking of innocent life. Thirteen people have been found to have been wrongfully convicted" (Ryan 2000).

[4] The ratio of private security personnel to sworn police officers tripled from 1970 to 1990. Shearing and Stenning (1981), p. 203; Cunningham and Taylor (1985), p. 112; Mangan and Shanahan (1990); Forst and Manning (1999), p. 16.

is essential to a well-functioning, citizen-supported criminal justice system, and while it involves matters other than errors of justice, it is largely about the processes that serve to minimize both types of justice errors.

It seems more than worthwhile to attempt to gain a sense of the likely effects of basic policy changes on two fundamental aspects of the legitimacy of the criminal justice system: the ability of those policies to bring offenders to justice and the ability of the policies to protect the rights of all citizens and minimize costs on innocent people. Such inquiry is likely to accomplish two useful objectives. First, it offers an important complement to conventional frameworks for assessing the criminal justice system, such as crime, recidivism rates, and cost. Second, it is likely to contribute more reliable and balanced knowledge of our ability to manage errors of justice than the sensational accounts of innocent people released from death row following the discovery of exculpatory DNA evidence and the equally sensational episodes that emerge from time to time in popular media accounts of dangerous people committing heinous crimes following lapses in mechanisms for bringing them to justice in prior cases. Political grandstanding has not infrequently followed such sensationalism. Prominent examples of victims whose names have been attached to legislative proposals for tougher sanctions include Megan Kanka (New Jersey, 1994), Polly Klaas (California, 1993), and Stephanie Roper (Maryland, 1982).

What Is an Error of Justice?

In general parlance, errors of justice are taken to mean errors in the interpretation, procedure, or execution of the law – typically, errors that violate due process, often resulting in the conviction of innocent people. In this book, we borrow from the perspective of welfare economics, using the notion of social costs[5] as the basis for defining errors of justice and assessing their consequences.[6] Thus, an error of justice

---

[5] Social costs, which include the costs of both crime and sanctions (Cook 1983; Cohen 2000), are discussed more fully in Chapter 5.

[6] The framework is consistent also with Herbert Packer's (1968) conceptualization of the due process and crime control models for assessing criminal justice sanctions.

occurs either when an innocent person (i.e., innocent of the crime in question) is harassed, detained or sanctioned, or when a culpable offender[7] receives a sanction that is either more or less than optimal – one that minimizes social cost – or escapes sanctioning altogether. In the former case, which we call an *error of due process,* the social cost of the error is the sum of the costs imposed on the innocent person and his or her dependents[8] and the costs imposed on society for failure to sanction the true offender. Due process errors include as well excessive intrusions against those who violate the law. In the case of an insufficient sanction or none at all where one is warranted, which we call an *error of impunity,* the social cost of the error is the difference between the total cost borne by society under the insufficient or absent sanction and the smaller social cost associated with an optimal sanction.

An error of justice is any departure from an optimal outcome of justice for a criminal case.[9] An optimal outcome is one that minimizes the total social cost of crime and crime control. An error is *systematic* when it is the product of a justice policy or policies that bias outcomes either toward errors of due process or errors of impunity. It is *random* when it results from the actions of individual criminal justice practitioners or private citizens, or from circumstances beyond the immediate control of the offender (e.g., an unforeseeable event or set of events that either inhibit or facilitate detection and conviction) or circumstances surrounding a matter that becomes a criminal case erroneously, without a true crime or offender.

This concept of justice error is quite unlike the notion of legal error that constitutes the business of our courts of appeal, such as questions

---

[7] We make the distinction "culpable" offenders in recognition that other offenders may be technically subject to formal sanctioning, but the social costs of administering a sanction in those cases may exceed the social benefit of the sanction. It is common practice for prosecutors and courts to drop such cases, often involving trivial offenses and first-time offenders, "in the interest of justice."

[8] This includes the exceptional case in which a person is convicted and sanctioned for a crime that did not, in fact, occur in the first place, as in the case of lost property officially reported as stolen or drug evidence planted on an unsuspecting person.

[9] The general model should apply as well to civil justice, a domain in which the need for error management is also great and the problems of analysis and implementation no less daunting than in the domain of criminal justice. I will leave it to others to work out the specifics of a framework for managing errors in that realm.

as to whether a search or a confession was proper. But it does not ignore legal errors. In the framework used in this book, legal (as distinct from factual) errors add to social cost to the extent that they impose costs on innocent people, offenders, victims, and taxpayers.

Our use of the term "error" to include failures to bring culpable offenders to justice is consistent not only with the notion of social costs and optimal sanctions but also with the bifurcated error structure of scientific inference. While the social costs associated with these justice errors are elusive empirically – they call for estimates of the full set of costs, tangible and intangible, associated with the stream of future crimes prevented by a sanction – we include them in the larger conceptual framework because they are important in the real world. I do not attempt to measure them here, yet they cannot be ignored.

If the costs of these errors are elusive, so too are estimates of their pervasiveness. Accurate counts of the extent of justice errors require knowledge of factual guilt and innocence, and such knowledge is unattainable. If it were otherwise, our elaborate procedures of jurisprudence to determine guilt and innocence would be superfluous. We can attempt, nonetheless, to make crude estimates of the extent of justice errors. Over 10 million felony crimes are reported to the police annually in the United States, and about as many are unreported. Only about two million persons are arrested for felony crimes each year, and about half of the defendants in those cases are convicted, leaving well over 10 million who escape conviction, errors of impunity. If one percent of all convictions are in error – a guess that could be too low, given that 1.3% of persons sentenced to death row since 1976 have been found innocent (Berlow, 1999), or too high given an estimate of 0.5% by Huff et al. (1996, p. xiv) – then some 10,000 people are convicted each year for crimes they did not commit, errors of due process.[10]

---

[10] The speculative nature of these estimates cannot be overemphasized. The estimate of 10,000 will be too high to the extent that some of the erroneous convictions reported are due to procedural errors in cases with true offenders rather than wrong-person errors. Also, some of the 10,000 may well have committed other felony offenses for which they were not brought to justice, a sort of canceling of errors over time,

We might wish to eliminate all such errors, or at least one type of error or the other. But many random errors of justice are both inevitable and even socially optimal. The cost of bringing some culpable offenders to justice may exceed the social benefit of doing so; for them, randomized enforcement to provide a degree of deterrence may be the preferred strategy. Some random errors of justice may be reduced through systems that structure the exercise of discretion of criminal justice practitioners. Such systems may, in the process, produce systematic errors of justice, as in the case of mandatory sentences that are set above socially optimal levels. Systematic errors of justice include policies and practices that are readily correctable under existing budgets and Constitutional constraints. These are precisely the sorts of policies that warrant rigorous policy analysis and correction, if the policies are found to produce systematic errors or interfere with other goals of justice. Such analysis should focus both on policies designed to reduce the risk of convicting innocent persons or reduce sentences that impose costs on society that exceed the crime control benefits, and on policies that aim to bring culpable offenders to justice.

Some policies may in fact have an effect that is opposite of what had been intended; or they may bring with them unacceptably large increases in the costs associated with failure to bring culpable offenders to justice. Even if we were to start with the most egregious errors on both sides of the justice balance scale and work our way to the less serious ones, at some margin the cost of reducing the errors further would exceed the social benefit of doing so. Given our complex world, we are not likely soon to be able to eliminate either type of error. In the meantime, we would be remiss not to work diligently to find ways of reducing both types, and to find coherent frameworks for resolving tensions between the two.

---

although an imperfect form of justice that threatens legitimacy along the way. The estimate will be too low to the extent that the rate of erroneous convictions is higher for run-of-the-mill felonies than for capital crimes. Juries may be less inclined to convict when they know that the death penalty may follow their finding of guilt, as Zeisel and Diamond (1974) have reported, or more inclined if prospective jurors are excluded from duty in death penalty cases if they say they are opposed to capital punishment.

Aim and Overview of the Book

This book aims to move that way, toward the development of a coherent framework for assessing criminal justice policies in terms of their effects on justice errors. Both types of errors undermine the legitimacy of the criminal justice system, yet their relationship to criminal justice policy is not well understood. The central thesis of the book is this: *Criminal justice legitimacy is largely about the ability of policies and procedures to reduce criminal justice errors; if criminal justice policies are to meet the test of this basic aspect of legitimacy, the assessment of those policies requires a coherent framework for relating the policies to justice errors.*

There is a long-standing precedent for such an undertaking. The quote that opens this chapter, from Sir Francis Bacon,[11] leads us to question prevailing orthodoxies that perpetuate errors. One of the dominant themes of his celebrated *Novum Organum*, the treatise on scientific method from which the opening quote was taken, is that knowledge is too readily reduced to "idols" of fear and fancy, at the expense of reason.[12] Another is that the use of inductive methods to derive general principles based on observation is preferable to syllogistic reasoning.[13] I make no claim here as to having Bacon's implicit blessing in the current enterprise. Rather, we can aim to follow his counsel that we would do well to scrutinize popular sentiments and work to overcome flawed thinking by taking full

---

[11] As both a lawyer and scientist, Bacon was an uncommon figure in his day, or any other. He achieved prominence as Britain's attorney general in 1613, but wrote that he considered himself to be primarily a scientist and philosopher (K.M.L., 1974, p. 564).

[12] "The idols and false notions which are now in possession of the human understanding, and have taken deep root therein, not only so beset men's minds that truth can hardly find entrance, but even after entrance obtained, they will again in the very instauration of the sciences meet and trouble us, unless men being forewarned of the danger fortify themselves as far as may be against their assaults.... There are four classes of Idols which beset men's minds. To these for distinction's sake I have assigned names – calling the first class Idols of the Tribe; the second, Idols of the Cave; the third, Idols of the Marketplace; the fourth, Idols of the Theatre... Idols of the Tribe... take their rise either from the homogeneity of the substance of the human spirit, or from its preoccupation, or from its narrowness, or from its restless motion, or from an infusion of the affections, or from the incompetency of the senses, or from the mode of impression." Bacon, Aphorisms 38, 39, and 52, from *Novum Organum*.

[13] See, for example, Aphorisms 13 and 14 from *Novum Organum*.

advantage of available evidence and systematic reasoning to reduce errors.

Chapters 2 and 3 spell out the nature of both types of criminal justice errors and give an overview of the sources of each type. Chapter 4 then describes analytic frameworks in other domains that may provide a basis for managing justice errors and for inquiring into the effects of changes in criminal justice standards, policies, and practices on the incidence of errors of justice: the logic of statistical inference and the associated system for managing errors in hypothesis testing, and principles of quality control and problem of managing errors in production processes and service delivery systems. Chapter 4 considers the parallels and critical differences between errors of justice and errors of inference in other settings. Next, Chapter 5 takes up the concepts of social costs and optimal sanctions, frameworks that permit a weighing of justice errors and assessment of the systemic costs of alternative criminal justice practices and policies.

Chapters 6 through 10 then describe the sources of justice errors in detail. Chapter 6 examines the effects of changes in standards of proof on both types of errors of justice by clarifying the relationships among three variables: the percentage of cases with true offenders, the conviction rate, and the percentage of defendants convicted who actually committed the crime. Chapter 7 focuses on the effects of police work on justice errors, including the effects of the quality and integrity of investigation, use of forensic technology, errors associated with witness identifications and use of informants, and the effects of alternative systems of profiling. Chapter 8 examines the effects of prosecution practices and policies on errors of justice, including the effects of alternative screening standards and plea bargaining practices, combining available data and estimates of current practices (case acceptance rates, plea-to-trial rates, and conviction rates) under a range of assumptions about factual innocence.[14] Chapter 9 looks at the jury,

---

[14] One might ask: Why no chapter on defense counsel? I take up the problem of weak defense representation at several points as a threat to due process. Strong defense counsel is assumed not to be a problem here, except to the extent that they may result in errors of impunity when matched with weak prosecution. A threat to the interest of crime control occurs also when the prosecutor is overburdened.

including the effects of jury size and decision rules on justice errors. Chapter 10 considers the effects of sentencing legislation and judicial decision-making, parole release decisions and related factors on errors of justice.

The last two chapters aim to synthesize the material of the preceding chapters. Chapter 11 applies the principles considered earlier to the problem of homicide. Chapter 12 considers the prospect of enhancing criminal justice legitimacy through the development and use of coherent systems for managing errors of justice. The book closes with a discussion of the limitations of the concepts and methods discussed in the earlier chapters and the prospects for future research and policy.

CHAPTER TWO

Errors of Due Process

...nor shall any person...be deprived of life, liberty, or property, without due process of law...
— Fifth Amendment to the U.S. Constitution (1791)

Introduction

The United States was founded on the principle that the people should be protected against an intrusive government. The Bill of Rights delineates those protections: the people will not be subjected to unreasonable searches and seizures, unwarranted interrogations, punishment without right to trial by a jury of peers, and other such invasions of life, liberty, or property. These distinctions were unprecedented as founding principles of governance when they were drafted and signed; the framers were sensitive to such intrusions after having freed themselves, at considerable expense, from more than a century of imperial rule. The United States is unique among common-law democracies for incorporating principles of due process explicitly in its constitution, overriding all legislation (Kiralfy, 1974). The basic protections, and the principles on which they were grounded, have survived for well over 200 years.

This chapter examines a class of fundamental problems that such protections aim to prevent: the unwarranted harassment, detention or conviction, or excessive sanctioning of people suspected of crime. The provisions are designed to protect the innocent, but they are designed to prevent excessive intrusions against everyone, including those who violate the law. Following the language of Chapter 1, we shall regard lapses of these protections in individual cases as errors of due process. All such episodes threaten the integrity of the justice system, and the public sector generally, by reflecting a government that overreaches its authority and strips citizens of basic rights. This type of error concerns all who cherish justice and the fundamental right of individuals to be free from tyranny.

Errors of due process are vexing for another basic reason: they often threaten *both* due process and the ability to control crime. If one person is wrongfully convicted and sentenced for a crime he did not commit, the real offender may not be brought to justice. It is, of course, virtually impossible to establish the proportion of errors of due process that also involve lapses in crime control. In some unknown proportion of cases involving the conviction of innocent defendants, the defendants may be convicted for crimes that were not in fact committed by anyone.[1]

In this chapter, we examine the nature of due process errors and their consequences. We begin with a discussion of the concept of due process.

What Is Due Process?

Due process is fundamentally about the rules and principles of law aimed at protecting individual private rights, although it has frequently come to mean both more and less. The concept is traceable to the Magna Carta, despite the fact that the words "due process" do not appear in any of the documents that have come to be known as the Magna Carta. King John's attaching his seal to those documents in 1215 was nonetheless an explicit commitment to the principle that no one, not even the king, was above the law, that the governed shall not be subjected to capricious rule.[2] This idea, unprecedented as an

---

[1] See Chapter 1, Note 8.

[2] An explicit expression of the due process concept is in the 39th article of the Magna Carta: "No freemen shall be taken or imprisoned . . . except by the legal judgment of his peers or by the law of the land." King John's personal commitment to the principle was clearly more a matter of necessity than enthusiasm. It was largely the product of a series of disasters, most notably the loss of French land and substantial wealth to King Philip II following defeat in battle at Bouvines and the capture of London by feudal barons protesting the King's capricious tax policies, which had been designed largely

act of law in the 13th century, was perhaps equally revolutionary as a founding principle of governance, as reflected in the U.S. Constitution and Bill of Rights. The expression, "due process," was used in the Fifth Amendment, excerpted at the head of this chapter, and again in the Fourteenth:

> No state shall make or enforce any law which shall abridge the privileges or immunities of citizens of the United States; nor shall any state deprive any person of life, liberty, or property, without due process of law; nor deny to any person within its jurisdiction the equal protection of the laws. (Section 1)

These two amendments established and fundamentally shaped the notion of due process in the United States. The Fifth Amendment had aimed to protect citizens against deprivation of life, liberty, or property in federal criminal proceedings by ensuring fair procedure, including the right to be notified of charges.[3] The Fourteenth Amendment, enacted in 1868, is significant for its extending the general protections of the Bill of Rights, including the Fifth Amendment, to the states. This was necessitated by the fact that the Bill of Rights had clearly not been honored by many of the states: vestiges of slavery continued even after the Civil War and passage of the Thirteenth Amendment, abolishing slavery; men were being forced into military service without pay; and states occasionally confiscated land and other property without due process.

The Fourteenth Amendment significantly advanced the incorporation of the criminal law provisions of the Bill of Rights into the due process clause of the Amendment: freedom from unreasonable searches protected under the Fourth Amendment, all of the protections

---

to restore financial order following the defeat to Philip. The phrase "due process of law" does appear in a 1354 statute of Edward III:

> ...no man of what estate or condition that he be, shall be put out of land or tenement, nor taken, nor imprisoned, nor disinherited, nor put to death, without being brought in answer by due process of law.

[3] The Fifth Amendment also specified that grand jury hearings be required in capital cases, it protected defendants against double jeopardy, and protected against compelling a defendant in any criminal case to "be a witness against himself, and ensured that private property shall not be taken for public use without "just compensation."

of the Fifth Amendment, and rights to speedy and public trial, with jury of peers, fair and impartial (prejudicial publicity prohibited), to confront witnesses (including the right to compulsory process to obtain supportive witnesses), to be heard in one's own defense, and to counsel assured under the Sixth Amendment, with the burden on the government to prove beyond a reasonable doubt that the accused committed the act with criminal intent.

Landmark Due Process Cases

The cause of due process was thus deeply imbedded in our system of law under the Fifth Amendment, and again more than 75 years later under the Fourteenth Amendment. The Supreme Court restricted the scope and sharpened the meaning of due process in the 1930s in the case of *Palko v. Connecticut* by ruling that the due process clause of the Fourteenth Amendment applies to the states only those provisions of the Bill of Rights that are "of the very essence of a scheme of ordered liberty" – those that involve principles of justice "so rooted in the traditions and conscience of our people as to be ranked as fundamental."[4]

The cause of due process was advanced significantly in the 1950s and 1960s under Earl Warren's tenure as chief justice of the Supreme Court. The Warren Court[5] decided several landmark cases that expanded the rights of the accused and revolutionized much of criminal procedure in the process. Here are five of the more significant of the Warren Court's rulings on due process:

- *Mapp v. Ohio* (1961) applied to the states provisions secured at the federal level under Weeks v. United States [232 U.S. 383

---

[4] 302 U.S. 319, 58 S.Ct. 149, 82 L.Ed. 288 (1937). Advocates of "selective incorporation" are quick to identify provisions of the Bill of Rights that are not incorporated as binding on the states under the Fourteenth Amendment: the right to bear arms, to grand jury indictment, and to a jury of twelve, among others (Alderman and Kennedy, 1991).

[5] The justices of the Supreme Court under Earl Warren (1953–69) included Hugo L. Black, William J. Brennan, Harold H. Burton, Tom C. Clark, William O. Douglas, Abe Fortas, Felix Frankfurter, Arthur J. Goldberg, John M. Harlan II, Robert H. Jackson, Thurgood Marshall, Sherman Minton, Stanley F. Reed, Potter Stewart, Byron R. White and Charles E. Whittaker.

(1914)] to protect individuals against unreasonable searches and
seizures, and provided for the blocking of the introduction of ille-
gally seized evidence from criminal trials under the "exclusionary
rule."[6]

- *Gideon v. Wainwright* (1963) guaranteed the right to counsel, requiring states to provide counsel to defendants who cannot afford
  it, in both capital and noncapital cases.[7]
- Under *Brady v. Maryland* (1963), the Supreme Court ruled that
  a prosecutor's suppression of exculpatory evidence violates the
  due process rights of the defendant.[8]
- Under *Escobedo v. Illinois* (1964), the Court ruled that any statements made by arrested persons in violation of their right to counsel prior to interrogation may be excluded from trial.[9]
- *Miranda v. Arizona* (1966) gave arrested persons the right to be
  told that they need not speak when asked questions.[10]
- *U.S. v. Wade* (1967) ruled that due process of law requires that
  procedures for identifying the offender be fair and impartial,
  free of "impermissibly suggestive" procedures.[11]

What prompted these decisions? Popular media accounts of the
Eisenhower Era tend to associate the times with the Yankees and
Dodgers, Lucy and Desi, and Ozzie and Harriet, but the period had
a deep, dark side as well. It was a period of entrenched racial and re-
ligious discrimination, Hollywood blacklists, and police brutality. The
Supreme Court's rulings in these landmark cases, often overcoming a
substantial minority dissent,[12] can be regarded as a deliberate response

---

[6] 367 U.S. 643, 81 S.Ct. 1684, 6 L.Ed.2d 1081 (1961). The exclusionary rule is exceptional by international standards; no nation other than the United States applies the
rule to illegal searches and seizures of physical evidence. While the exclusionary rule
allows culpable offenders to go free, several studies have found that the proportion
of arrests that are either rejected or dismissed under the rule is quite small, less than
one percent of all felony arrests, with most of those in drug arrests (Forst, Lucianovic,
and Cox, 1977; Brosi 1979; Boland, Mahanna, and Sones, 1992).

[7] 372 U.S. 335, 83 S.Ct. 792, 9 L.Ed.2d 799 (1963).

[8] 373 U.S. 83, 83 S. Ct. 1194, 10 L.Ed.2d 215 (1963).

[9] 378 U.S. 478, 84 S.Ct. 1758, 12 L.Ed.2d 977 (1964).

[10] 384 U.S. 436, 86 S.Ct. 1602, 16 L.Ed.2d 694 (1966).

[11] 388 U.S. 218, 87 S.Ct. 1926, 18 L.Ed.2d 1149 (1967).

[12] Justices Harlan, Stewart, and White (a Kennedy appointee) made up the core of the
dissenting opinion in several of the landmark due process cases.

to a populist and virulent strain of repression embodied in the McCarthyism of the 1950s. The legislative and executive branches were less well-situated politically to deal effectively with such oppressive and divisive forces. The Court's rulings in these cases attempted to respond to injustices in criminal processing generally and in policing in particular, much as the Court's ruling in *Brown v. Board of Education of Topeka*[13] responded to segregation, and its ruling in *Watkins v. United States*[14] responded to Senator Joseph McCarthy's Red-baiting interrogations.[15] A narrow majority of the Court was inclined to see matters along civil libertarian lines. Most had been selected ("packed" was the term in common use) by Democratic Presidents Roosevelt and Truman from 1932 until 1952, the year prior to Warren's appointment, with four additional Warren Court justices appointed by Presidents Kennedy and Johnson in the 1960s.[16]

The decisions of the Warren Court did more than alter criminal justice procedure. They represented a significant shift of the Supreme Court to the political left; they were controversial across broad sectors of the public (Powe, 2000). The star player did not come from the left, he came from the blue. Chief Justice Earl Warren had been Republican District Attorney of Alameda County, California, and California Attorney General from 1939 to 1943, then Governor of California from 1943 until 1953, when he was appointed to the Court by the Republican President Eisenhower. The Supreme Court, and Earl Warren in particular, came under increasing attack during the 1960s, especially as crime rates escalated and civil disturbances reached epic

---

[13] 347 U.S. 483 (1954).

[14] 354 U.S. 178 (1957).

[15] The ruling granted witnesses the right not to be held in contempt of Congress for refusing to answer questions concerning other people's involvement in the Communist Party following their disassociation from the Party. The witness, John T. Watkins, felt that the information was irrelevant, and the Court concurred.

[16] The four were Justices Fortas (appointed in 1965), Goldberg (1962), Marshall (1967) and White (1962). The majority opinion in *Mapp* was written by Justice Clark, a Truman appointee; in *Gideon v. Wainwright* it was written by Justice Black, a 1937 Roosevelt appointee; the majority opinion in *Escobedo* was written by Justice Goldberg, appointed by John F. Kennedy in 1962; Chief Justice Warren wrote the opinion for the majority in *Miranda*; and the majority opinion in *U.S. v. Wade* was written by Justice Brennan, a Democratic labor lawyer appointed by President Eisenhower in 1956. These landmark cases were often sharply divided – both *Escobedo* and *Miranda* were 5–4 decisions, *Mapp* was 6–3.

levels in response to an increasingly unpopular war in Vietnam. By the time of his retirement in 1969, assaults on the Court from the right were accentuated by the widespread distribution of Warren Impeachment Kits and Impeach Earl Warren bumper stickers (Powe, 2000).

The Warren Court's rulings fueled political divisions in the 1960s. The decisions were popular among civil libertarians, but reviled by conservatives and many in the political mainstream. They were especially despised in the law enforcement community. Police officials expressed grave concerns about their ability to do their jobs, seeing themselves as becoming increasingly handicapped by the Supreme Court in their ability to serve and protect lives and property, especially in the mid-to-late 1960s, when crime started spinning out of control (Fogelson, 1977; Powe, 2000). These concerns eventually subsided as police departments around the country came to understand that the rulings were both real and permanent, that in the end their work would be more credible if they honored the Constitution and its interpretation by the Court.

The Sources of Due Process Errors and Their Social Significance

Erosions of due process protections have more than symbolic consequences; they touch everyone. As these protections falter, innocent people are more likely to be harassed, detained, and convicted, and actions taken against offenders, from interrogation to the terms of incarceration, may become needlessly harsh, with avoidable external costs imposed on taxpayers, the punished, and their dependents. Subsequent crimes, and costs associated with civil unrest, may be imposed on society as the system becomes viewed increasingly as corrupt.

The sources of due process errors fall on a spectrum from honest mistakes to venal acts. On the innocent end of the spectrum, the errors may be inadvertent and random, such as due to mistaken eyewitness identification even following reasonable police precautions to prevent such error[17] (Huff et al., 1996; Scheck et al., 2001, pp. 53–8), or cases in which strong circumstantial evidence conspires coincidentally to point to an ill-fated bystander, often with a prior criminal record, who happened to show up at or near the crime scene at precisely the wrong time. Or they may be due to overloaded criminal justice resources. Although most of these errors appear avoidable, some are bound to occur even in a criminal justice system scrupulous about the need to protect due process rights, given over 10 million felony crimes annually (Federal Bureau of Investigation, 2000).

Less honest errors appear all too common. These include systematic errors of due process spawned by excessive pressure to solve cases or reduce crime, and by the absence of professionalism among criminal justice officials. False confessions were reported in nearly a quarter of all DNA exonerations studied by the Innocence Project.[18] Flawed systems of police accountability have been reported to lead to extreme pressures on police officers, investigators, and supervisors to solve crimes, make arrests, and reduce the crime rate in their jurisdictions (Flynn, 2000). Legislators may feel similarly pressured to secure reelection by promoting dubious legislation with get-tough-on-criminals slogans (e.g., "Three-strikes-and-you're-out" laws, "drug kingpin" laws) and draconian mandatory sentences, thus elevating self-interested politics over the public interest. The sentences may be legal and not technically in violation of Eighth Amendment protections against cruel and unusual punishments, but they may nonetheless be excessive under both utilitarian and pure justice frameworks of sentencing. (These are dealt with in more detail in Chapter 10.) Due process errors associated with the absence of professionalism are exemplified by police placed in positions of significant authority without adequate training or experience (dealt with in Chapter 7), reliance on information provided by

---

[17] Mistaken identifications by eyewitnesses or victims have been cited as "the single most important cause of wrongful imprisonment" by Scheck et al. (2001). Such identifications were cited in 86% (24) of the 28 convictions overturned by DNA evidence in a 1996 study sponsored by the Department of Justice (Connors et al., 1996, pp. 16–17). A similar number (82%) was reported in exonerations attributed to the pro bono Innocence Project of the Cardozo School of Law in New York (Scheck et al., 2001).

[18] Scheck et al., 2001, p. 120.

informants of questionable credibility (Scheck et al., 2001, pp. 163–
203),[19] the incompetent or unenthusiastic defense lawyer, and discrimination by race or class, conscious or otherwise. These are more than
innocuous problems, since they are often spawned by deeper frustra-
tions and social divisions. They are more dangerous as well; they can
aggravate the underlying problems. In city after city, police overreac-
tions to minor disturbances have been known to ignite major urban
riots, with substantial losses of life and property.

The worst case is the error associated unambiguously with more
sinister motives. The extreme case is the avoidable police killing of a
person, producing the same end result as capital punishment while
short-cutting all elements of due process. Some police killings are justifiable as defensive acts resorted to only when all other attempts to
perform a legitimate policing duty failed. However, many, if not most,
appear to be preventable (Fyfe, 1986; Geller, 1982). Some, such as
the sensational killing of Amadou Diallo, turn out to involve police
shootings of unarmed, innocent people identified as suspects. The
prospect of assembling reliable data that might permit an assessment
of police behaviors in the cases in which these errors occur is daunting. A valid assessment would require not only estimates of the relevant
social costs of the errors of various actions (including inaction), but
also an identification of all episodes in which the potential for such
errors is present (Fyfe, 2001). Other examples of error associated with
serious breaches of due process protections include the police or lab
technician tampering with or fabricating evidence (Scheck et al., 2001,
pp. 138–62; Connors et al., 1996, pp. 15–18), the overzealous prosecutor who withholds exculpatory evidence from the defense (Bedau and
Radelet, 1987, pp. 57–60; Gershman, 1999; Huff et al., 1996; Scheck
et al., 2001, pp. 222–36),[20] and conscious discrimination by police,
prosecutors, judges, juries, and correctional officials. (These are discussed in Chapters 7 through 11.)

---

[19] The informant may be either a collaborator in the offense in question or a prison
or jail "snitch" who claims to have incriminating information. In both instances, the
informant generally receives a lessened sanction in return for the information.

[20] As noted earlier, a prosecutor's suppression of exculpatory evidence violates the due
process rights of the defendant under *Brady v. Maryland.*

Managing Due Process Errors

No clear lines have been drawn between these classes of due process errors. They lie on a continuous and somewhat arbitrary spectrum between innocuous and egregious. What is common to all is that much has been proposed to reduce them. They are not likely to be eliminated, as I have noted, but some interventions are bound to be much more effective than others.

One thing is clear: errors of due process cannot be managed in a vacuum. Interventions that aim to reduce these errors must be weighed against their impacts on our ability to maintain peace and order in the community, and on costs. The experience of the Warren Court's rulings may be instructive here. While unpopular among large segments of society, the strengthening of due process protections under the rulings of the Warren Court did much to bring integrity to a justice system that had been regarded by many as a system by and for the rich and powerful. In making government intrusions against citizens and noncitizens more difficult, the rulings almost surely also worked to reduce the numbers of innocent people convicted.

At the same time, however, the possibility cannot be ignored that the rulings may have contributed to increases in the number and rate of offenders not brought to justice. A range of prospects present themselves here. One is that the premise is simply wrong, that the crime rate would have increased as much in the absence of the rulings of the Warren Court. The increase in crime in the 1960s and 1970s was primarily a product of an increase in the number of males in the crime-prone ages of 18-to-24 and alienation associated with the social upheaval of the period, rather than the decisions of the Supreme Court. The police became less able to respond to inner-city crime, where the bulk of the increase occurred, primarily because the number of crimes relative to the number of sworn officers increased substantially during the 1960s and 1970s.

A second prospect is that the effects were indirect, largely a product of needless police malaise. The police did not have to respond to the Court's rulings by complaining of being "hamstrung" by the rulings and neglecting all but the most serious inner-city crimes. Had the police established a more sensible set of policies during the 1960s rather than isolate themselves from the inner cities with a why-bother attitude, they could have done much to head off the increase in crime long ago. The expansion of the community policing movement in the 1990s appears to have contributed to the decline in crime in the 1990s, but the police were some 25 years too late in discovering the need to build closer ties to the communities they had been sworn to serve.

Another possibility is that the expansion of due process protections did have a direct effect on the number of crimes not cleared by arrest and conviction, but that the effect was small. Empirical evidence supports the claim that due process problems have been overrated as a cause of crimes falling through the crack. Arrests rejected for prosecution because of due process violations have represented less than one percent of all felony arrests (Forst, 2002).

The fourth prospect is that the rulings of the Warren Court really did shift the balance of power from the police to the marginal offender; they may have significantly reduced the ability of the police to bring culpable offenders to justice. The small proportion of arrests rejected by prosecutors because of due process problems overlooks the much larger number of episodes in which the police do not bother to arrest the offender and bring the case to the prosecutor because they know that search or confession problems would cause the prosecutor to reject the case. Cassell and Fowles report that "crime clearance rates fell precipitously immediately after *Miranda* (1966–69) and have remained at lower levels ever since." They conclude that *Miranda* did "handcuff" the police, and that alternative approaches to regulating police interrogations should be explored.[21]

---

[21] Cassell and Fowles (1998), p. 1062. Their conclusion is based on a multiple regression time-series analysis that controlled for crime rates, expenditures on police, percent of the population in crime-prone ages, and other factors. They found effects for violent crime in the aggregate and property crime in the aggregate, as well as for the individual crime categories of robbery, vehicle theft, and larceny, and a marginal effect for burglary. They found no effects for three of the four categories of violent crime – murder, rape, or assault – which raises questions about how one should interpret their finding an effect for violent crime generally. Feeney (2000) questions the validity of the Cassell and Fowles analysis, observing that the sharp decline in clearance rates may have been due primarily to factors other than those controlled by Cassell and Fowles, such as the epidemic of urban riots that occurred in the mid-1960s. See Leo and Thomas (1998) for a more comprehensive assessment of *Miranda*.

Regardless of which of these prospects is closest to the truth, one aspect of the relationship between liberty and security remains a critical paradox. It is reflected in a popular aphorism: "Wise restraints make us free."[22] It would be extremely useful to know more about this relationship. Which restraints are wise, and under what circumstances? What precisely is the effect of those restraints on our freedoms?

Conclusion

Clearly, much remains to be done to properly balance the interests of due process with those of crime control. Greatly needed are analyses that will allow us to better understand the full effects of any particular intervention to protect the rights of defendants not only in reducing due process errors, but as well on our ability to control crime and costs, a measure of the extent to which these interventions draw resources away from other important public and private demands.

A serious barrier must first be dealt with: such analyses cannot be conducted without reliable and relevant data. Citizens are expected to put up with stops, detentions and other intrusions with little systematic police accountability, much as people have become accustomed to put up with airport security procedures. Data on the incidence of these intrusions and the distribution of costs imposed on citizens under each major type of intrusion would serve both the interests of police accountability and the need to estimate the social harms associated with those intrusions.

We must, of course, work diligently to minimize errors of due process. But we should aim to do so mindfully of other legitimate social interests. None of the great thinkers has yet discovered a way to eliminate due process errors without incurring unacceptably high crime and resource costs. The challenge is to find ways to reduce both crime and errors of due process under a framework that accounts for the social costs of both.

[22] This anonymous aphorism was used in 1987 by Supreme Court Justice Anthony M. Kennedy. It has been invoked since by Senator Edward M. Kennedy, former Harvard President Neil L. Rudenstine, Supreme Court Justice Stephen Breyer, and others.

CHAPTER THREE

Errors of Impunity

Bringing to justice those who violate human rights is essential to end impunity and to the effective prevention of further violations.

– Amnesty International (1997)

Introduction

Many are inclined to regard errors of justice exclusively as ones that cause innocent persons to be arrested and convicted. Much of what has been written on justice errors, indeed, is restricted to this type of error. But the Goddess of Justice holds a balance scale with *two* plates, one of which supports the interests of domestic tranquility, the right of the people to be protected against crime, to ensure that justice is served by sanctioning those who violate the law. Failure to take sufficient action to prevent and respond to crime imposes costs, tangible and intangible, on victims individually and on society at large. Increases in crime tend to increase the demand for public and private interventions, at the expense of other important social goods and services: education, health care, and so on.

This chapter examines errors on this other side of the scale, and their costs. It begins with a description of "errors of impunity" and a discussion of their sources, considers their consequences, and concludes with a discussion of measures that might be taken to manage those errors more effectively, balancing them more consciously than we have in the past with errors of due process and the costs of managing the two.

What Is an Error of Impunity?

We shall refer to a lapse of justice that allows a culpable offender to remain at large as an "error of impunity."[1] This is not a crisp definition; many offenders are at the margin of culpability. Juveniles, emotionally disturbed offenders, and people who injure others while in states of diminished capacity due to circumstances beyond their control – all these are examples of acts that often go unpunished despite the fact that the other elements of a crime have been met. We might regard these as disasters akin to car accidents or tornadoes. The community may be able to do more to prevent them, but we generally prefer to consider it beyond the reach of the criminal justice system to do so.

In other cases, errors of impunity are real, unambiguous, and significant. As the number of culpable offenders set free increases, public safety and the quality of life are compromised, the credibility of deterrent effectiveness is lost, and citizens become increasingly inclined to perceive injustices to victims and alienation from the police and courts, if not from government generally. The integrity of the justice system thus becomes threatened both by the reality and perception of ineffectualness. These lapses can run through the entire justice system, from ineffective policing and prosecution to weak sentencing and corrections (as when inmates escape).

The Sources and Consequences of Errors of Impunity

There are several sources of these errors. All are barriers to the successful investigation and prosecution of crimes, barriers that allow offenders to go free. We will discuss them in detail in subsequent chapters, but provide an overview of them and their consequences here.

Skillful Offenders

The first, and perhaps most difficult to manage barrier to effective crime control is the *skillful offender*. The offender who evades

---

[1] Here is a standard definition of impunity: exemption from punishment, penalty, or harm. Source: *American Heritage Dictionary of the English Language*, fourth edition (New York: Houghton Mifflin, 2000)

detection and arrest is an archetype of both the classical criminology and neoclassical economic theories of crime, which portray offenders as rational decision makers, choosing to commit crimes after weighing their alternatives in the legitimate and illegitimate sectors. Having elected to commit crime, they then proceed to find ways of committing those crimes that maximize their expected net gains from criminal activity, taking into account the likelihood of getting caught, the expected consequences of arrest and conviction, and the expected gains of particular crimes if they do not get caught.

The most skillfully committed offenses leave little for the investigator to work with to solve the crime: no witnesses, little or no readily accessible evidence, and crime scene unknown in murder cases. Some serious crimes go unwitnessed, such as the homicide victim reported as a missing person, suicide, or accident. Many other crimes are known by the public but not reported to police. The rate at which victims report crimes has increased over the decades since the public has been surveyed about victimizations, but the overall reporting rate is still below 50 percent (Duhart, 2000, p. 10). Even in crimes known to the police, many have no known eyewitnesses. They are reported either because they have been discovered by the victim ("My car has been stolen") or a body has been found, sometimes away from the crime scene, perhaps discarded at a roadside or in a wooded area or river. These offenses usually present limited opportunities for successful investigation and identification of the offender.

Ineffective Policing

Lapses in policing are a second barrier to crime control. In most large metropolitan police departments, such lapses can usually be traced directly or indirectly to insufficient resources and intractably large crime loads. In many metropolitan areas, urban police departments have moderate budgets, measured on a per resident or per officer basis, and large crime loads, while departments in more affluent neighboring communities have large per capita budgets and much smaller crime loads. It is surely no coincidence that the rates of clearance by arrest are consistently higher in suburban and rural areas than in urban places – both for violent and property crimes (Sourcebook, 2000,

Table 4.19). As resources must be spread over a larger set of demands, the amount of time and effort that can be allocated to each case diminishes, with a corresponding decline in successful outcomes.

Police-related lapses in crime control may be attributable to other sources, sometimes themselves a product of thin resources. Investigative work is hampered by police officers who have been inadequately screened and trained in effective techniques for securing, collecting and processing physical evidence, interviewing witnesses, and interrogating suspects. The first investigator at a crime scene is typically a patrol officer, and some police departments prepare both patrol officers and detectives much better than others in the essentials of preserving crime scenes, identifying and collecting evidence, and obtaining useful information from witnesses and suspects. The ability of the police to solve crimes depends also on the cooperation of the public, and some police departments appear to be more successful in currying such support than others, quite possibly the product of effective community policing programs in those jurisdictions.

Lapses in Prosecution and Adjudication
The problem of insufficient resources and high crime rates is not unique to big-city police departments. District attorneys' offices and courts in most urban areas are similarly stressed, limiting the amount of attention available to each case. The problem tends to be especially acute in misdemeanor courts, involving less serious cases, but it is common in most metropolitan felony courts as well. Unfortunately, the absence of a comprehensive national reporting program on the screening and prosecution of arrests limits opportunities to gain systematic insights about the impact of specific prosecution practices and policies on case outcomes in court.[2] It is nonetheless possible to assess

---

[2] On at least one critical dimension – prosecutors' decisions whether to file charges in felony arrests brought by the police – we actually know *less* today than we did in the 1970s and 1980s. Detailed information about the decisions made about whether to accept cases, reasons for rejections, extent of charge reductions, diversions, and related matters – collected through the Prosecutor's Management Information System (PROMIS) from Manhattan, Los Angeles County, Washington, DC, Wayne County (Detroit), Marion County (Indianapolis), Multnomah County (Portland, OR), and a

the effect of screening and plea bargaining policies and strategies on errors of impunity and due process, as we shall see in Chapter 8, as well as the effects of changes in conviction rates (Chapter 6) and jury size and rules (Chapter 9) on these errors.

Weak Sanctions

Convicting the offender provides no assurance against errors of impunity. Under either the utilitarian ("consequentialist") or the pure justice ("just desert") model, the sanction that follows conviction could be less than optimal. In the utilitarian framework, the sanction will be insufficient if the social costs associated with a more severe sanction are lower. (See Chapter 5, Figure 5.1.) Under a pure justice ("just desert") model, the sanction will be too weak if it is less than commensurate with the severity of the crime committed (Kleinig, 1974; von Hirsch, 1976). Such sanctions may be the product of prosecutors who concede too much in plea negotiations or judges who sentence offenders without sufficient attention to either utilitarian or pure justice considerations.

Flawed Correctional Practices

Crime costs may exceed socially optimal levels also if parole boards release offenders prematurely, without adequate concern to the likely crime costs of their release decisions, or if correctional facilities are too lax in preventing offenders in confinement from committing crimes prior to their official release dates, in the form of crimes committed against other inmates, crimes following escapes from confinement, or crimes associated with lax parole or probation officer supervision practices. Evidence of errors attributable to some combination of weak sanctions and flawed correctional practices is provided by the finding that over 800 inmates serving time for homicide in 1984 had previously been convicted of murder (Cassell and Markman, 1988).

host of other jurisdictions – was, for about 15 years, documented and published by the Bureau of Justice Statistics (BJS). Unfortunately, this series was quietly discontinued in 1992, despite the proliferation of PROMIS-like data systems in district attorneys' offices throughout the United States, as part of a revealed BJS preference for aggregate national estimates over local area data.

Managing Errors of Impunity

How can errors of impunity be managed without interfering excessively with errors of due process, and without diverting resources excessively from other publically valued demands? Let us first consider the problem of the skillful offender, for which two strategies are available: more effective crime prevention and deterrence. Crime prevention can be achieved through public and private efforts to harden targets and design public spaces that are more defensible (Jeffrey; Newman, 1972). Surely one of the more prominent examples of costly inadequacies in preventive design is the 1995 truck bombing of the vulnerable Murrah Federal Building in Oklahoma City, in which 168 were killed in the second most devastating terrorist incident in the United States to date. Prominent examples of effective preventive strategies include the open design of the Washington Metro and the low crime rates associated with that design, in contrast with the hidden corners and dark passageways of the New York and Philadelphia subway systems and their much higher crime rates (LaVigne, 1997),[3] and the reduced crime for the Five Oaks Redesign Project in Dayton, Ohio, in contrast to its predecessor and to the hopelessly failed design of the Pruitt-Igoe housing project in St. Louis decades earlier (Newman, 1997). Crime prevention also may be promoted through the installation of surveillance and detection devices, information to the community about neighborhood crime prevention programs, effective antistalking programs, and community bridge-building programs to encourage victims to report crimes and cooperate with the police and prosecutors.

A complementary strategy for dealing with the skillful offender is tough sanctioning under the theory of deterrence. We may not catch most skillful offenders, especially those who limit their exposure by committing very few crimes, but we may be able to discourage participation in illegitimate activity by giving tough sanctions to those who are caught and convicted. While such punishments may seem unfair and excessive to the hapless few who are caught, the strategy is justifiable

---

[3] I thank Jim Fyfe for noting that some of the difference in crime rates may be because the Washington Metro system is closed for several hours late at night, while the New York and Philadelphia subways are open around the clock.

to the extent that the reduction in social costs associated with the deterrent effect of each sentence exceeds the marginal social cost of the punishment itself.[4] Both the strategies of prevention and deterrence aim to raise the cost of committing crimes to the prospective offender, but they must be done in a way that is mindful of other social costs.

Lapses in policing, prosecution, and adjudication may be reduced in several ways. One is the development and enhancement of systems of accountability that encourage practices that are more effective and discourage those that are ineffective or counterproductive. Substantial gains in policing in the 1990s have been attributed to one such system – Compstat in New York, New Orleans, and Philadelphia (Silverman, 1999). These experiences have inspired the development of similar systems in police departments in Minneapolis (CODEFOR), Seattle (COMPASS), and elsewhere (Anderson, 2001). The better police accountability systems incorporate measures of both effectiveness and due process (e.g., complaints against officers), to ensure that lapses in effectiveness are not countered by procedures that violate individuals' rights to due process (Alpert and Moore, 1993).

Systems of accountability in prosecution have been much less visible. Many prosecutors' offices appear to have them, but these systems have remained below the horizon, largely to assure that the information is not used as part of embarrassing exposés by media and political opposition (Forst, 2000b, pp. 137–8). Ironically, community prosecution programs that have become popular since the late 1990s, aimed largely at improving the visibility of the prosecutor in the community, have done virtually nothing to enhance formal systems of accountability that might cast a brighter light on the operations of the prosecutor, from the initial stage at which arrests are screened to final disposition. What we know about the prosecutor in most jurisdictions is restricted to the sensational cases in the news. Most citizens have no clue as to how the prosecutor's operations in their jurisdiction compares with those in other jurisdictions, or how it has changed over time in its measured

---

[4] Deterrence may be achievable through interventions other than tough sentences. Uviller, for example, has suggested the use of sophisticated communication technology to permit police officers to obtain search and arrest warrants more quickly, without jeopardizing due process protections.

ability to bring offenders to justice. Doing so by neighborhood could surely support the community's understanding of prosecution and thus serve the community in a substantive way that is overlooked by conventional community prosecution programs, which may serve primarily to elevate political popularity over prosecution effectiveness by diverting resources from the court to the street. Public access to systematic information about prosecutor performance is, in any case, an area with considerable room for improvement.

Improved systems of accountability enrich the prospects for a second approach to enhancing the effectiveness of the criminal justice system's ability to control crime: more research, and better research. One of the most important and least appreciated breakthroughs of the past 30 years has been our ability to dispel myths about what works in criminal justice and find more productive paths to crime control through the collection and analysis of data on criminal justice interventions and their impacts on crime. The research is often conducted using experimental or quasi-experimental designs. We have witnessed sea changes in criminal justice policies and practices – especially in policing and corrections – and these changes have been, to a large extent, the immediate product of research findings (Sherman et al., 1999). This research has paved the way for a less obstructed view of systematic errors in justice and programs to reduce those errors.

A third way to increase effectiveness is to make more resources available. Citizens and commercial establishments routinely raise resources privately as they perceive the needs, while the public sector attempts to do so through the legislative and electoral processes. In both the public and private sectors, the communities that are best protected are those that can most readily afford effective protections, and the crime rates tend to be lower as a consequence. Federal programs subsidize high-crime areas, but federal funding often goes to the jurisdictions that have better connections to the federal establishment and write the best grant applications, which are not always the neediest jurisdictions. The insights gained through research can serve, nonetheless, as a light to guide the development of new programs for improving criminal justice effectiveness.

Conclusion

Scholars of the justice system, while concerned about security, are often inclined nonetheless to produce many more lines of thoughtful text on the problem of violations of rights to due process and privacy than on the problem of preserving order and protecting public safety.[5] The voting public, by contrast, fed by media distortions of the crime problem and pandering politicians, tends to take a less nuanced position, showing more concern about a criminal justice system that they see as too permissive. Since 1980, the public has been more willing to increase its spending of scarce public resources on the police, jails and prisons than on most social programs.

All factions, scholars and the voting public alike, may be short-sighted in focusing on one side of the scale of justice to the exclusion, and often at the expense, of the other. It will be more enlightening, and quite possibly more productive, to explore frameworks for policy assessment and error control that embrace both sets of legitimate justice interests and incorporate the errors that correspond to each. In the next two chapters, we consider such frameworks.

[5] This book is not exceptional. The word count for Chapter 2 is 48 percent higher than for Chapter 3.

CHAPTER FOUR

Frameworks for Analyzing the Incidence of Justice Errors

A mature science, with respect to the matter of errors in variables, is not one that measures its variables without error, for this is impossible. It is, rather, a science which properly manages its errors, controlling their magnitudes and correctly calculating their implications for substantive conclusions.

– Otis Dudley Duncan (1975)

Introduction

We can begin the search for a system of managing errors in criminal justice by considering systems of error management in other domains. Several domains provide tools that have potential value as components of a system for managing justice errors. We focus here on two, with no presumption to have exhausted the relevant prospects. First is the domain of statistical inference, in which a logic and set of tools derived from that logic have been developed to test research hypotheses and estimate parameters of interest in such a way that is mindful of both random and systematic errors of inference. Second is that of quality control analysis, in which frameworks such as simulation modeling have been developed to manage errors in the production of goods and delivery of services. In Chapter 5, we will focus on a third, that of welfare economics and its concept of social costs, aimed at finding public policies and programs that minimize the sum of the cost of social harms and the cost of interventions designed to counter those harms.

Of particular interest in this chapter are methods that open an inquiry into the effects of changes in criminal justice standards, policies, and practices on the incidence of justice errors. This chapter reviews essential elements of statistical inference and quality control analysis and explores the prospects of applying each element to the problem of managing errors of justice.

Managing Errors of Statistical Inference: The Problem of Reliability

Researchers routinely test theories by restating the theories as testable hypotheses,[1] drawing data from samples designed to the extent practicable to represent the populations about which the theories apply, measuring variables in the sample in a way that corresponds as closely as possible to the central elements of the theory, and using appropriate statistical reduction techniques to carry out the test. To test a research hypothesis – for example, that a drug treatment program reduces subsequent drug use and criminal behavior – the scientist calculates the distribution of results that would ordinarily occur just due to chance if in fact that hypothesis were untrue, if the reductions observed in a particular sample were just a random fluke. The results are said to confirm the research hypothesis if they fall outside the range of ordinary occurrence – typically, if they are outside the range that would occur 95 percent or 99 percent of the time if the hypothesis were untrue. The use of a replicable procedure allows the researcher to conclude that the result obtained is either within an interval of results that would normally occur due to chance or that it is outside that interval. Such results cannot prove the research hypothesis, but they can provide a confirmation of it.

In drawing inferences about the population from the sample, the researchers face threats to *reliability*, the risk of making erroneous inferences associated with random variation endemic to small samples. They also face threats to *validity*, risks of making systematic errors

---

[1] The hypotheses may involve questions about the outcome for a single observation drawn from a population with a known probability distribution (e.g., binomial, Poisson, normal), about the value of a parameter based on observations made on a sample drawn from the population, or about a relationship between two, or among several, variables observed in the sample.

associated with biased samples of the population or with data that fail to reflect accurately the concepts in the theory.[2] We will focus on those threats to accurate inference in statistical research that have parallels with problems in drawing inferences about the guilt or innocence of an offender, toward the development of a framework for managing justice errors (as defined in Chapter 1) and assessing criminal justice policies and procedures in terms of their effects on such errors.

Threats to Reliability

Reliability refers to the consistency of observation, the ability of an instrument or sample to measure each element observed in precisely the same way. Random errors in the measurement or recording of observations are a common threat to reliability.[3] Such errors are generally uncovered either by measuring and recording observations twice to find discrepancies or to build in to the data collection process internal consistency checks that reveal such errors.

These kinds of threats to statistical inference can occur as well in the collection of evidence at crime scene investigations and in witness interviews and suspect interrogations. Use of multiple investigating officers, detailed and comprehensive photographs of crime scenes, tapings of interviews and interrogations, and repeated measures in the forensic analysis of physical evidence are standard procedures aimed at minimizing all such errors.

Small samples are another important threat to reliability in statistical inference. As the sample size diminishes, often a product of budgetary or logistical constraints, random errors tend to grow large and the statistical results grow unreliable. The most unreliable sample is

---

[2] "Threat to internal validity" is generally defined in such a way as to include any factor that jeopardizes the accuracy of a test of a theory; reliability thus qualifies as a threat to internal validity. We shall follow here the statistical convention of regarding accuracy as the composite of validity and reliability, with departure from accuracy (measured as mean square error, the square of the difference between an estimator and the parameter estimated) equal to the sum of departure from validity (measured as the square of bias, the difference between the mean of the estimator and the parameter estimated) and reliability (measured as the variance of the estimator about its mean).

[3] Nonrandom errors, the product of improper calibration of an instrument or different interviewers using different procedures, are more common in many settings. These are examples of threats to validity, discussed in the next section.

the sample consisting of a single observation – the anecdote or case study. While anecdotes and case studies are often rich in details that provide important insights into behaviors and processes of interest that are otherwise unavailable, they are inherently unreliable, often atypical of the population at large. Large samples and straightforward data elements that are not subject to interpretation generally pass the test of reliability.

The problem of small sample unreliability has parallels in the criminal justice problem of establishing guilt. When the amount of evidence, both physical and testimonial, obtained from an investigation is scant, the results may be unreliable, much like small samples. In more serious cases investigators tend to collect more tangible evidence, interview more witnesses, and do more work checking out leads, telephone and bank check records, and other information sources to establish whether the suspect really committed the crime. The prosecutor's burden to prove beyond a reasonable doubt that the defendant committed the crime offers a basic standard for protecting innocent people and ensuring the reliability of findings of guilt. This protection is threatened by defense lawyers who do too little work to ensure that the court hears exculpatory evidence on behalf of their client.

Managing Threats to Reliability

In any particular study, the errors of inference associated with small samples – problems of reliability – may be either of two types: (1) that of accepting the research hypothesis (e.g., the drug treatment program is effective) based on a sample result when in fact the hypothesis is false, known as the Type I error; or (2) that of rejecting the research hypothesis based on a sample result when in fact it is true, known as the Type II error. Researchers can manage those errors by selecting the risk of committing the Type I error, designated as α and typically set at .05 or .01, and by exercising options about the sample size and design – the larger the sample or more efficient the design,[4] the smaller

---

[4] Examples of design efficiencies include the use of stratified or cluster sampling rather than simple random sampling to make use of known characteristics of the population to ensure representativeness.

the likelihood of committing a Type II error, with the probability of committing a Type II error denoted as β. While challenges have been raised against the basic logic of this "classical" system of statistical inference, the fundamental approach is well-established, coherent, widely used, and objective.[5]

Statisticians have developed tools to help in this process of managing errors of inference associated with reliability. One such tool is that of *statistical power analysis*, which permits an assessment of the effect of sample size on the risk of a Type II error, with power defined as the probability of accepting the research hypothesis when it is true (1-β). The result of such an analysis is commonly presented in the form of a graph depicting the relationship between 1-β and the value of the parameter tested for a wide array of sample sizes.[6] It can be used as well to assess the errors associated with alternative classification systems, which have parallels in criminal justice policy that are addressed below. This general approach has been applied to medical diagnosis, aeronautical fault analysis, weather forecasting, and credit scoring (Swets et al., 2000; Leape, 1994).

The approach may be equally useful for examining relationships between criminal justice policies and justice errors. In subsequent chapters we will explore prospects for combining available estimates of criminal justice practices (rates relevant to police profiling systems, case acceptance rates in screening decisions, plea-to-trial rates, conviction rates, etc.) with a range of assumptions about factual innocence,

---

[5] The principal challenge to the classical system of statistical inference has come from the "Bayesian" school, which holds that the classical system is deficient for its dismissal of opportunities to integrate valid subjective (*a priori*) information with empirically derived frequencies. The Bayesian system does not fundamentally alter the logic of error management considered here for the criminal justice system. It is likely to complicate the prospect of managing errors of inference, however, through the potential misuse of subjective information in an adversarial setting.

[6] A common variant of the power curve is the *operating characteristic* curve, which traces the relationship between the probability of committing the Type II error (β) and the value of the parameter tested for various sample sizes. Another increasingly popular variant is *receiver operating characteristic* analysis, which traces the relationship between the rate of true positives (positives accurately identified as positive as a percentage of total actually positive) and the false positives rate (negatives falsely identified as positive as a percentage of total actually negative). This analysis, initially designed for signal detection systems, typically aims to assess alternative systems of diagnosis and classification in terms of their error rates (Swets et al., 2000).

to estimate the effects of policy on both types of errors: innocent people detained or convicted and true offenders either not detained or set free. A statistical tool will be especially helpful in these applications to the extent that it permits assessment of the effects of alternative policies on justice errors under a broad range of assumptions about true innocence. Such an application is illustrated in Chapter 6.

Managing Errors of Statistical Inference: The Problem of Validity

Biased Samples

Validity is threatened by biased samples. Samples are biased when they have been designed in such a way that, for large samples, statistics that describe the sample tend not to represent the population of interest. This can result from sampling designs that are nonrandom (e.g., convenience sampling, quota sampling, purposive sampling, snowball sampling), or through the use of lists of the population ("sampling frames") from which samples are drawn that fail to cover the entire population of interest, or as a result of nonresponse errors that are concentrated among certain classes of units sampled.

One of the most common sources of bias in sampling are *selection effects*, the selection of individuals or jurisdictions for study based on desirable attributes (Heckman, 1990).[7] Selection effects occur when, for example, a correctional authority hand picks inmates or probationers as eligibles for a rehabilitation program based on their perceived potential for rehabilitation, or when the candidates volunteer themselves for the program, a process known as self-selection. In both instances, persons in the program may end up with lower subsequent rates of arrest because of the attributes that induced them to be in the program rather than because of the effect of the program itself.

Intentionally random samples are rare in criminal justice practice. They may be intended in traffic stops or tax audits, or in jury selection,

---

[7] Fyfe (1996, 2002) gives an example of selection bias at the jurisdictional level: studies of policing appear to be biased to the extent that the agencies that consent to be studied tend to be more progressive.

but these are exceptions, and they are often corrupted in spite of initial design specifications. Selection effects are built intentionally into most crime-solving efforts of law enforcement, in the selection of suspects and in decisions to arrest and convict. Questions of legality and social costs associated with controversial selection processes known as "profiling" are taken up in Chapter 7.

Unmeasured Factors

Even when the samples are representative of the population, statistical research can yield invalid interpretations. A common threat to validity occurs when the data collected for analysis fail to account for key factors that influence the dependent variable of primary interest. When those omitted factors precede both the observed independent variable (i.e., presumed causative factor) or variables and the dependent variable (i.e., presumed effect), and are correlated with both, the findings that show up will be spurious to the extent of the unmeasured correlations between the omitted variables and the ones included. The result will be an effect erroneously attributed to an independent variable (or variables) included in the analysis that in fact is attributable to an omitted factor or set of factors.[8]

This problem can create systematic errors in criminal justice. Sentencing guidelines based on findings of the effect of prior record on recidivism, for example, should be adjusted to ensure that the effects observed control for age. Failure to do so could unduly penalize older offenders, who tend to have long criminal records relative to their likelihood of reoffending than younger offenders. Three-strikes laws have been known to produce such errors (Kleiman, 2000; Skolnick, 1994).

Statistical inquiry can be led astray also when the omitted factors mediate the effect of an independent variable on a dependent variable, when two independent variables are said to "interact." A negative interaction indicates that the combined effect of the two variables is less than the sum of the independent effects of each; a positive

---

[8] A standard textbook example is the finding of a correlation between shoe size and spelling ability among grade-school children when age is omitted from the analysis.

interaction indicates the existence of a symbiotic relationship between the two, so that the whole is greater than the simple sum of the parts. A series of experiments on the effect of arrest for domestic violence on subsequent episodes of the crime have revealed that arrest tends to deter employed offenders from committing the crime again, but to provoke unemployed batterers to reoffend – a negative interaction between arrest and employment status (Sherman, 1992). Mandatory arrest policies may be justifiable on ethical grounds, but they may put certain populations in jeopardy, endangering victims of unemployed offenders and inducing them to be less inclined to notify the police in times of harm. Initial evidence on the effect of arrest on subsequent episodes of domestic violence failed to account for the interaction between employment status and arrest – the mediating effect of employment – and may thus have led to legislation and policy that imposed excessive costs on victims of crime, in the name of serving them.

Unmeasured factors have been known to create other errors in policing and adjudication. Due process errors can result when police and prosecutors pursue innocent people who fit offender profiles and happen coincidentally to show up at the wrong place at the wrong time. Unmeasured factors such as prior record and employment status can be critical in these cases, and justice errors can result from failures to consider exculpatory evidence, especially when witness identification, crime scene, or evidence processing procedures are flawed and the police and prosecutor feel compelled to achieve closure through arrest and conviction. By contrast, lapses in crime control may be attributed to bad fortune or skillful offenders when an ineffectual investigation is really the problem, when the police have overlooked incriminating evidence or witness accounts that are in fact available.

Other Threats to Validity

There are a host of other threats to validity in statistical research.[9] Two that are loosely parallel to systematic justice errors are testing effects

---

[9] Common threats to validity not dealt with here include regression effects, history effects, Hawthorne effects, instrumentation effects, experimental contamination, circular relationships among key variables ("simultaneity"), and Pygmalion effects (Babbie, 1995).

and experimental mortality. The *testing effect* occurs when a subject performs differently after having been exposed to an intervention or other independent variable of interest. Experiments designed to establish whether an intervention works to improve test scores typically measure a panel of experimentals and a panel of controls before and after the intervention, but some of what emerges after the intervention may be the ability of subjects to answer the questions more accurately the second time simply because they have seen the questions before.[10] This problem has its counterpart in criminal justice practice: both prosecutors and defense lawyers may coach their witnesses before trial to ensure that the witnesses do not volunteer statements favorable to the other side. This could reduce errors by minimizing thoughtless testimony, but might more often create errors by allowing witnesses for one side or the other to conceal critical elements of the whole truth more credibly.

Panel attrition (or *experimental mortality*) is another problem in many longitudinal studies in which the same group of individuals is measured over time. The problem arises when some individuals start off as panel members and then either drop out or cannot be found after some point during the study. This poses a threat to validity, introducing systematic error when the ones who drop out differ from those who do not in some important way. Even when the dropouts are like the others, panel attrition poses a threat to reliability when the number of dropouts reduces the number of subjects remaining to a statistically unstable level.

The problem of panel attrition has approximate parallels both in errors of due process and errors of impunity. Due process is jeopardized when exculpatory evidence is found and then ignored or discarded, either inadvertently or intentionally. Inadvertent errors can be minimized through the use of systematic crime scene and evidence collection procedures, and intentional errors can be minimized through strict administrative control and no-nonsense disciplinary and legal

---

[10] The testing effect can be analytically disentangled from the effect of the intervention through the use of a four-group "Solomon" design, in which two groups (an experimental and a control) are pre-tested and the other two are not, while all four groups are post-tested (Babbie, 1995, p. 245).

action. The ability of the criminal justice system to control crime is threatened, by contrast, when large caseloads of investigators and prosecutors limit follow-up work or when witnesses who are inclined initially to support the prosecutor and victim are threatened by the offender. The solution to these problems is essentially the same as in empirical research: track subjects and remain sensitive to their needs in order to encourage continuing participation.

Parallels between Errors of Statistical Inference and Errors of Justice

Table 4.1 summarizes parallels between errors of inference in statistical research and errors of justice noted earlier.

While parallels are apparent, some closer than others, an equally apparent difference emerges from these comparisons: the means for dealing with errors differ considerably across the two domains. Threats to the accuracy of the results of statistical inference are countered by research designs that aim to ensure that the results are valid and reliable, whereas threats to due process and crime control are more

Table 4.1. *Parallels between Errors of Inference and Errors of Justice*

Errors of Inference	Errors of Due Process	Errors of Impunity
Threats to Reliability:		
Sampling error	Defendant in wrong place, wrong time, circumstantial case	Evidence collected turns out not to be the strongest available
Threats to Validity:		
Selection bias	Discriminatory profiling	Sticking with wrong suspect
Omitted variables	Withheld exculpatory evidence	Weak investigation
Testing effect	Coaching government witnesses to avoid certain responses	Coaching defense witnesses to avoid certain responses
Panel attrition	Exculpatory evidence observed, not documented or collected	Witness intimidation

likely to be countered by attempts to ensure the victory of one side of the case over the other, often at the expense of accuracy. If there is an imbalance of power, as is often the case with indigent defendants, biased presentation of the facts may be guaranteed. Researchers have been known to operate as advocates, selecting research design options guaranteed to produce a desired set of results, but such practices are usually discovered when other researchers fail to either replicate the results or produce similar results under sound alternative research designs. Lack of objectivity is no virtue in research. Prosecutors and defense counsel, by contrast, may not be praised so much for their objectivity as for their reputation for pursuing their respective sides as vigorously as possible, for achieving victory over the other side.[11]

A basic principle common to both research and the law is that purposefulness and follow-through can reduce errors in both domains. Otherwise, the standard responses to threats to validity and reliability in statistical applications have limited relevance for the criminal justice system under the adversarial model. Random samples that aim to eliminate selection effects have especially limited applications in criminal justice practice, except for the occasional use of random stops as an alternative to profiling to intervene against prospective offenders – for example, along common drug trafficking routes and to deal with drunk driving on New Year's Eve. Removals of jurors for cause and peremptory challenges guarantee that jury selection is anything but random. Principles designed to ensure dispassionate scientific inference may be more at home in most Continental European courts of civil law than in the adversarial common law setting that characterizes criminal courts in the United States and England.

Managing Errors in Production and Service Delivery Processes

The twentieth century was marked by extraordinary productivity growth, much of it fueled by two revolutions: unprecedented

---

[11] Courtroom joke: When the law is against you, argue the facts; when the facts are against you, argue the law; when both are against you, pound the table.

technological advances in production processes in the first two-thirds of the century and unprecedented advances in information technology in the last third. Much of the productivity gains, especially in the former, can be attributed to the development of quality control systems developed and promoted by Frederick W. Taylor, W. Edwards Deming, and other pioneers of scientific production management. Quality control systems were applied as well to the service delivery sector that mushroomed in the latter half of the century. Accreditation services are now available for firms that wish to advertise that they are certified as having met standards of quality management systems in place.[12]

At the heart of these systems is a commitment to quality and a toolkit that aims to improve quality by analyzing the risks and errors associated with alternative policies, strategies, and organizational approaches. The tools in the kit include deterministic models that solve relationships among inputs and outputs algebraically, optimization models that find solutions involving the maximization of effectiveness subject to capacity and budget constraints (or minimization of costs subject to minimum standards of performance), simulation modeling when the systems are too complex to solve otherwise, and charts that display the effects of selected inputs and configurations on error rates under a variety of assumptions and settings (Banks, 1989; Kolarik, 1999; Evans and Olson, 1998; Vose, 2000).

One standard approach for managing errors in both production processes and service delivery settings (hospitals are a prime example) is the use of check sheets that record and organize data on errors. The Japanese led in much of the development and uses of these tools in the 1980s (Ishikawa, 1985; Taguchi, 2002). In a criminal justice setting, the use of such a tool to manage errors might begin by specifying the dimensions of the check sheet, following the consideration of these sorts of questions: What are the major sources of errors in a department or office (police, prosecution, adjudication, sentencing, and corrections)? How do these vary by crime situation, type of

---

[12] Organizations such as BMI Management Systems and QMS International are authorized to register, certify, and accredit companies around the world for quality control in product and service delivery under the ISO 9000 and ISO 14000 (International Organization for Standardization) series standards.

neighborhood setting, time of year, day of week, and time of day, type of personnel involved (e.g., patrol officer or investigator, experience level of prosecutor), and so on? How can we more systematically obtain information documenting errors in each major category of these dimensions? An analysis of these check sheets over a period of, say, a year could help to establish how resources might be redeployed to reduce the most frequent and costly types of errors.

Parallels between the problem of quality control in the production of products and delivery of services and the problem of criminal justice errors are readily apparent. While trends in quality control such as Total Quality Management (TQM) may have limited value for the criminal justice system,[13] the idea of transporting quality control principles and tools of proven effectiveness in production and service delivery processes to another domain – to assess criminal justice policies in terms of their effects on errors of justice – seems a worthy prospect. We will explore this prospect by using tools of quality control to consider the effects of different criminal justice policy options on errors of justice in subsequent chapters: standards of evidence (Chapter 6) and the prosecutor's choice between an emphasis on quality or number of convictions (Chapter 8). It is not difficult to imagine the use of such approaches as well in the assessment of alternative investigative profiling strategies, parole release guideline systems, and other complex decision processes involving errors of both due process and crime control.

Conclusion

Most criminologists and scholars of the criminal justice system embrace the scientific method, not only out of their appreciation for the coherence and rigor of science, and the power it brings to the goals of achieving predictive accuracy and explanatory validity, but to a degree also out of a desire to elevate their status within the academy. James Q. Wilson, in his landmark 1974 essay, "Thinking About Crime," which

---

[13] See, for example, Peter Manning's critique of TQM applications as fad in policing (Forst and Manning, 1999, pp. 80–91).

was expanded into one of the most widely read books ever written in the field, suggests that criminologists had abandoned scientific analysis when it was most needed. He wrote that, in the 1960s, "when social scientists were asked for advice by national policy making bodies, they could not respond with suggestions derived from and supported by their scholarly work" (p. 44–45). He went on to say that they "were speaking out of ideology, not scholarship" (p. 62) and that the focal concerns of their tradition were largely "beyond the reach of science" (p. 63).

In the intervening years, long strides have been made to bring the rigor and respectability of science to the work of criminology and criminal justice scholarship. We still do not attempt to persuade physical scientists that analyses of human behavior and policy lend themselves neatly to the theoretical and empirical frameworks of inquiry that are used routinely in particle physics, organic chemistry, and cellular biology, but we have made progress. Still, we are not yet a mature science, not in the way that Otis Dudley Duncan asserts in the quote that opens this chapter: a science that properly manages its errors. Duncan is speaking primarily of managing errors in variables rather than errors in policies, and the differences are important. They are not so great, however, that we should abandon opportunities to examine the commonalities and improve our ability to manage errors in both domains, at least for the sake of science.

CHAPTER FIVE

Assessing the Cost of Justice Errors

It is better that ten guilty persons escape than one innocent person suffer.

– Blackstone (1765, Book IV, Chapter 27)

Introduction

It is often said that it is better to free several true offenders than to convict an innocent person, with "several" typically taking on numbers like 2, or Blackstone's famous "10," or 99.[1] But what are the justifications for such numbers? Should the ratio be the same for people charged with shoplifting and those charged with serial rape or child molestation? If not, why not? Do the ratios apply equally to cases that come to trial, cases filed in court, and to larger pools of suspects?[2] Blackstone's dictum places an arbitrary lower bound on the tradeoff, leaving open the question, "How *much* better?," thus side-stepping an assessment of the respective social costs of each type of error.[3] It can be safely

---

[1] Voltaire (1749) may have been more interested in crime control than Blackstone and others: "It is better to risk saving a guilty person than to condemn an innocent one" (*Zadig*, Chapter 6).

[2] Recall from Chapter 1 that some nine million felonies reported to the police each year do not end in conviction, while a 1 percent rate of erroneous convictions implies some 10,000 innocent persons convicted annually, a ratio of 900 to 1 from the perspective of crimes reported to the police. The ratio is likely to be substantially smaller for cases that go to trial.

[3] One can infer that Blackstone meant "only very slightly better," reasoning that he would have given a larger number had he meant "much better." Alternatively, one can infer that he meant "much better," offering the number 10 as a conservative assessment of the proper tradeoff. Oliver Wendell Holmes was even less specific: "We have to choose, and for my part I think it a less evil that some criminals should escape than that the government should play an ignoble part" (*Olmstead v. U.S.*, 277 U.S.438 [1928]).

said only that civil libertarians tend to prefer large numbers, while law-and-order conservatives tend to prefer smaller ones.

Such preferences are based largely on opposing ethical positions. The civil libertarian places a higher premium on the need to protect the innocent, and the offender as well, against wrongful intrusions by police and prosecutors. The law-and-order conservative generally places a high premium on the need to protect citizens against offenders. These positions are often justified by the selective use of data: civil libertarians and progressives are more inclined to express concern over wrongful convictions and conservatives more inclined to express concern over "super-predators" who commit a disproportionate number of crimes and are then allowed to commit further crimes by a system that releases them from custody too soon.

The tools discussed in the previous chapter may be useful for estimating the incidence of such errors, but knowing the effect of decisions, policies and laws on the incidence of errors does not provide a sufficient basis for assessing those acts. We should also wish to know the harms and consequences of those errors. To what lengths should we be willing to go to prevent each type of error and the associated harms? To provide the basis for developing a calculus of decision making and policy assessment that considers those consequences, it is necessary first to have a coherent logic for weighing the errors and the costs of reducing them. The field of welfare economics provides the foundation for such a framework in the concept of social costs. In this chapter we shall consider the prospect of assessing errors of justice in terms of social costs and the difficulties associated with making such assessments.

What Are the Social Costs of Crime and Justice?

The *social cost* of any act – for the present purposes a crime, a public or private intervention, an erroneous conviction, a misallocation of police resources and the crimes that result, and so on – is the net reduction in aggregate wealth associated with the act (Posner, 1981, pp. 60–115). Because the theft of money involves a transfer from victim to thief, resulting in no immediate aggregate loss of wealth, some prefer to use *external costs* rather than social costs as the metric of choice, ignoring the offender's gains (Cohen, 2000; Cook, 1983; Trumbull, 1990; McChesney, 1993). The theft of nonmoney property is more complicated, since the value of the property to the victim is usually higher than to the thief, who must either bear transaction costs to convert the property to cash or live with a good that is often the product of opportunity rather than thoughtful selection.[4] For our purposes, the use of either social costs or external costs will be suitable.[5]

Social costs have two primary components: costs associated with crimes and costs associated with private and public actions to prevent and respond to crime. The *crime costs* include the costs associated with injury or death (medical costs, costs of pain and suffering), losses and damages to property, and lost income. Most of these costs are borne by the victim, often over a lifetime,[6] but some – including insurance coverage of medical costs and property losses, productivity losses covered by employers, victim service agency costs, and increased fear of crime in the community – are borne by society at large. The *costs of prevention and response* include expenditures for the criminal justice system (sworn officers, civilians, capital, fuel, supplies, and so on), expenditures for security personnel, security and surveillance systems (locks, hardened targets, protected parking facilities, cameras, movement sensors, alarms, etc.) purchased by private citizens and commercial establishments, costs incurred by dependents of incarcerated offenders[7] and by witnesses whose time is taken up with police interviews and court obligations, and costs associated with

---

[4] Value to the victim often includes unrecoverable sentimental value that exceeds replacement cost of the property. Insurance effects further complicate the calculus.

[5] The question of whether to include the offender's gain from crime is a moral one, outside the development of a general framework for assessing errors. Our interest is in developing a framework that will accommodate either treatment of the offender's gains. Accordingly, we will use the term "social cost" loosely as though it either includes or excludes the offender's gains, as the reader prefers. The question of whether to consider the offender's utility is another such concern in sanctioning policy, one that is taken up in Chapter 10.

[6] Macmillan (2000) reports substantial reductions in lifetime earning streams for adolescent victims of crime.

[7] Piehl, Useem, and DiIulio (1999) report that most inmates are parents, with about 65 percent of inmates helping to support at least one dependent at the time of arrest.

Table 5.1. *Public and Private Costs of Crime and Crime Interventions*

	Incurred Privately	Incurred Publicly
Costs of Crime	Property stolen or damaged, not covered by insurance Pain, suffering (physical, emotional) Medical expenses, uninsured Lost income Loss of life Missed school	Insurance costs for theft Victim service agency costs Insurance costs for medical claims Lost productivity of victims Lost commerce in high-crime areas Increased fear of crime in the community
Costs of Prevention and Intervention	Private security personnel Locks, hardened targets, surveillance and alarm systems Community crime prevention participation (labor, outlays) Dependents deprived of incomes, services of incarcerated people Lost income, freedom for innocent suspects detained by CJS Victim and witness time lost in interviews, testimony	Criminal justice system personnel Capital equipment, buildings for police, prosecutors, courts, jails, and corrections Public support of crime prevention programs Lost productivity of incarcerated offenders, witnesses while interviewed, in court

community crime prevention activities.[8] These costs are summarized in Table 5.1.

Difficulties in Assessing the Social Costs of Crime and Justice

Many of these costs are extremely elusive. Even reported estimates of tangible losses to crime, such as the value of property stolen, are suspect. How accurate are recollections of the amount of cash stolen? Some victims might have reasons to understate those amounts (e.g.,

---

[8] I do not address here whether expenditures on crime prevention activities are optimal, that is, whether they are allocated to resources that minimize the expected present value of the stream of future crimes against the persons and properties of interest.

embarrassment), others to overstate them (e.g., insurance claims). Should property stolen be assessed at original cost, depreciated cost, or replacement cost? Should we ignore the sentimental value to the victim of stolen family keepsakes? Here are two particularly vexing questions regarding the problem of assessing the social costs of crime:

- How can we estimate the dollar cost equivalent of a victim's *pain and suffering*, especially with crimes such as rape or child abuse?
- How can we estimate the social costs associated with failures to convict crimes in which the *victims* are *difficult to identify*, such as drug use and trafficking offenses and white collar crime?

Thoughtful people disagree about the answers to these questions. That the assessments are debatable and elusive, however, does not mean that they ought to be ignored. To have an imperfect sense of the social costs of the justice errors associated with alternative interventions, or to have to deal with the complexity of multiple assessments based on different sets of values and assumptions, is likely to be better than to have no sense at all. Some decision rules and policies may turn out to be superior or inferior under *any* reasonable approach to assessing an elusive social cost, and we should like to know which decision rules and policies are thus dominant or inferior. Let us consider these two questions in more depth, to provide a basis for assessments that are mindful of the difficulties and internally consistent.

Pain and Suffering

Intangible costs of crime can be assessed in a variety of ways. One way is to survey victims and prospective victims, asking what they would be willing to pay to avoid the discomforts of crime. Another is to impute such values from revealed preferences, such as amounts spent on crime prevention resources and the higher cost of homes in low-crime areas. Still another is to use the values arrived at by juries that have deliberated on the worth of such elusive harms. Each of these approaches has its strengths and weaknesses. A thorough assessment system might well draw from all three approaches.

Asking people what they would be willing to pay to avoid being victimized by crime has the virtue of directness, but the weakness of abstraction. This approach typically involves a battery of questions designed to elicit responses to a variety of aspects of crime, including the type and amount of property stolen or destroyed, physical harm, emotional harm, diminished capacity, and harm to loved ones. Can such responses be trusted? Since the questions are hypothetical, what guarantee do we have that the payments stated are not either exaggerated or understated? Should the amounts offered by actual victims be assigned more weight than the amounts offered by prospective victims? How much more? Can we really expect an actual victim of a crime like rape or child abuse to think about an amount that they would pay to avoid having been victimized by the crime? What sort of adjustments, if any, should be made to deal with the fact that poor respondents are less able to make such expenditures and are likely to offer smaller amounts than wealthy respondents?[9]

Imputing the intangible cost of crime from revealed preferences, the actual amounts spent on crime prevention devices and services, has the virtue of credibility, overcoming the dubiousness of responses to hypothetical questions, but brings another set of difficulties. Actual expenditures are likely to reflect flawed assessments of the likelihood of being victimized by various types of crimes. They are likely to reflect flawed estimates of the deterrent effect of each type of expenditure on crime. Do homeowners have any idea what effect an additional $250 for a more substantial front door will actually have on the likelihood of break-in and, in turn, on the likely amount of property or violence thus prevented? What portion of such expenditures were actually made for reasons other than security, such as design or improved performance? Higher expenditures to prevent crime, moreover, will not distinguish between the tangible and intangible costs of crime. They will reflect ability to pay, with poor people spending less, in spite of the fact that the inner-city poor are subject to the highest rates of victimization. They will reflect different degrees of risk aversion. The estimates will be confounded as well by externalities, such as my benefitting from or

---

[9] Frank and Sunstein argue that estimates of willingness to pay tend to be understated because of reluctance to make voluntary payments when those payments lower one's living standard. If relative living standards matter, individuals will value collective increases in safety more highly than they will increases in safety that they alone purchase.

being harmed by my neighbors' having guns and dogs. It is unclear that one can meaningfully extract assessments of the cost of pain and suffering, or even valid assessments of tangible costs, from such an amalgam of difficulties.

Juries have assigned values to intangibles in arriving at awards to victims and their dependents for harms caused by crime. These have the obvious advantages of explicitness, deliberation, and consensus, but they bring another set of problems. They may include punitive assessments, even in the face of instructions to ignore such considerations. They are subject to extreme variation, by jurisdiction and the unique mix of jurors making the assessment.[10] They are typically designed to "make the person whole" rather than to assess the cost of pain and suffering, and the two may be quite different.

Offenses with Hard-to-Identify Victims
Estimating the social costs of individual crimes, essential for assessing lapses in bringing offenders to justice, is difficult enough for crimes such as burglary, and more difficult still for crimes involving large intangible costs, such as rape. It may be even more problematic for crimes without immediate victims, like drugs, prostitution, gambling, and many white collar offenses. Since drug crimes account for a larger percentage of correctional populations than any other crime, it will be especially useful to examine the difficulties in assessing the social costs associated with drug crimes. Our drug laws are justified largely on the grounds that drugs harm society by producing higher levels of street crime, due partly to drug users committing crimes to support drug habits, partly to pharmacological effects of drugs, and partly to complex drug-crime culture effects. The nature and magnitude of these effects appear to vary substantially by drug type.[11] But the laws have been justified on other grounds as well: drugs impose costly health problems on society; drugs hinder productivity and social well-being; if drugs were legal they would be in more homes, hence more accessible to children.

---

[10] Cohen (2000) has noted that jury awards are more predictable than is widely asserted, especially for common case categories (p. 286).
[11] These effects are explored in some depth by Boyum and Kleiman (2002).

A major difficulty in assessing the social costs of drug offenses is that
a significant portion of the costs may be attributable to *interventions*
against drug use rather than to drug use itself. One example: Drugs
might not be so pharmacologically dangerous if they were made available as a controlled substance. Another example: Drug-turf-war crimes
 would be sharply reduced if drugs were available through legitimate
sources. Yet another: Supply-side drug strategies raise the retail price
of illegal drugs, increasing the number of crimes committed in order
to raise the money needed to support drug habits. And this: Drug enforcement tends to corrupt the police. Many of these effects and the
associated costs are elusive. Attempts to estimate them may nonetheless provide a basis for determining levels of each type of enforcement
mechanism for each type of drug that minimize the total social costs
of drug use and interventions designed to curtail drug use (Harwood,
Fountain and Livermore, 1998; Cohen, 2000).

White collar crimes present a different set of difficulties. They are,
for one thing, an assemblage of crimes ranging from fraud, in which
the victims are often readily identifiable, to bribery of a public official, in which some victims will be harmed more than others and we
cannot know precisely who they are, or how many. These crimes are,
moreover, an assemblage in which some, like bribery and consumer
fraud, are much more difficult to detect and measure than others, like
embezzlement.

Optimal Levels of Interventions Against Crime

Regardless of whether we have estimates of the costs of crime and
interventions that can be regarded as suitable for policy purposes, it
is useful to have a conceptual framework for determining "optimal"
sanction levels for each type of crime, sanctions that minimize the total
social cost of crime and the sanctions themselves. Such a framework
can provide a basis as well for determining, at least conceptually, optimal levels of each major component of the criminal justice system –
policing, prosecution and courts, and corrections – and the aggregate
level of expenditure on the criminal justice system.

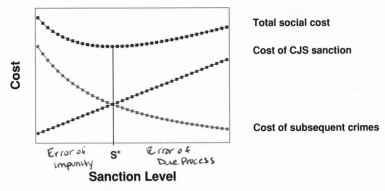

Figure 5.1. Optimal Sanction Level

The notion of an optimal sanction level presumes that as a sanction becomes more severe and more costly, at least over some range, it will reduce crime and its associated costs. A large body of theoretical and empirical information on the deterrent and incapacitative effects of sanctions offers some support for this presumption (Blumstein et al., 1978; Levitt, 2002). At some point, however, the marginal increase in the social cost of the sanction will not be offset by the marginal decrease in the social cost of crime produced by the sanction. At that point, the social cost of the sanction will equal the social cost of the amount of crime associated with that sanction. This is depicted in Figure 5.1.

The basic framework can be used, at least conceptually, to assess a particular sanction, a component of the criminal justice system, or the level of spending for the criminal justice system as a whole.[12] Departures in either direction from the optimal level, S*, will produce systematic errors of justice. For a given sanction or intervention, say random traffic stops by the police or a mandatory sentencing law for a particular type of offense, the intervention will be biased toward errors of impunity if the level of the intervention falls below S*, and will be

---

[12] An important corollary set of problems has to do with complementarity and substitutability among criminal justice inputs. An increase or decrease in a particular sanction cannot validly be assessed independently of the effect of the change on other inputs. Drug treatment programs, for example, are likely to be both a substitute for and complement of prosecution and conviction.

biased increasingly toward errors of due process as the intervention level rises above S*. For interventions that are ineffective at any positive level of use, the cost of crimes function will not decline as the intervention increases, and in some cases the intervention might well aggravate matters and cause crime to increase.

Initial Estimates

The difficulties discussed above have not prevented adventuresome attempts to estimate the social costs of crimes, and to do so by crime category. For many offense categories, the range of estimated costs per crime is not, in fact, as broad as one might expect. Cohen documents three estimates of the average cost of an index (felony, essentially) crime, ranging from $1200 to $2300 in 1993 dollars (Cohen 2000, p. 291). These estimates provide the basis for estimating the total social cost of crime in the United States – the sum of all four quadrants of Table 5.1 – with similar variation in the assessments. Miller, Cohen, and Wiersema (1996) estimate the total cost at $450 billion annually in 1993 dollars for all victimizations from 1987 to 1990, with tangible costs (value of property stolen, medical costs, lost income) accounting for 25 percent of the total. Laband and Sophocleus (1992) estimate $450 billion in 1985 for the cost of crime and insurance against crime and another $180 billion for public and private expenditures for crime prevention and intervention resources. Anderson (1999) estimates that the total burden of crime in the United States exceeds $1 trillion.[13] While the estimates for individual crime categories offered by Miller, Cohen, and Wiersema suggest a degree of precision that belies the difficulties in making such estimates – sexual abuse of children ($99,000), physical abuse of children ($67,000), emotional abuse of children ($27,000), rape ($87,000), arson ($38,000), and so on – such estimates nonetheless provide a starting point for weighing lapses in crime control against errors of due process.

---

[13] Even this high estimate may be too small, if we include the opportunity costs associated with existing policies, practices, and laws that are substantially less than optimal.

Conclusion

These estimates of the social cost of individual crimes leave several critical pieces of information unanswered: What are the social costs of the detention, conviction, and incarceration of an innocent person? What is the social cost of an excessive term of incarceration for a culpable offender? How do we assess culpability?[14] When do ethical considerations trump utilitarian ones? For example, is a policy of mandatory arrest for domestic violence justifiable even if it raises the incidence of subsequent crimes for certain classes of offender? How can we know whether a term of incarceration is excessive or insufficient in terms of its social costs if we do not have reliable estimates of the deterrent and incapacitative effects of confinement for various classes of offenders?

One of the more critical prospective uses of the framework proposed here is to assess the value of various types of criminal justice data.[15] Statistical decision theory offers concepts and constructs for estimating the cost of imperfect information,[16] and it should be possible to build on such notions to provide estimates of the social costs associated with parameter values that are either missing or of questionable accuracy. Such estimates could help to shape the priorities and policies of federal, state, and local criminal justice statistics agencies.

At this point, we can say safely that integrating elements of the notion of social costs with elements of the logic of statistical inference will not eliminate prospects for ideology to trump objectivity in the development of an error-sensitive justice policy. In the domain of scientific inquiry, the development of an elaborate system of theoretical and empirical methods aimed at minimizing opportunities for ideology to drive the results of analysis has not eliminated all prospects for

[14] There are several ways to build this desert-based concept into a utilitarian framework, either to assess sentence terms or manage case processing errors. A utilitarian approach might be to regard the social cost of a crime as a measure of its culpability. Alternatives involve the use of consensus-scaling approaches such as the Sellin-Wolfgang method (Blumstein et al., 1986, Volume I, p. 401), or statutory maximum or minimum sentences. See also Chapter 1, Note 7, supra.

[15] I thank Joan Petersilia for pointing this out.

[16] Such estimates have been made in other domains, such as the value of weather forecasting (Costello, Adams, and Polasky, 1998; Hamlet, Huppert, and Lettenmaier, 2002).

research mischief. The use of such a system is likely, however, to have reduced the risk of such mischief in research; such a system could similarly reduce opportunities for mischief in the justice system as well. Surely, it can't hurt to try. In the process, we may be able to examine more consciously the barriers that block the path to criminal justice policies that are mindful of errors of justice and their social costs. That could be a significant step forward.

CHAPTER SIX

Standards of Evidence

Proof beyond a reasonable doubt is proof that leaves you firmly convinced of the defendant's guilt. There are very few things in this world that we know with absolute certainty, and in criminal cases the law does not require proof that overcomes every possible doubt. If, based on your consideration of the evidence, you are firmly convinced that the defendant is guilty of the crime or crimes charged, you must find him guilty. If, on the other hand, you think there is a real possibility that he is not guilty, you must give him the benefit of the doubt and find him not guilty.

– 133 Sample Jury Instructions [18 U.S.C. §§ 241 (1997)]

Introduction

Our criminal courts work to achieve justice by establishing guilt and, for defendants found guilty, sanctioning them in accordance with the law. Establishing guilt involves a fact-finding process that aims to determine whether the evidence is sufficient to prove beyond a reasonable doubt that the defendant is guilty of the crime charged. This rule is actually invoked only for the relatively few cases that go to trial – some 85 to 90 percent of all felony convictions are by plea[1] – but the interpretation of the rule by juries and judges (not all trials use juries, and judges may influence the jury's interpretation in those that do) lies at the heart of the problem of finding a balance between the error of convicting an innocent person and that of failing to convict a true offender.

---

[1] See Forst (2002), p. 511.

Here is the central question in this interpretation: What precisely is meant by "proof beyond a reasonable doubt"? The model instructions to juries quoted at the head of this chapter provides a sense of an answer, but where precisely the line is drawn between "firmly convinced" and "less than firmly convinced" is itself less than firm. This chapter examines the effect of different placements of that line on errors of justice. It considers, specifically, the effects of changes in standards of proof both on what we call due process errors and errors of impunity by establishing relationships among three variables: the percentage of cases with true offenders, the conviction rate, and the percentage of defendants convicted who actually committed the crime. It then qualifies the results in terms of threats to validity related to adaptive behaviors of criminal justice practitioners and real-world circumstances that lie outside the assumptions on which the estimates are made.

Varying the Parameters

Let us now consider the effects of increases and decreases in the threshold of evidence needed to convict a person in trial on justice errors: proof beyond a reasonable doubt. Available data from state and local prosecutors and courts suggest that the current standard of evidentiary proof results in about 75 percent of all persons whose cases come to trial being found guilty (Boland and Sones, 1986; DeFrances and Steadman, 1998; Forst, 2002). We do not know how many of those found guilty actually committed the crimes for which they were convicted and how many did not; if we had an independent, inexpensive, and just way of knowing which offenders were truly culpable and which were not, we would not need our elaborate system of justice to attempt to make such determinations.[2] We can nonetheless examine the effects of changes in those standards by assuming different levels of factual guilt under current conviction rates and calculating the ratio of

---

[2] Reversals of convictions associated with DNA evidence provide a unique opportunity to discover errors; the Innocence Project at the Benjamin N. Cardozo School of Law had reported 110 as of late 2002 (Associated Press, 2002). But these cases are anything but a random sample of all convictions – for example, a disproportionate number involve sexual assault (Connors et al., 1996, p. 12) – and there is no independent measure of the extent of bias in this unique sample of cases.

Table 6.1. *70 Percent Conviction Rate, 80 Percent True Offenders, 1 Percent Conviction Error Rate*

	Factually Guilty	Factually Innocent	Total
Convicted	693	**7**	700
Acquitted	**107**	193	300
Total	800	200	1000

exonerated true offenders to convicted innocent persons under each set of assumptions.

Scenario 1 uses a threshold of proof beyond reasonable doubt that produces a conviction rate of 70 percent of all trials and the assumptions that 80 percent of all persons who go to trial actually committed the crime and 99 percent of those convicted are factually guilty.[3] For a pool of 1,000 persons who go to trial under this scenario, the errors – the number of guilty offenders exonerated and number of innocent persons convicted – are shown in bold in all tables.

We see for this first scenario that 10.7 percent of all persons who go to trial are erroneously acquitted, while 0.7 percent are erroneously convicted, a ratio of about *15* offenders set free for each truly innocent person convicted, with a total error rate of 11.4 percent of all cases.[4]

---

[3] The 1.3 percent exoneration rate among death row inmates noted earlier would seem to suggest that the 99 percent assumption is too high. Huff et al., 1996 (p. xiv), estimate that only 0.5 percent of all persons convicted of felonies are innocent of the charges. Moreover, a number of these exonerations were based on procedural errors that do not necessarily imply factual innocence in the crime. On the other hand, it is conceivable that more than 80 of the 6,000 death row sentences may be factually innocent and not exonerated. Moreover, the standard of proof is likely to be higher in capital cases than in others. Accordingly, half of the calculations reported here assume the much higher error rate of 5 percent.

[4] These results can be derived from the assumed information using basic laws of probability. If we denote P(G) as the probability that a defendant is factually guilty, P($^\sim$G) as the probability that he is not factually guilty, P(C) as the probability of conviction, P($^\sim$C) as the probability that the defendant is not convicted, and P($^\sim$G|C) as the conviction error rate, the number of offenders set free per innocent person convicted will be

$$\frac{P(G) - P(C)[1 - P(^\sim G|C)]}{P(C) \cdot (^\sim P(G|C))},$$

and the total error rate will be: $P(G) - P(C) [1 - 2P(^\sim G|C)]$.

Table 6.2. *50 Percent Conviction Rate, 80 Percent True
Offenders, 1 Percent Conviction Error Rate*

	Factually Guilty	Factually Innocent	Total
Convicted	495	5	500
Acquitted	**305**	195	500
Total	800	200	1000

Table 6.3. *40 Percent Conviction Rate, 80 Percent True
Offenders, 1 Percent Conviction Error Rate*

	Factually Guilty	Factually Innocent	Total
Convicted	396	4	400
Acquitted	**404**	196	600
Total	800	200	1000

Now suppose the threshold of proof beyond a reasonable doubt
is raised so that only half are convicted rather than 70 percent. Assuming everything else the same as in Scenario 1, this scenario produces a
substantially higher ratio of offenders set free for each truly innocent
person convicted: *61 to one* (see Table 6.2). Notice also that the shift
from Scenario 1 to 2 reduces by two the number of innocent persons
convicted while increasing the number of offenders who escape conviction by 198, a ratio of 99 to one, thus increasing the total error rate
from 11.4 percent to 31.0 percent of all cases.

Now suppose the threshold of proof beyond a reasonable doubt is
raised further so that only 40 percent are convicted. Assuming all else
the same as in Scenarios 1 and 2, this scenario produces a still higher
ratio of offenders set free for each truly innocent person convicted: *101
to one* (see Table 6.3). The total error rate increases to 40.8 percent
of all cases under this scenario.

Suppose next that the evidentiary standard of proof beyond a reasonable doubt were lowered from Scenario 1 rather than raised, so that
four-fifths of all persons who went to trial were convicted. Assuming
that all else were the same as in Scenarios 1 through 3, this scenario
produces a ratio that might make Justice Holmes and most of the rest

Table 6.4. *80 Percent Conviction Rate, 80 Percent True Offenders, 1 Percent Conviction Error Rate*

	Factually Guilty	Factually Innocent	Total
Convicted	792	8	800
Acquitted	8	192	200
Total	800	200	1000

of us quite uncomfortable: now, for each offender set free we end up with one truly innocent person convicted (see Table 6.4). Of course, the increase of 99 convicted offenders associated with the 10 percent higher conviction rate seems like decent compensation for the additional innocent person convicted, as does the associated reduction in the total error rate from 11.4 percent to 1.6 percent. Still, the eight innocent persons convicted somehow seems to loom larger when the errors of allowing offenders to escape conviction are also at eight.

We can organize the above information in the form of a table showing the effect of a change in the standard of evidence on the ratio of offenders set free per innocent person convicted for different assumptions about the percentage of cases in which the accused is a true offender. This summary is shown in Table 6.5, with the results shown graphically in Figures 6.1a and 6.1b.

We also can summarize the total error rate across the various scenarios. The results are shown in Table 6.6.

The results of Tables 6.5 and 6.6 reflect the confluence of three important factors that shape errors of justice: wrongful arrests, wrongful convictions, and the conviction rate. Within the range of assumptions considered, a decline in the conviction rate produces increases both in the number of offenders freed per innocent person convicted and in the total percentage of cases erroneously decided.

1. the percentage of defendants who actually committed the crime decreases,
2. the percentage of cases with true offenders increases, and
3. the conviction rate declines.

The obvious problem with the numbers used in these scenarios is that we don't know which set is nearest to the truth in any jurisdiction.

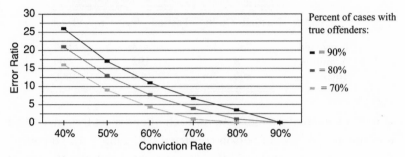

Figure 6.1a.

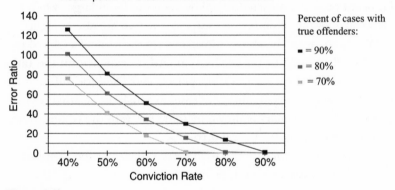

Figure 6.1b.

Conviction rates differ from one jurisdiction to another (Boland and Sones, 1981, 1986), as do the percentages of cases involving true offenders, which is likely to be driven by the nature and mix of crimes in the community, local police practices, standards for case acceptance by the prosecutor at the intake stage (Boland and Forst, 1985), and other factors. The percentage of those convicted who did not commit the crime will be based largely on police and prosecution practices, as well as the inclinations of judges to protect the rights of the defendant and the willingness of juries to decide on verdicts of guilt. The latter

Table 6.5. *Number of Offenders Acquitted per Innocent Person Found Guilty*

| Conviction Rate | 95 Percent of All Convicted Committed Crime | | | 99 Percent of All Convicted Committed Crime | | |
| | Percent of Cases with True Offenders | | | Percent of Cases with True Offenders | | |
	70%	80%	90%	70%	80%	90%
40%	16.0	21.0	26.0	76.0	101	126
50%	9.0	13.0	17.0	41.0	61.0	81.0
60%	4.3	7.7	11.0	17.7	34.3	51.0
70%	1.0	3.9	6.7	1.0	15.3	29.6
80%	*	1.0	3.5	*	1.0	13.5
90%	*	*	1.0	*	*	1.0

* Assumption: Number convicted will not exceed number of true offenders.

Table 6.6. *Percentage of Cases Erroneously Decided*

| Conviction Rate | 95 Percent of All Convicted Committed Crime | | | 99 Percent of All Convicted Committed Crime | | |
| | Percent of Cases with True Offenders | | | Percent of Cases with True Offenders | | |
	70%	80%	90%	70%	80%	90%
40%	34%	44%	54%	31%	41%	51%
50%	25%	35%	45%	21%	31%	41%
60%	16%	26%	36%	11%	21%	31%
70%	7%	17%	27%	1%	11%	21%
80%	*	8%	18%	*	2%	12%
90%	*	*	9%	*	*	2%

* Assumption: Number convicted will not exceed number of true offenders.

two percentages will, in any case, be unknowable in any jurisdiction. The number of offenders freed per innocent defendant convicted and corresponding total error rate are likely to be affected also by the quality of defense counsel in the jurisdiction and the willingness of each side to engage in plea negotiations.

Conclusion

Questions about the accuracy of the assumptions about factual guilt
and innocence notwithstanding, the techniques used here permit estimates of the effect of any given change in the evidentiary threshold for determining guilt on the number of true offenders set free
per innocent person convicted. *For most sets of assumptions depicted in
Tables 6.5 and 6.6, raising evidentiary standards to an extent that produces a ten percentage point reduction in the conviction rate approximately doubles the number of true offenders set free per innocent person
convicted and increases the total error rate by about 10 percentage points.*
Stated conversely, lowering those standards to a degree that produces
a 10 percentage point increase in the conviction rate approximately
halves the number of true offenders set free per innocent person convicted and decreases the total error rate by about 10 percentage points.

Although certain findings are robust to a wide variety of assumptions, questions about the accuracy of those assumptions remain. The
findings are limited also by the prospect that changes in the standards
of proof are likely to be met by adaptations by prosecutors, defense
lawyers, and the police. A raising of the standard of evidence for conviction and the associated lowering of the conviction rate is likely to
be met by the prosecutor's rejection of marginal cases that would have
previously been accepted; prosecutors would then be inclined to spend
more time with the remaining cases. Stricter screening standards are
likely in turn to increase the percentage of true offenders and the conviction rate, and additional time spent on the remaining cases might
also cause the new conviction rate to rise, perhaps to previous levels.
And the police might become less inclined to bring marginal cases
in the first place. One can only speculate on the full set of adaptive
behaviors and the net effect of this complex combination of such behaviors on the ratio of freed offenders to innocent persons convicted
and corresponding total error rate; these cannot be determined with
any degree of reliability.

Based on these results alone, one cannot say whether a jurisdiction
should raise or lower its standard of evidentiary proof, thus lowering or raising its conviction rate. As we saw in Chapter 5, the matter

depends on the costs associated with each type of error, and those costs will vary by crime category and jurisdiction. Other factors matter as well. A jurisdiction in which the prosecutor receives from the police arrests with stronger evidence, the determinants of which are the focus of the next chapter, should have a higher conviction rate than one in which the prosecutor receives arrests that are less convictable, other factors held constant. A jurisdiction in which the community's foremost problem is paralysis from fear of crime may be less inclined to free culpable offenders than one in which the community is hurt, first and foremost, by having a large fraction of its citizens behind bars. It is useful to know the effect of a change of evidentiary standards on the number of offenders freed per innocent person convicted and on the overall error rate, but such information provides just a single piece of the large and complex puzzle of criminal justice policy.

CHAPTER SEVEN

Police-Induced Errors

If the police do not (develop and refine standards), legislators, judges, and jurors, who know far less about policing, will do it for them, often at great expense and after great pain.

– James J. Fyfe et al.[1]

Introduction

Criminal justice errors typically begin with a police response to a call for service. What the responding officers and investigators do (or fail to do) and how well they do it can have a profound impact on the ability of the police both to solve crimes and reduce mistaken detentions and arrests. What are the key factors that distinguish effective from ineffective police responses to crimes, and accurate assessments of the identity of offenders from inaccurate ones that lead to arrests of innocent persons? Under what circumstances are police-initiated contacts appropriate and inappropriate, especially those involving profiling? What, in short, is the nature of justice errors attributable to the police and what are their sources? How do we find out about them, and how might we discover them more quickly? Can accountability systems be established to induce the police to substantially reduce the combined social costs associated with the two basic types of justice errors identified in Chapters 2 and 3? How might the goal of error management be balanced with other policing goals? These are the central questions of this chapter.

[1] Fyfe et al. (1997), p. 522.

Making Sense of Policing Errors

In February 1999, four members of a New York Police Department special crime unit, assigned to a predominantly minority neighborhood of the Bronx, shot and killed Amadou Diallo, a 22-year-old immigrant from West Africa. Diallo was unarmed and unconnected to the criminality that prompted the officers' assignment to the area. He happened to be where the officers were looking and acted furtively; when commanded to freeze, he reached in his pocket for his wallet. Thinking he was reaching for a gun, the four officers fired a hail of 41 bullets in his direction, 19 of which hit Diallo. Mayor Rudolph Giuliani and Police Commissioner Howard Safir called the incident a tragic error, and in February 2000 the four officers were found innocent in court of any criminal act. Four months later, the United States Commission on Civil Rights, a body appointed by the President and Congress, issued a report finding that racial profiling, the practice of routinely stopping and interrogating minorities, contributed to Diallo's death.

The Diallo incident is criminal justice error in its most extreme form. In recent cases of persons sentenced to death row and later found innocent and released, factual errors were uncovered, but the defendants at least received their days in court and came away alive and, eventually, free. Diallo was deprived of both due process and his life. His killing also failed to solve the crimes that prompted the officers' assignment in the first place. It may even have interfered with the ability of the police to act effectively toward solving other crimes. The case, moreover, drove a sensational wedge between the police and the public in New York and elsewhere. It raised serious questions about the legitimacy of the criminal justice system. The simple fact that four white officers were not held criminally responsible for killing an unarmed black man added a tanker-load of fuel to racial fire in New York and other urban centers.

Something useful may yet emerge from this tragedy. It has cast a bright light on several questionable police policies and practices. The police obviously erred in shooting an unarmed man, but they appear to have thought he was reaching for a weapon; he might not have done so had they been trained to approach him more effectively. They erred in thinking that he may have been the offender, but they might not have done so had they been more familiar with the neighborhood and its members in the first place. Assigning four armed officers of one ethnicity to a neighborhood consisting predominantly of people of a different culture in an already racially volatile setting is, on its face, dubious. The New York Police Department has made several adjustments in training and policy to minimize the likelihood that such episodes will happen again.

The problem with this manner of reflection as a basis for policy reform is that the Diallo case represents but a single datum, the dubious practice of policy assessment by an exceptional episode.[2] The adjustments made may intrude excessively on the ability of the police to control crime in the city's most crime-plagued neighborhoods, and their impact on civil liberties is unclear. The episode and prospective interventions can permit truly useful, comprehensive insights into weaknesses in police policy and practice generally when combined with a representative sample of known episodes of policing successes and errors that occur under given circumstances. We should prefer to know the implications that can be drawn from the facts of this case when combined with the facts from a representative sample of the many thousands of other cases involving the interrogation of rape suspects, taking into account the safety of prospective victims of rape offenders.

Diallo's sensational death overwhelms our ability to use that case as a sufficient basis for balancing his needs against those of prospective, unidentifiable rape victims, just as the death of a known rape victim overwhelms our ability to balance her needs against those of prospective, unidentifiable rape suspects. Authorities are not of one view as to how officers should be trained in approaching and questioning suspects of serious crimes, and they can be effectively guided both by insights gained from individual cases and by systematic analysis of a large sample of representative cases.

Even if data from such cases *were* assembled, however, our ability to make sense of them collectively would be limited by the fact that cases

---

[2] About 400 other people were killed by police in the United States in the same year – Brown and Langan (2001) report an average of 370 per year from 1976 to 1998 – but even those are not the relevant pool of cases in the Diallo matter: opportunities to find and interrogate crime suspects.

with known errors in identifying and interrogating suspects may be quite different from those with unrevealed errors. We have information about suspects who turn out to be innocent and data on unsolved crimes, but no data on persons interrogated, arrested, and convicted who are never revealed to be innocent in fact. The police label cases as "solved" or "unsolved," but we have no clue as to the error rates for "solved" crimes, nor do we know how many unsolved ones could or should have been readily solved. The conventions for labeling cases as solved vary from one police department to the next, and even for departments with similar labeling conventions the error rates depend on the competencies of the investigators and inherent difficulties presented by the cases.

These overwhelming complexities make the task of arriving at a sensible set of police interrogation and evidence collection procedures, ones that balance due process rights with the rights of victims of serious crimes, extremely difficult, and doing so based systematically on empirical information virtually impossible. We are left to piece together reasonable conjectures about justice errors from an assortment of sensational anecdotes and data on victimizations, reported crimes, arrests, convictions, and sanctions.

We can nonetheless go about the task of dealing with what we know and making plausible conjectures about what we do not know more systematically than we have. We can begin by attempting to identify the nature and sources of justice errors associated with police practices and policies and identifying solutions, in a manner that is mindful of both types of error and their social costs and the larger goals of policing and interests of the community.

Nature and Sources of Justice Errors Associated with the Police

Suspect Identification Following Calls for Service

Justice errors frequently begin with a call for service: a 911 call, an automated or manual alarm signal, or an in-person summons to the police. The police can err either by overresponding, imposing needless costs on innocent people, or by underresponding, imposing avoidable crime costs on victims.[3] Overresponse occurs when the police dispatch a patrol unit away from a more important activity to respond to a call for service that could be fully handled telephonically or otherwise, such as in a follow-up contact, perhaps by a parapolice officer or civilian. Failure to service the activity from which resources are pulled can interfere with crime-prevention, crime-solving, and other legitimate goals of the police. Underresponse may take the form of the police not responding at all, allocating resources to less important tasks, or in responding and then failing to take action that leads to the arrest and conviction of an offender.

Even when the response to a call for service is appropriate, the police frequently misidentify suspects, often soon after arrival to a destination. Whether and when to designate a person officially as a suspect varies from jurisdiction to jurisdiction; there is no uniform standard under the law. The patrol report filed by the officer who responds to a call for service typically includes the names of any and all suspects identified by the officer.

The nature of uncertainty dictates that some people identified as suspects will turn out to be innocent, even when the police operate optimally. For high visibility unsolved cases, the pressure on the police to find a pool of candidate suspects, sometimes starting with police modus operandi (MO) files and vague offender descriptions, and deal aggressively with them can be especially high. While such efforts can yield accurate offender identifications, each suspect thus identified may have an extremely low likelihood of having actually committed the crime in question – Captain Louis Renault's (played by Claude Rains) immortal "Round up the usual suspects" line from the movie classic *Casablanca* comes to mind. Among a pool of initial suspects, one

---

[3] The police may, of course, commit errors with regard to policing goals other than the minimization of social costs associated with justice errors. For example, rude behavior and ambiguous communications can undermine the public's satisfaction with police service and quality of life in the community. These are likely, in turn, to interfere with the ability of the police to manage errors of justice, but these second-order effects and effects on other policing goals take us beyond the immediate task at hand, to understand how police practices and policies contribute directly to errors of justice.

person may emerge as the leading suspect, but a *leading* suspect does not automatically qualify as a *likely* suspect.

The designation of "suspect" – or, more recently, "person of interest" – can impose costs on the persons so named and is likely to impose other costs as well. The police waste their own scarce resources, and may impose avoidable costs on such persons when the designation is made in the face of insufficient justification, or when compelling exonerating information known to the officer disqualifies the person in question as a legitimate suspect. When all leads are weak, any particular leading suspect is likely not to be the offender. The FBI's erroneous identification of Richard Jewell as the prime suspect in the fatal bombing at the 1996 Olympic Games in Atlanta had a chilling effect on the police practice of naming individuals as official suspects in major cases, for better or worse. The FBI had been under intense pressure to report progress in the case – and in the investigations of Wen Ho Lee and, following the extraordinary anthrax murders of 2001, Steven Hatfill as well – but the FBI's eagerness to report progress in each of these cases proved costly to their already tarnished reputation. Mistakes may be a natural and common consequence of decision making under uncertainty, making sensational failure commonplace in complex cases in the news, and the FBI has been responsible for at least its fair share of those. Still, high visibility cases call not only for good judgment in the identification of suspects but discretion in the information given to the media.

The court has determined that the police do indeed occasionally designate persons as suspects prematurely based on calls for service. In the case of *Florida v. J. L.*,[4] the United States Supreme Court refused, in a unanimous decision, to allow a stop-and-frisk, or "Terry stop" (*Terry v. Ohio*, 392 U.S. 1, 1968), of a person based on nothing more than an anonymous tip. In that case, the tip was that a 15-year-old Miami boy wearing a plaid shirt and standing at a particular bus stop was carrying a gun. The police frisked the boy and seized a gun from his pocket. The Supreme Court held that the tip provided no predictive information and created no reasonable suspicion because it was reliable only

---

[4] (120 S. Ct. 1375, U.S. 2000).

in terms of identification and not in terms of illegality. The Supreme Court specifically refused to create a "firearm exception" to the reasonable suspicion requirements of a Terry stop. While the court does not base such decisions explicitly on the framework used here, a reading of such decisions generally reflects central concern for pertinent social costs and for need to balance errors of due process and crime control.

Police Profiling: Police-Initiated Contacts

Justice errors occur also following contacts initiated by the police. Police often operate to catch offenders in areas in which crimes are known to be committed frequently – without attempting to clear any particular crime, without responding to a call for service – to deter criminal activity. This may take the form of a drug, prostitution, or gambling bust, a gang bust, a campaign to remove vagrants or other "undesirables" from an area, or the investigation of a suspected terrorist. Given the virtually limitless demand for policing of such problems in many jurisdictions, the police often attempt to organize their activity through profiling.

The central purpose of profiling is to prevent crimes through targeting, although profiling may also reduce errors for crimes not prevented by having resources ready to respond more quickly and effectively when needed to solve crimes previously committed. In both its police-initiated preventive and reactive crime-solving applications, profiling aims to organize scarce law enforcement resources in a way that is purposeful and efficient rather than random or arbitrary. Profiling is especially common in areas in which the police have a wide variety of options for resource allocation and moderate to high levels of crime.

The decision to initiate a police interrogation or search in the absence of a call for service may be based on time and place, on situation, on the characteristics of frequently offending individuals or, more typically, on combinations of the three.

Geographic Profiling

When based on *time and place*, perhaps the product of "hot spot" policing (Sherman, 2002, pp. 387–91) or geographic profiling (Rossmo,

1997, 1999), crime might be more effectively controlled, but possibly at the expense of imposing inconvenience costs on innocent people in the area at the time. Arrests that follow this sort of targeting are useful when they reduce crime, provided that the inconvenience costs to others are not excessive. When they do not reduce crime, the police should seek alternative interventions (Sherman, 2002, p. 392).

Kim Rossmo's system of geographic profiling aims principally to use mapping information and sophisticated computer systems to identify, track, and apprehend specific serial predators, both to deal with prior crimes and prevent further ones. Rossmo's approach, which he refers to as a "strategic information management system" (1997, p. 174), combines crime analysis methods to link unsolved cases to individuals, and mapping and crime analysis to predict the location of an offender's residence given the characteristics of a series of related offenses, based on data from previously solved cases.[5] Rossmo's approach includes a typology of methods that serial killers use to search ("hunt," "poach," "troll," "trap") and attack ("raptor," "stalker," "ambusher") their victims (1997, p. 167–70). The information that emerges from such analysis has been used to manage resources assigned to solving high-profile crimes such as serial homicide, rape, and arson, and to inform decisions involving neighborhood canvasses aimed at catching major offenders.

While designed to apprehend specific individuals, information about the distribution of distances traveled by offenders to their targets, for various crime categories, has wide applicability for informing policing strategy in crime prevention. Geographic profiling systems appear generally capable of reducing errors in solving crimes. These systems may introduce some due process errors in the short term, especially if the data on which the systems are based are seriously flawed

---

[5] Reliance on inferences only from solved cases is likely to produce biased information regarding the most difficult-to-solve cases, ones that may differ systematically from the cases that make up the geographical profiles. One important factor here is the number of offenses committed. Other factors constant, each offense committed increases an offender's exposure to apprehension. One might be able to get a sense of this aspect of the bias from a population of solved cases by examining the extent to which the geographical profiles for offenders with high rates of offending differ from those with low rates.

(Ainsworth, 2001, pp. 92–4) or if police use the systems injudiciously, but geographic profiling appears capable of reducing errors over the long term.

Situational Profiling

When police interrogations and searches are based on *situation* – for example, people behaving suspiciously just outside of a bar that is occasioned by frequent assaults, or in a parking lot that is the scene of a rash of thefts – the conditions observed must satisfy the legal standard of "reasonable suspicion" in order for the police to have legal justification for a search without a court-issued warrant. The reasonable suspicion standard is less stringent than that of "probable cause," needed for the police to make an arrest or search an automobile without a warrant.

Several police practices done under the rubric of situational profiling are controversial. One is the use of field interrogations of suspicious persons under the Supreme Court's 1968 ruling in *Terry v. Ohio.* In that landmark case, the Supreme Court upheld the right of the police to conduct "field interrogations," brief inquiries of suspicious individuals or groups, when they see reason to suspect those persons may be armed and dangerous to the police or others. The Terry rule represents an exception to the Fourth Amendment provision that a search warrant shall be required to conduct searches, but the Court ruled explicitly in *Terry* that the police cannot use the stop-and-frisk exception to conduct exploratory searches or harass citizens.

The courts have ruled that the Terry frisk is permissible in another common example of situational profiling: to justify the search of a person fitting the profile of a drug courier or terrorist at airports and other points of entry into the country. The profiles, based on information about the behaviors of people previously captured, include persons who are last off the plane (looking for agents), who take circuitous routes from origin to destination, often on different airlines, pay for their tickets in cash, have heavy baggage, are young and show signs of nervousness. Note that these descriptors exclude reference to personal characteristics – for example, that drug couriers are usually in their late teens or early to mid-20s or that young Arab males are more likely to be terrorists than most other subgroups – which in situational profiling is of secondary importance.

Another controversial situational policing intervention is the policy of mandatory arrest in misdemeanor domestic violence cases. Typically, the police can exercise discretion whether or not to arrest a misdemeanor offender. In jurisdictions with mandatory arrest policies for domestic violence, or under mandatory arrest statutes, the police have no discretion; they must make an arrest if there is probable cause that the suspect committed a misdemeanor domestic assault.[6] Research findings from experiments conducted in several jurisdictions suggest that mandatory arrest policies tend to deter subsequent episodes of domestic violence when the offender lives in an area of high employment, but they tend to have a counterdeterrent effect in cases in which the offender lives in an area of low unemployment (Sherman, 1992, 2002). To the extent that those findings are generalizable, mandatory arrest statutes and policies could well *raise* crime costs in the community. As in the case of many other dubious policing policies – including "zero tolerance" arrests for crimes of disorder and Drug Abuse Resistance Education programs, in which police officers lecture to kids about drugs in schools – the policy of mandatory arrest for domestic violence could be more politically attractive than socially optimal.

More is involved in situational profiling, however, than whether or not a policy applied to a particular class of offender tends to deter a particular crime. The question of how much discretion to give the police officer in any situation, whether profiling or not, has elements that are independent of the crime effects of the policy in question. Other factors held constant, errors may be reduced if discretion is given to officers who have been screened, trained, and monitored in such a way that they can be trusted to exercise it wisely. In jurisdictions or cases involving officers who are inexperienced or inadequately screened and trained, hence poorly prepared to conduct situational profiling

---

[6] A misdemeanor assault, punishable for no more than a year in jail, is less serious than a felony assault, punishable for at least a year in prison. It does not involve the use of a deadly weapon and usually does not involve injury requiring hospitalization.

with the prudent exercise of discretion, mandatory arrest policies and other such restrictions on discretion could lower aggregate social costs.[7]

Suspect Profiling

Easily the most controversial practice in contemporary policing is the search or interrogation based primarily on characteristics of the *individual*, often for a minor infraction without probable cause that a more serious crime was committed, a practice commonly known as suspect profiling.[8] It is controversial largely because the vast majority of people who happen to have characteristics that fit a profile – including ethnicity, gender, and age – are usually innocent of the crime under suspicion. Police who engage in suspect profiling generally develop a set of sociopsychological characteristics designed to provide focus to the detection of offenders. Suspect profiling is often done in response to a glut of crimes in an area, and sometimes in response to a specific crime. To the proponents of profiling, it is a "multidisciplinary forensic practice" (Turvey, 2001) that has revolutionized the ability of investigators to solve serious crimes by restricting the suspect pool to manageable proportions (Holmes, 1998) and identifying offenders more quickly, and using the profile information subsequently to guide the suspect interrogation and other aspects of the investigation (Douglas and Olshaker, 1995; Miethe and McCorkle, 2001). To most scientists, profiling is charlatanism when based purely on intuition or unconfirmed speculation, devoid of systematic empirical validation (Canter, 2000; Muller, 2000). To civil libertarians, profiling is especially toxic when police action is based on ethnicity rather than behavior, when it results in the arrest and harassment of disproportionate numbers of

---

[7] The Metropolitan Police Department of the District of Columbia lowered its screening standards in the late 1980s to such an extent that even recruits with significant criminal records were allowed to join the force. The 1989–90 classes accounted for half of the 200 officers arrested during the subsequent three years on charges from shoplifting to rape and murder (Rowan, 1995). The policy of mandatory arrest for domestic assault introduced in the mid-1990s in the District may have been preferable to the alternative under these circumstances.

[8] It is important to distinguish this practice of targeting people with particular sets of characteristics from the practice of police targeting of specific high-risk individuals, repeat offenders or "career criminals" (Martin and Sherman, 1986).

persons from disadvantaged minority groups, a practice that has come to be known as "racial profiling" (Kennedy, 1997).

In the extreme, profiling is either an effective crime-solving approach or a sure-fire way to multiply due process errors, institutionalize racism, and reduce police legitimacy, thus further limiting the ability of the police to get support from the community in solving crimes. As is the case with most criminal justice practices, the truth is more complicated. Confusion about profiling has been exacerbated by the fact that the term "profiling" has several different connotations, depending on whether used to prevent crimes or apprehend a particular offender, or whether used to develop a psychological picture of a particular offender, usually an intuitive process, or to fit a particular pattern of offending with a more general criminal archetype, which is more conducive to empirical methods.

Profiling is widely regarded as to have originated with the work of Howard D. Teten, often referred to as the "grandfather" of profiling, although essentials of contemporary profiling were applied in the 19th-century murders committed by Jack the Ripper (Turvey, 2001), and many of the nonpsychological essentials of profiling can be traced to the work of Cesare Lombroso.[9] Teten came to the FBI in 1962 and developed profiling soon afterward as an investigative tool for homicide cases, in collaboration with colleague Pat Mullany. Teten regarded profiling as "applied criminology."

For Teten, profiling was an arcane investigative tool. He does not appear to have attempted to popularize or glamorize it. A disciple of Teten, John E. Douglas, changed Teten's dry approach, almost single-handedly. Douglas came to the FBI in 1970 and, over the course of a 25-year career with the Bureau's Behavioral Science Unit (later called the Investigative Support Unit), became legendary for his pursuit of some of the most notorious and sadistic serial killers of the latter part of the 20th century, including Wayne Williams, known to have killed 27 boys in Atlanta, Robert Hansen, who murdered prostitutes for sport in

---

[9] Both contemporary profiling and Lombroso's criminal anthropology are based on the assumption of criminal archetypes, that some people are naturally more inclined to aggression and misbehavior than others, and that society can be protected against such people through identification of patterns of personal attributes.

the wilds of Alaska, and Seattle's Green River killer, a case that Douglas says nearly cost him his life.[10] Douglas advanced Teten's development by distinguishing between organized offenders, who are planners, usually better educated, more stealthful, and disorganized offenders, who are more opportunistic, usually less intelligent, and less socially skilled (Ainsworth, 2001, pp. 100–1; Petherick, 2003). Douglas also developed more in-depth personality profile archetypes. His reputation reached celebrity status when he became the model for the Jack Crawford character in Thomas Harris's 1988 classic *The Silence of the Lambs*, later made into the even more popular motion picture.

A central feature of Douglas's method for developing detailed personality profiles was his in-prison interviews with several infamous serial killers, including Charles Manson, Ted Bundy, and David Berkowitz ("Son of Sam"). Douglas created a mystique about his work by role-playing as both predator and prey, on site at each crime scene, reenacting both killer's and victim's actions in his mind, and then imagining their habits and predicting what they would do next.

Is Douglas's brand of profiling more entertainment than science? Missing from the hype about the psychological profiling of individuals is systematic evidence that it actually contributes to the ability of investigators to solve crimes more effectively, with fewer errors. In a rare inquiry into the success of subjective profiling, Copson found that it had helped to solve just 14 percent of the cases studied, and to identify the offender in only 3 percent of the cases. It is unclear what share of those would have been solved and identified without the profiling

---

[10] Douglas dishes up a dramatic sense of profiling, dripping with macabre imagery. In *Obsession*, he appears on the book cover wearing a dark suit, crimson tie and silk pocket hankie, half his face starkly shaded by a studio lamp. Inside, he is unashamedly self-promotional: "the Green River killings remain unsolved. For that reason, as well as the nearly deadly role the case played in my own life, it has continued to obsess me and probably always will. Someone or more likely several predators are still out there hunting.... And so are we." Douglas's coauthor, Mark Olshaker, is a novelist and filmmaker. Douglas gets additional help from his publisher. Here's Simon and Schuster's promotional blurb for his best-selling book, *Mindhunter* (1995): "Now, in chilling detail, the legendary *Mindhunter* takes us behind the scenes of some of his most gruesome, fascinating, and challenging cases – and into the darkest recesses of our worst nightmares." This aspect of Douglas's approach to profiling has quite possibly contributed to keen interest in the subject among more than a handful of criminology students (Fuller, 2001).

studied by Copson. The fact that the FBI's heralded profilers deter-mined in 1993 that the Unabomber was a "neat dresser who leads a meticulously organized life," is likely to be "an almost ideal neighbor" and "probably has had menial jobs" should make one hesitate before calling psychological profiling a science,[11] as should profiler assess-ments that the sniper who terrorized the Washington, DC, area in 2002 was a white male loner with a day job.[12] According to Eli Lehrer, "Even within the FBI – by far the leading proponent of psychological profiling – the notion that this is a 'science' has become the butt of jokes. What began in the 1970s as the Bureau's Behavioral Sciences Unit soon was widely known as the 'Bull S–t Unit'" (2002, p. 13).

Ethnic Profiling

The most controversial question of all is whether race or ethnicity should be used as a factor in profiling. The American Civil Liberties Union (2002) defines racial profiling as follows: "'Racial profiling' oc-curs when the police target someone for investigation on the basis of that person's race, national origin, or ethnicity." The ACLU gives these as common examples of profiling: "the use of race to determine which drivers to stop for minor traffic violations ('driving while black') and the use of race to determine which motorists or pedestrians to search for contraband." Even conservatives such as U.S. Attorney General John Ashcroft have professed to be opposed to police action based purely on race. In February 2002, President Bush said, "It is wrong, and we must end it" (Cloud, 2001). African Americans have been the dominant targets of racial profiling, especially "driving while black" or "DWB" (a play on the official police designation, "DWI," or stop for driving while intoxicated), at least until September 11, 2001. Since then, Arab-Muslims have become a prime target of profiling for ter-rorists, not only at airports and other U.S. entry points but virtually

[11] A 2002 *Washington Post* editorial quipped: "If the science of profiling is inexact enough to confuse a Berkeley math professor living in a shack in Montana with a well-dressed menial laborer, it is probably capable of confusing an American biological weapons scientist with, say, an al Qaeda operative" (Editorial, 2002).
[12] Several columnists had a field day after the arrests of John Allen Muhammad and John Lee Malvo, citing the earlier predictions of television talking-head experts in their erroneous profiles of the sniper (Goldberg, 2002; Alter, 2002; Lehrer, 2002).

everywhere else as well, as were white males in profiling for spree killers prior to the sniper attacks that petrified the Washington, DC, area in the fall of 2002 (J. Leo, 2002).

Profiling that includes race as a factor is controversial principally because it is inherently discriminatory, yet to the extent that ethnicity may actually predict certain classes of criminal activity, profiling that combines ethnicity with suspicious activity may serve to reduce crime, a conflict between crime control and the civil liberty of affected minorities.[13] This issue has been and will continue to be tested in the courts. The Supreme Court has not been strongly opposed to profiling systems that use race as a factor, even when the stops that result are used as pretexts for searches.[14]

Law enforcement authorities generally distance themselves from the expression, "racial profiling." They may acknowledge using race as a factor in attempting to solve a crime or prevent crimes in which a targeted race is known or suspected to be disproportionately involved, but the police generally combine race with gender, age, and other factors that are known or believed to be associated with the crime. While the agencies that do this might regard that simply as smart policing rather than racial profiling, it does fit the ACLU definition of racial profiling.

Suppose ethnicity does show up as a predictor of certain types of criminality, that a particular ethnicity is in fact disproportionately represented among offenders. Does that justify using it as a factor in profiling? Many say, "No." Randall Kennedy has argued persuasively that even when race is a systematic predictor of criminality, it should not be part of a profiling system: "Don't draw racial distinctions, except under extraordinary circumstances" (1998, p. 49).

---

[13] It is tempting to frame this as a conflict between the races or classes, but doing so may overlook the tendency for victims of crime to be disproportionately from the same groups that are targeted by profiling systems that include race, class, and age as elements for targeting.

[14] In the 1996 case of *Whren vs. U.S.* (116 S. Ct. 1769), the Supreme Court ruled in support of the police using a traffic stop as a pretext for a vehicle search. The *Whren* decision involved police stopping a car for a traffic violation and, after observing a bag of drugs in the car, arresting the occupants on narcotics charges. The Court held that even if the traffic stop was a pretext for the search, the officers' intent was irrelevant. Id. at 812–13, 819.

Kennedy's argument is based primarily on our history, on a deep and troubling legacy of discrimination (1998, p. 41), but his position is justifiable on other grounds as well. Race is a socially constructed variable, very much in the eyes of the beholder, unlike age and gender. It is less precisely measured than variables that can be far more relevant theoretically and ethically, such as number of prior felony convictions. Two profilers may not agree about the ethnicity of a particular person, and both may disagree with the ethnic self-designation preferred by the person in question. The U.S. Census Bureau offered five categories for ethnicity on the 1990 census form and 64 in 2000, allowing respondents to check as many boxes at they like.[15] Individuals who fill out the forms also change over time: given individuals sometimes change their own self-designations from one census to the next, sometimes in the spirit of assimilation, sometimes in the spirit of group identity (Skerry, 2000, pp. 200–1; Etzioni, 2000, p. 11). The relationship between a research finding on race and its application to searching a particular person is, in short, both methodologically and morally dubious.

It can lead, moreover, to wasteful delays in the solving of serious crimes. Several hundreds of white males driving white vans were stopped and searched by the police in major dragnets following the seriously flawed profiling of the Washington, DC, area "sniper" of 2002, who turned out to be a black man and a black juvenile working in tandem out of a blue sedan. Kennedy's expressed concern was about the profiling of minorities, but one cannot ignore the crime opportunities that police profiling opens up for people who do not fit a particular ethnic profile.[16]

Rigorous analysis has produced reliable evidence of racial disparity against minorities in the exercise of police discretion (Black, 1980; Reiss, 1971; Smith and Visher, 1981). Numerous lawsuits have been

---

[15] The Office of Management and Budget, which supervises the census, issued Directive 15 (*Race and Ethnic Standards for Federal Statistics and Administrative Reporting*, May 1997) to accompany the release of the 2000 census, outlining the racial/ethnic categories for the Census. The first paragraph of the directive includes this: "These categories have no scientific validity."

[16] Similarly, the initial profile of the Oklahoma City bomber was a person or persons of Middle East descent. The offender, Timothy McVeigh, turned out to be a right-wing U.S. Army veteran of European descent.

filed charging police departments with racial discrimination in traffic stops, field interrogations of pedestrians, and other discretionary actions (American Civil Liberties Freedom Network, 2003). Many of these appear to have been "DWB stops" or "pretext stops," the pretext being that the stop is for a minor driving infraction, such as a burned out taillight or license plate bulb, or a speeding violation in which the vast majority of the cars on the road at that place and time are also traveling over the limit.

The basis for these cases is often evidence that the number of stops or arrests of specific minorities, usually blacks, is disproportionate to their numbers as residents in the population. There are, of course, reasons other than discrimination for why the number of police stops of a group in question could be disproportionate to their numbers in the population. With regard to traffic stops, their presence on the road could be disproportionate to their numbers in the population because they drive more often, or over longer distances per drive, or both. If they drive less, yet are stopped more, that could suggest even more strongly either discriminatory policing or higher rates of traffic offending, or both. Either way, it would be important to know the driving exposure rates of the group or groups in question. To the extent that minorities are more likely to be poor, they may be more likely to have taillight and license plate bulb lights unrepaired. Any number of other factors omitted from the analysis – education, type of vehicle, and so on – could cause ethnicity to be spuriously related to the rates of stops, citations, and arrests. And if the vast majority of drivers travel over the speed limit, which is typically the case in many jurisdictions, we should like to know the rates at which different groups drive *substantially*, say at least 15 or 25 miles per hour, over the limit.[17] A

---

[17] Volokh observes that an ethnically blind solution to traffic stops is the expanded replacement of police officers exercising discretion with cameras, computers, and mailed citations. He notes that this spares society not only the obvious labor cost of police officers, but also the not insignificant costs associated with drivers trying to sweet talk police officers into issuing warnings rather than fines, including the "demeaning pressure to be especially submissive to the policeman in the hope that he might let me off the hook ... [and avoid] any possibility of being pulled out and frisked, or my car being searched." It would, of course, also reduce the potential for corruption. One might have good reason to worry, however, that this solution carries with it risk of abuse, for example, the temptation for jurisdictions to set the thresholds

more relevant basis for assessing the disproportionality of traffic stops on interstates, in any case, might be the rates at which different groups are involved in serious accidents on the highway in question. Accident reduction should, after all, be the primary goal of traffic stops and citations, consistent with the overarching police mission of protecting life and property.

Similarly, the number of field interrogations and arrests of minority groups could be disproportionate for reasons other than either higher offending rates or police racism.[18] Suppose, for example, that police of all races are inclined to demand compliance more sternly when a person on the street is perceived to be uncooperative or show disrespect for the officer, regardless of the race of the civilian. To the extent that the behaviors that induce such perceptions are related to race, one would expect arrests to turn up as more common for that group. We should prefer, in any case, that the police be screened and trained in such a way that they treat everyone respectfully, so as to minimize the risk of such unpleasant episodes and cross-cultural misunderstanding generally, but even imaginative and sensitive policing cannot guarantee that all street encounters will be pleasant.

Using ethnicity as a factor in profiling is, in short, unjustifiable when its relationship to a crime is unfounded, or when it is used in place of factors that are related to a crime. It is especially unjustifiable when used as a ruse, as when a trivial traffic violation is invoked arbitrarily as a lever to allow the police to search the member of a minority for weapons or drugs. These assertions are based on fundamental notions of justice, on ethical rather than utilitarian considerations. Still, police departments that permit such practices risk losing legitimacy in the community and exposure to elevated risks to the safety of its officers, so the elimination of such practices may be justifiable on utilitarian grounds as well. Eliminating racial profiling is likely to reduce

for violations arbitrarily low, with tendencies to overemphasize the safety costs of any particular speeding limit and ignore the time costs. The police are rarely sued for imposing time costs on citizens.

[18] Engel, Calnon, and Bernard put it bluntly: "The literature on racial profiling is misleading, fails to include crucial explanatory variables, and provides a limited understanding of the phenomenon. Accordingly, no firm policy implications can be derived from this research" (p. 269).

the disproportionality of stops and arrests of previously targeted minorities, but the gains to attitudes toward the police widely held in the community that follow the ending of racial profiling could have a more profound impact on the willingness of the public to support the police than do the results of statistical tests confirming nondiscriminatory policing.

These issues have been elevated to a new level in the era of terrorism. The tension between the basic crime control and due process goals raised by racial profiling in less perilous times tests the limits of any analytical framework. What can be said about social costs when an error made to avoid a cost associated with due process contributes to what Yale law professor Peter Schuck has called a "social calamity of incalculable proportions"? Now we confront a new set of difficult questions: Should airport security officers not subject young Arab men to greater scrutiny in airports than, say, elderly Japanese women? If profiling based on ethnicity is unjustifiable in enforcing drug laws, is it equally unjustifiable in preventing acts of terrorism? How do we resolve the tension between ethical and utilitarian considerations raised by ethnic profiling when the social costs of errors are vastly greater than under more ordinary circumstances? Does this qualify as a bona fide extraordinary circumstance under Randall Kennedy's (1998) rule of not drawing racial distinctions except under extraordinary circumstances?[19]

Soon after the airlines tightened their security procedures in response to the attacks of September 2001, Arab-American groups filed lawsuits in federal courts protesting the discriminatory nature of the new procedures. In each of the instances cited in the lawsuits, the

---

[19] An important related question is this: What mix of public and private security arrangements minimizes errors of justice in flight security? Commercial air carriers are responsible for air security, as are airports and the Federal Aviation Administration. Government intervention is warranted to the extent that air security is a public good; that is, to the extent that unregulated markets provide insufficient protection against victims of air terrorism (such as the people killed in the World Trade Towers and the Pentagon on September 11, 2001). Such intervention can impose burdensome costs on society, on the other hand, to the extent that government agents may be more inclined to operate as monopolists insensitive to the costs of enforcing security, including time costs, inconvenience, intrusions on privacy, and monopolistic inefficiency. These issues are raised in other matters of commerce as well, including shipping and trucking.

passengers had cleared security and were later pulled from their flights or denied the right to board after other passengers or crew members expressed discomfort with their presence. All were given seats on later flights, but their suits claim damages associated with humiliation, time lost, and other discomforts (Associated Press, 2002).

These matters are likely to be resolved through a mix of the court's interpretation of the law and common sense. One commentator has suggested that minorities singled out and seriously delayed for security checks should be compensated with frequent flier miles (Kinsley, 2001). The decisions made under any framework are bound not to satisfy everyone. One can only hope that the resolution process does not ignore the relevant social costs and probabilities associated both with errors of due process and those that undermine safety to society.

Common sense should tell us at least this: *Many of the restrictions to liberty imposed in the name of preventing terrorism do nothing at all to reduce the risk of terrorism.* Some may even increase it by displacing security resources from more productive activities and alienating marginal individuals. A prominent *Newsweek* reporter has noted: "the greatest obstacle to fighting terror is not our freedom but government inefficiency" (Zakaria, 2002, pp. 28–9). Former Senator George McGovern has written compellingly of the wasteful "grip of bureaucratic devotion" that too often causes people to miss flights needlessly, cripples operations at airports, and frustrates most everyone involved.

The problem is compounded by the arbitrary nature of many of the new restrictions and by sheer incompetence. The public's sense of security can only be diminished by reports of airport screening tests conducted by the Transportation Security Administration in which the testing agents are instructed not to artfully conceal simulated bombs and other weapons as terrorists might, but rather to pack their bags in ways that would test whether screeners could spot basic items they had been trained to recognize. In spite of this lower and clearly less relevant standard, 58 percent of the screeners failed to pass such a test at the international airport in Cincinnati, 50 percent failed in Las Vegas, 50 percent in Jacksonville, and 41 percent in Los Angeles. Overall, 25 percent of the screening tests conducted at 32 airports failed (Morrison, 2002). Even people of extreme tolerance cannot be comforted to learn of the Immigration and Naturalization Service sending student visa approvals to a flight school in Florida for two men responsible for the 9/11 attacks six months after the attack.

Incompetent screening procedures were all too evident in the case of failed suicide airplane bomber Richard Reid. His name and ethnicity (his parents were British and Jamaican) did not suggest an obvious link to terrorism, but his behavior, appearance, and prior record certainly did. The profile Reid presented at the airport in Paris should have warranted a careful search of the sort that would have uncovered the lethal explosives in his shoes. His suspicious behavior and a record of 10 prior convictions were conspicuous, yet he was given a seat on the airplane, and the jet took off for Miami. Only the prompt action of a perceptive flight attendant thwarted Reid's intention to blow up the airplane. Her quick response appears to have saved over 300 lives.

Fareed Zakaria (2002) has called the crazy-quilt assortment of federal, state, and local authorities involved in protection "the single greatest threat to America's safety." He adds:

> The FBI is finding out all it can about the 1,200 people rounded up since September 11 – except whether they have ever bought firearms. It's not that the government doesn't have that information, but the Justice Department will not share it because of an NRA-sponsored law that says that information about people buying guns – even illegal immigrants! – can never be shared with anyone. (p. 29)

From an errors-of-justice management perspective, it is clear that some varieties of profiling are more acceptable than others. Profiling to expedite the solving of serious crimes, when based on valid factors, is likely to reduce errors that permit culpable offenders to remain at large, and could reduce due process errors as well. Profiling that targets minorities and harasses them in the process is likely to increase both due process errors and errors of impunity, and clear evidence of harassment by a police or security officer should be grounds for dismissal. In between, we can do no wrong to ensure that assessments of profiling systems are based more explicitly on the extent to which they reduce errors that allow offenders to commit crimes *and* the extent to which they either raise or lower the risks of due process errors, and the associated social costs of both sets of errors. An effective profiling system will reduce both sets of errors, and a just system will work to minimize harm on targeted minorities.

Witness Identification

Easily the most pervasive cause of erroneous convictions is mistaken witness identification (Donigan and Fisher, 1980, p. 205; Huff, Sagarin, and Rattner, 1996, p. 66). This has been strongly confirmed in the exoneration of over 100 people sent to death row over a 25-year period starting in 1977, based on reliable DNA evidence (Scheck, Neufeld, and Dwyer, 2001; Connors, Lundregan, Miller, and McEwen, 1996). How do such errors emerge? How extensive do they appear to be?

Interviews with Victims and Witnesses

Two ingredients are especially common in cases involving mistaken witness identification. First, victims and witnesses are more likely to err when they did not get a good look at an offender they do not recall ever having seen prior to the crime. Second, they are more likely to identify the wrong person when the police have a strong interest in solving the crime, typically because it is serious or involves an offender the police have developed a stake in getting convicted.[20]

On the other side, errors of impunity tend to occur when the witness feels intimidated by the offender, fearing reprisal if she or he testifies. This is especially common when the police are unable to persuade the person that they will be able to protect the individual from reprisal.[21] Other factors have been found to contribute to both types of error. The accuracy of a witness's memory of events tends to decay over time (Baddeley, Thompson, and Buchanan, 1975). Witnesses have more difficulty recalling specifics accurately when the event at

---

[20] According to Elizabeth Loftus, a path-breaking researcher on the accuracy of eye-witness testimony, "pressure ... comes from the police [who] want to see the crime solved, but there is also a psychological pressure that is understandable on the part of the victim who wants to see the bad guy caught and wants to feel that justice is done" (DNA Testing, 1995, p. 10).

[21] It is not difficult to imagine cases in which the witness may intentionally identify the wrong person in a lineup in order to avoid confrontation with the actual offender.

issue was violent (Clifford and Scott, 1978; Loftus and Burns, 1982). Even in nonviolent crimes, the presence of stress, fear, and anxiety may disrupt normal perception processes and cloud subsequent memory (Huff et al., 1996, p. 87). Research findings to date on inhibitors to accurate memory recall give us reason not to accept every witness claim of having been so frightened that the offender's face is forever etched in the witness's memory.[22]

Police Lineups

Police lineups can be useful for confirming a witness's identity of an offender, but they can also introduce error when the witness either identifies a wrong person as the offender or fails to identify the actual offender standing in line. The witness may identify the wrong person either by chance or because the police led the victim to the selection of a particular suspect. Police-induced identifications can occur, for example, when the police ask a witness to find the person in a file of mug shots, and then put the person selected by the witness in the lineup. The person selected may only resemble the actual offender, and then be selected by the witness in a subsequent lineup from a recollection of the picture rather than the criminal event. Or the police may give facial or other cues suggesting to the witness that a particular picture is the "right guy" (Eysenck and Eysenck, 1994, p. 160). Or it can be the result of a "suggestive one-man showup," in which a witness is shown a single suspect and asked, "Is this the guy?"[23] Systematic errors can occur also when the lineup consists largely of people who do not fit the physical description of the offender, increasing the risk of selecting a particular person in the lineup who is in fact innocent of the crime in question, who just happens to fit the description.

---

[22] Here is an example of courtroom testimony of erroneous identification expressed with conviction that appears in the news from time to time: "'He is the man who raped me,' she said. She had never been so sure of anything." (From reporter Helen O'Neill's account of Jennifer Thompson's mistaken identification of Ronald Cotton in a 1985 in Burlington, North Carolina. Cotton served 11 years in prison for the alleged crime. DNA evidence subsequently led to the identification of Bobby Poole, who closely resembled Cotton, as the actual offender.)

[23] *Williams v. State*, 546 So. 2d 705, 706 (Ala. Crim. App. 1989) (quoting *Biggers v. Tennessee*, 390 U.S. 404, 407, 88 S.Ct. 979, 981, 19 L.Ed. 2d 1267, 1269 (1968) (Douglas, J., dissenting).

And once a witness has identified the suspect in a lineup, she may convince herself that that person was indeed the offender.[24] Defense counsel, especially those appointed by the court, cannot always be counted on to know of and reveal these various improper procedures in trial.

Other Sources of Erroneous Testimonial Evidence
The police have been known to produce other sorts of testimonial evidence that has led to wrongful convictions and failures to bring offenders to justice. One is the improper use of informants. People who offer unsolicited information about a crime may do so for a variety of reasons ranging from unselfish public service to vengeance-motivated lying. At the benign end of this spectrum is the samaritan, good neighbor, or altruistically motivated professional (e.g., doctor, UPS delivery person) who witnesses a crime or extremely suspicious event, act, or object and notifies the police about it. Even reliable people sometimes give less than reliable information. At the other extreme are the offender who makes a plausible accusation against an innocent person (Huff et al., 1996, pp. 77–9) and the jailhouse snitch, a criminal eager to find a way of getting lenient treatment for a crime previously committed, often by attempting to gain credibility by using an item of privileged information obtained from another offender in exchange for a favor (Scheck et al., 2001, pp. 163–203). Wrongful convictions have been documented at this disreputable end of the spectrum, but errors can occur as well when an apparently disreputable or incredible person actually has important, accurate information that the police reject. Between these extremes is an assortment of semi-reliable informants ranging from the jealous spouse, to the meddling bystander, to the James Bond wannabe, to the drunken or disreputable person with unclear intentions. The police are responsible for sorting through this nest of ambiguity to separate fact from fiction, and breakthroughs in forensic technology in the late 20th century have revealed that combinations of excessive zeal to solve crimes and incompetence occasionally get in the way (Connors et al., 1996; Scheck et al., 2001).

[24] *U.S. v. Wade*, 388 U.S. at 228–9, 87 S.Ct. at 1933, 18 L.Ed. 2d (1967) at 1158–9.

Another source of erroneous testimonial evidence is the false confession, which can result from police interrogation procedures that run afoul of the Fifth Amendment protection against self-incrimination. In comparison with other sources of erroneous convictions, extant assessments of the rate of erroneous convictions due to false confessions suggest that it is quite low, based on interviews with inmates (Cassell, 1998; Huff et al., 1996). In overturned convictions involving false confessions, the police almost invariably are certain that the suspect was in fact culpable, and work purposefully and often for long periods of time to wear him down in order to extract a confession, sometimes combined with good-cop, bad-cop routines and other psychological tricks common to popular TV cop shows, methods of coercion that do not leave bruises or other physical marks. The suspect is often well below average intelligence. When exculpatory evidence is present, the police often dismiss it as a dodge or gimmick (Huff et al., 1996, pp. 110–41; Scheck et al., 2001, pp. 101–37).

Tangible Evidence

Excessive police zeal to clinch a case against a particular suspect sometimes manifests in the form of physical evidence. This appears to occur most commonly in drug cases, in which the officer either finds evidence in violation of Fourth Amendment protections against illegal searches or plants evidence on a "known offender." Well over 90 percent of all felony cases dropped by prosecutors has been found to be associated with evidence wrongfully seized in drug cases (Forst, Lucianovic, and Cox, 1977; Brosi, 1979; Boland, Mahanna, and Sones, 1992).

Evidence planting by the police is far more serious, a criminal act. What we know about it is based more on anecdote than on systematic evidence, but it does occur – again, mostly in drug cases – as has been documented by several investigative bodies, including the 1972 Knapp and 1994 Mollen Commission inquiries into corruption scandals of the New York Police Department, and the 2000 Rampart Independent Review Panel investigation into corruption in the Los Angeles Police Department (*Report*, 2000, p. 5). The motives are mixed, associated typically with desires to get drug money, to punish undesirables, and to satisfy thrill-seeking interests.

Fraud also occurs in the processing and laboratory analysis of evidence. Two of the more notorious names in the world of forensic specialists known principally for their extensive associations with overturned convictions, if not fraud, are Joyce Gilchrist and Frederick Zain. Gilchrist was fired by the Oklahoma City Police Department following findings of numerous irregularities and convictions overturned by DNA evidence, all cases in which she had been responsible for the forensic analysis of physical evidence supporting conviction in the original case. Zain, previously a state trooper, became a police chemist in West Virginia 1979, in spite of a remarkably thin record of relevant academic accomplishment.[25] He became a popular expert witness for the prosecution nonetheless, testifying in dozens of rape and murder convictions about tests he had never done and results he had never obtained (Kelly and Wearne, 1998; Berlow, 1999). The judge presiding in a habeas corpus inquiry following a conviction supported by Zain's testimony concluded that there was "overwhelming evidence of misconduct on the part of Zain" (Holliday, 1993). Other prominent figures in the netherworld of shady forensic specialists include Texas pathologist Ralph Erdmann, Mississippi forensic dentist Michael West, Illinois serologist Pamela Fish, and FBI special agent Thomas Curran, who managed to do considerable damage before an internal FBI investigation revealed an extensive pattern of perjury, incompetence, and falsification of reports (Kelly and Wearne; Scheck et al., 2001).

The FBI's problems have not been restricted to Agent Curran. The Bureau manages the largest forensic operation in the world, with a staff of some 700 forensic specialists that conduct upwards of a million examinations annually involving federal cases and local crimes that cross state lines. In 1997, the Department of Justice issued a report documenting a variety of shoddy practices, "significant instances of

---

[25] Zain's college transcripts show several grades of "F" and "D" in relevant courses in basic chemistry, zoology, botany, genetics, and algebra. Zain ended up with a total of 10 hours of chemistry courses in which he received a grade of "C" or better, including make-ups of previously failed courses (Holliday, 1993, Note 33).

testimonial errors, substandard analytical work, and deficient practices" (Office of the Inspector General, 1997). Others see these problems as a natural manifestation of a deeper problem: the FBI is run hierarchically in the interest of helping U.S. Attorneys to win convictions, in a manner consistent with presumption of guilt, not to process evidence in an open and fully objective manner to determine whether suspects are guilty or innocent (Kelly and Wearne, 1998).[26]

Managing Justice Errors Attributable to the Police

There are countless ways for police to reduce errors of justice, some more effective and readily available than others. We can begin to prioritize these ideas under an organizing principle that is rarely considered in police academy training or criminal investigation textbooks, a principle that is especially difficult to maintain in an adversarial culture: the police should focus not just on incriminating information, but should be equally interested in exculpatory information, especially after a suspect or suspects have been identified. This is a challenge given that the police are the first line of defense against crime, with a primary mission of protecting life and property rather than liberty. They are held accountable primarily for controlling crime in a common law, adversarial system of justice. But if they pay too much attention to catching criminals and not enough to minimizing errors of due process, they run the risk of losing credibility in the community and ending up actually less able to control crime than if they find a balance that minimizes the social cost associated with both sets of errors. Adherence to this principle is not only good science, consistent with

---

[26] This is not a new problem. The columnist Robert Novak observes that even conservatives have been appalled by the FBI's willingness to harm innocent people, a tendency that has ultimately done severe damage to the reputation of an organization that is, in other respects, extremely professional and capable:

> The day is long gone when knowledgeable conservatives worshiped at the FBI's altar. As chairman of the House Government Reform Committee, (Dan) Burton was stunned when he learned of FBI complicity in the wrongful conviction in 1968 of four men (two of whom died in prison) for murder committed by FBI informants in Boston. To protect these sources, Director J. Edgar Hoover sent innocent men to prison. Before the current congressional recess, Burton introduced a bill to remove Hoover's name from national FBI headquarters.

Popper's falsification principle,[27] but also in the interests of justice and police legitimacy.

Connecting the Dots

The crime of our lifetime, resulting in nearly 3,000 homicides on September 11, 2001, has been characterized as the product of a failure to "connect the dots" that were known to the FBI and other law enforcement and intelligence agencies. Connecting dots is a serviceable metaphor for thinking about how to make effective use of available information.

Collecting the dots first, and then making sense of them, are equally essential. A *New Yorker* cartoon by Robert Weber (2002) shows a private investigator telling a prospective client: "We're talking fifteen hundred to find the dots, then another fifteen hundred to connect them." The cartoon accompanies an article by Seymour Hersh on government failures to make sense of information that could have served to prevent the 9/11 terrorist attack. Hersh notes that the attack was partly the product of a failure to produce more pertinent dots to facilitate the prospects for connectability, no less the product of an abundance of too many extraneous dots,[28] and especially the product of extraordinary bureaucratic failures. These obstacles proved to be too great, despite the need for extraordinary coordination among 19 men to successfully hijack four large commercial jet airplanes simultaneously. Connecting the right dots is difficult enough when the ratio of extraneous dots to relevant ones is extremely large,[29] and can be impossible

---

[27] "If the degree of falsifiability is increased, then introducing the hypothesis has actually strengthened the theory; the system now rules out more than it did previously; it prohibits more" (Popper, 2002, text at Note 6).

[28] The situation is far worse today. The FBI responded to 300 calls about suspicious packages from January 1 to September 10, 2001, and received 54,000 calls and responded to 14,000 of them in a much shorter period following September 11 (Hersh, 2002, p. 48).

[29] The problem is exacerbated by language problems. One of the 19 hijackers was Saeed Alghamdi. Hersh reports at least four other men with the same name on the books of the Florida flight school Alghamdi attended. The school reported that it had trained more than 1,600 students with the first name Saeed and more than 200 with the surname Alghamdi (2002, p. 44). Alternate name spellings further complicate matters. Here are 10 alternative spellings of the Libyan leader's surname that have appeared in print: Qadhafi, Qaddafi, Qatafi, Quathafi, Kadafi, Kaddafi, Khadaffi, Gadhafi, Gaddafi, Gadafy (Diamond, 2002).

when the machinery responsible for making the connections is not up to the task.

The central point here is not so much about terrorism as it is about making sense of available information. In order to prevent serious crimes in the future, and to solve the ones that are not prevented – to reduce the social costs of errors associated with those crimes – the law enforcement community must work to collect pertinent data, ensure and protect its reliability, and develop computerized systems and effective cooperative networks to draw useful inferences about crimes and crime patterns from the data. These systems should make use of information about the nature and sources of the errors that have impeded crime prevention and crime solving over the years.

Certain prospects appear prime for reducing both errors of due process and errors of impunity. The field of criminal investigation offers especially rich opportunities to reduce both types of error. Much of the failure to correctly solve crimes is attributable to skillfully committed crimes and inadequate investigative resources, but surely some of the approximately nine million felonies reported to the police that do not end in conviction are attributable as well to deficiencies in the work of investigators. In a landmark 1975 study, researchers at the Rand Corporation found that only about 7 percent of all investigative time is spent on activities that lead to the solving of crimes (Greenwood et al., 1975). Even the much of 7 percent that leads to solutions could surely be better spent. Careful perusal of the literature of criminal investigation and textbooks on the subject reveals the absence of a coherent framework for drawing conclusions and taking effective action in criminal investigation, and decision-support tools to make such a framework accessible to investigators on the ground. Conventional treatments of criminal investigation cover essential elements of criminal investigation without providing an underlying logic for determining what to do next in any particular investigative context. Criminal investigation textbooks present a wide range of pertinent information on the subject and checklists for specific situations, but not within a coherent framework for drawing inferences and taking effective action in any situation.

Tools to support such decision making have been effectively applied to a range of problems from medical diagnosis and treatment to defense logistics to production and operations management. Those tools have proven to be especially critical as advanced societies everywhere continue their shift from production-oriented economies to predominantly service, communication, and information technology economies. Yet, except for significant advances in forensic and information technologies and related scientific developments that have improved our technical ability to solve crimes, the field of criminal investigation has not experienced the same degree of progress in resource management and fundamental case processing decision support that has transformed the delivery of services throughout the private economy. Most investigators are competent and hard-working professionals, but the sort of reasoning prowess that one finds in a Sherlock Holmes or Agatha Christie novel remains largely fictional. Not all investigators today make systematic use of data on prior solved and unsolved crimes to inform the investigative process on the effectiveness of alternative investigative procedures in specific situations. Little formal training is given on how to link seemingly unrelated incidents to individual offenders. For all of its reputation for selectivity, professionalism, and development and use of advanced forensic technologies, the Federal Bureau of Investigation was widely criticized following the 9/11 attack for its extraordinary backwardness in the use of computers for crime prevention and crime solving (Kessler, 2002; Wilke, 2002).[30]

Low rates of crime solving can be attributed largely to factors beyond the control of the police, but they are attributable as well to the fact that investigators receive little or no instruction in basic skills of drawing accurate inferences about suspects and making decisions that contribute to solving crimes. Many investigators have developed effective skills and keen intuitive instincts following years of experience and more than a few miscalculations, but many have not. The community stands to benefit substantially from a compression of this learning curve.

[30] Wilke reports that e-mail and internet access was unavailable to many FBI agents on September 11, 2001, that photographs of the 19 hijackers had to be mailed overnight to the Bureau's 56 field offices after the attack because they could not be transmitted electronically. Ronald Kessler lays much of the blame for the FBI's cyber-backwardness squarely on the shoulders of ex-Director Louis Freeh, whose aversion to technology extended to his own unwillingness to use e-mail.

Some of the errors in investigation are attributable to fact that the initial investigator at the scene of a crime is usually a patrol officer, not a person trained first and foremost as a professional investigative scientist. Research on variation in crime clearance rates has found that the information gathered by patrol officers during the preliminary investigation stage is the most important factor driving variation in clearance rates (Isaacs, 1967; Ward, 1971; Folk, 1971; Eck, 1983; Wellford and Cronin, 2000). Some police officers have been found to be systematically much more successful than others in producing cases that end in conviction (Forst et al., 1977, 1982), and the sources of this variation may contribute no less to differences in the error rates from one officer to another. Investigative effectiveness has been found also to be associated with the detective's caseload: increases in caseload reduces effectiveness (Ward, 1971). Organizational structure and detective procedures have been found also to affect clearance and arrest rates (Elliot, 1978; Bloch and Bell, 1976; Schwartz and Clarren, 1977).

Modus Operandi Files

One of the most important assets in the dot-connection business is reliable information about incidents and offenders (Skogan and Antunes, 1979, p. 219). The source of such information in most police departments is the *modus operandi* (MO) file, a data base describing prior crimes, solved and unsolved, used both to identify patterns that can help in the identification of known offenders in currently unsolved crimes and to link unsolved crimes by elements that implicate the same offender. For solved crimes, the MO file provides information about an offender's methods of preparing for and committing a criminal act, and evidence of his behavior afterward. Police departments have used MO files since around 1900.[31]

Some agencies rely more heavily on MO files than others, however, and within a given agency some detectives rely on them more than others (Morgan, 1990; Forst, 1994). A part of this variation is due to

---

[31] The general structure of the MO file was developed by Sir Llewelyn Atcherley, in Yorkshire, England. Atcherley surmised that offenders tend to commit the same crime in a habitual fashion (O. Wilson, 1951, p. 131). August Vollmer is credited with adopting and revising Atcherley's MO scheme in the United States (Wilson).

the crime mix and rate of offending unique to each community. Not all crime circumstances lend themselves to the use of MO files – crimes that are unpremeditated and easily solved, for example, involving an offender who was previously known to the victim. It was noted earlier that MO files can be misused in identifying a pool of candidate suspects; they can also be overlooked as a useful crime-solving resource. Crimes for which the MO file is more likely to be a useful tool include homicide, stranger rape, arson, robbery, and burglary. Modus operandi files have been found to be more likely to contain information on and identities of people committing new unsolved cases in communities that have offenders who commit more crimes and police departments that manage to solve a high percentage of crimes (Forst and Planty, 2000).

Variation in reliance on MO files from department to department is attributable as well to the orientation of the investigative units and individual investigators. Some investigators are introspective problem-solvers who appreciate the need to collect and connect dots. Others are more sociable and intuitive than analytical; they are more inclined to work with victims, witnesses, and other investigators to solve crimes.[32] We may be less likely to hear complaints about "paperwork" and the often tedious work associated with developing and maintaining MO files from detectives who are more inclined to make use of the files and be aware that reliable information contributes to their usefulness. Some investigative units, in any event, place a higher priority than others on the need to gather and nurture reliable information, with procedures and accountability systems that provide greater incentives to produce and preserve reliable MO information. These differences are bound to have a self-fulfilling quality: offices that work to ensure that the MO files are reliable will find them more useful for solving crimes than offices that neglect them.

One solution to this problem is greater reliance on civilians for the more tedious aspects of the business of creating and connecting dots. The ratio of full-time civilians to sworn officers in law enforcement

---

[32] For more on personality archetypes generally, see Jung (1971); Eysenck (1971).

agencies increased by a factor of three from 1965 to 1995, and much of this transformation has occurred in investigative operations, including the use of civilians as crime scene technicians, forensic laboratory scientists, and computer specialists. Civilians are usually less costly than sworn officers, and they are often more effective, especially in routine, highly specialized tasks (Harring, 1981; Forst, 2000a). The use of civilians, together with incentive systems that induce sworn officers to make better use of MO files, could go a long way toward increasing the rate at which culpable offenders are apprehended and convicted, and could reduce due process errors along the way by diverting investigative resources away from innocent suspects.

Reducing Mistaken Witness Identification
Improved police procedures to establish whether a suspect is the real offender can be effective both for removing innocent people from suspicion and for confirming that a suspect is the real offender. To the extent that existing procedures are flawed, both types of errors result: real offenders remain free and innocent people are convicted. Many of the existing flaws have been revealed in cases overturned due to breakthroughs in forensic technology.

The courts have helped to keep these errors in check. In *U.S. v. Wade*, the Supreme Court ruled that the defendant's right to due process is violated if the procedures used to identifying the offender are "impermissively suggestive" rather than fair and impartial, free of opportunities that induce the witness to pick out a particular suspect as the offender. The wording of the Court in the *Wade* decision was sharp:

> The identification of strangers is proverbially untrustworthy. . . . The influence of improper suggestion upon identifying witnesses probably accounts for more miscarriages of justice than any other single factor – perhaps it is responsible for more such errors than all other factors combined. . . . Suggestion can be created intentionally or unintentionally in many subtle ways. And the dangers for the suspect are particularly grave when the witness' opportunity for observation was insubstantial, and thus his susceptibility to suggestion the greatest. . . . Moreover, [i]t is a matter of common experience that, once a witness has picked out the accused at the line-up, he is not

likely to go back on his word later on, so that in practice the issue of identity may... for all practical purposes be determined there and then, before the trial.[33]

Other solutions have been proposed to minimize errors that derive from information provided by victims and other witnesses. Most of these are designed to reduce the risk of erroneous convictions, but some are likely to reduce errors of impunity too, in part because an erroneous conviction generally means that the true offender goes unpunished, but for other reasons as well, including greater citizen support of the police. Some of the most basic principles are these:

1. Investigators must be skilled in assessing the competence of witnesses and credibility of the information they give. Young children, witnesses intoxicated at the time of the crime or when interviewed by the investigator, and witnesses who appear to have participated in the crime or provoked the suspect tend to be among the more questionable of witnesses, but what they say may nonetheless be absolutely accurate. Other witnesses often bring biases and interests to a case that interfere with the accuracy of the information they provide. The credibility of all such information depends also on the witnesses being present at the event, in control of their senses, and conscious of what was happening, who was involved, and pertinent specifics about the involvement of each person. Investigators who are perceptive, skilled in making the witness comfortable, and able to draw out information logically are better equipped to assess the credibility of the information provided by a witness and, of primary importance, whether their identification of the offender is accurate.

2. Lineups should aim to provide an objective identification of the offender, not strengthen a case against a particular suspect. Lineups can be useful for minimizing both types of justice error, but they must be conducted in a way that eliminates opportunities for preconceived police notions about the identity of the offender to influence the results of the lineup. The witness or

---

[33] 388 U.S. 218, 87 S.Ct. 1926, 18 L.Ed.2d 1149 (1967) at 228–9.

witnesses should not be allowed to see the defendant in custody prior to the lineup, nor should she or he be shown a photograph of the defendant in advance. The lineup should be administered by an independent person, not aware of the case or the identity of any suspects. All persons in the lineup, usually consisting of no fewer than six to eight persons, should be of the same ethnicity and about the same age, with similar physical characteristics (height, weight, etc.), and wearing similar clothing, all consistent with the description provided earlier by the witness and documented for the record.[34] If statements are made by individuals in the lineup, each person should say the same words. The police should not be allowed to say or suggest anything to provide cues to the witness. The lineup should be videotaped for possible subsequent use in court. If more than one witness sees the lineup, they should do so separately to minimize prospects of contamination. Many police departments follow these procedures routinely, but the evidence on wrongful convictions reveals that too many do not.

3. Informants should be checked out to ensure that the information they give is reliable and their motives for giving it are clear and credible. Police should not offer promises to informants they do not intend to keep, should treat the informant respectfully, and should protect the source of the information so that the informant is not exposed to reprisal. The Attorney General of the United States issued a useful set of guidelines in 1981 on how the police and prosecutors should deal with informants; police departments would do well to establish procedures and policies consistent with these guidelines.

4. Huge opportunities to reduce errors in offender identification are available through greater use of smart identification

---

[34] Research by Lindsay and Wells (1985) suggests that identification errors may be reduced when eyewitnesses see the suspects one-by-one, sequentially, rather than simultaneously in a lineup. It is plausible that some circumstances may warrant the sequential option, while the conventional lineup may be more accurate in other cases. Much research on the issue has been done since Lindsay and Wells's landmark study; more is needed to establish more precisely those circumstances that warrant each type of identification procedure.

technologies. These technologies can be used both to prevent and solve crimes, often much less invasively than through conventional body searches. Advances in facial recognition technology (especially when imbedded in video surveillance systems), biometric systems for eye scanning, facial and hand geometry, electronic fingerprint identification, X-ray and heat-sensing technologies for weapon and bomb detection, and ID cards with computer chips – all present prospects for reducing crime and terrorism, and substantially reducing the labor-intensive options that have made street searches, airport searches, and traffic stops so intrusive and corresponding errors so pervasive. Many of these technologies are of course also intrusive, but at least they are less conspicuous. The invasions of privacy they pose cannot be dismissed, in any case. The technologies ought to be more controversial when used to detect marijuana than when used at airports to detect terrorists. In between, their use could be determined following less contentiousness and more thoughtful discussion based on a thorough accounting of the respective effects of each on safety and security, privacy and civil liberty.

Improved Coordination with the Prosecutor

The agent with primary responsibility for checking the procedures used by the police to ensure that they minimize erroneous witness identifications is the prosecutor. This is but one aspect of a much larger responsibility of the prosecutor, to validate the accuracy of police work generally and the quality of arrests brought forward for court processing in particular. If procedures used in a lineup are invalid, or other procedures used by the police to obtain testimonial or physical evidence violate the arrestee's constitutionally protected rights, the prosecutor has a responsibility to reject the evidence. Pertinent elements of this role are discussed in greater depth in the next chapter.

A related responsibility is critical systemically rather than constitutionally. If the criminal justice system is to operate coherently, the police and prosecutor have a shared responsibility to ensure that information about problems in the collection and processing of tangible and testimonial evidence is routinely provided by the prosecutor so

that the police can identify patterns of problems and use the information to improve the quality of the arrests they make, toward the end of
reducing errors of justice. A large body of research has found that arrests are rejected by the prosecutor principally due to insufficiencies in
the amount and quality of tangible and testimonial evidence brought
by the police (Forst, Lucianovic, and Cox, 1977; U.S. Department of
Justice, 1977; Davies, 1983; Feeney, Dill, and Weir, 1983). Police accountability systems do not generally provide incentives for the police
to improve the quality of the arrests brought forward for prosecution
(Forst, 2002). This virtually assures that errors of justice will be needlessly large.

Dealing with Ethnic Discrimination in Profiling
It was noted earlier that police profiling based on race or ethnicity
is often misguided – both ineffective and unjust – especially when
ethnicity is used in substitute for factors that are related to a crime.
Suspicious behavior and prior record should take precedence over
ethnicity in any profiling system. Stephen Flynn (2002) of the Council
on Foreign Relations recommends a variant of conventional profiling,
which he calls "reverse profiling":

> If you could go, as we must go, towards the point of origin controls
> we can do 'reverse profiling,' taking a very controversial term and
> turning it on its head. What we need is a system that accurately
> profiles legitimate as legitimate. Legal identity, legal purpose, up-
> front efficiency and integrity through the system will permit waving
> it through. In fact, if you had confidence that the origin is in fact
> secure, you actually would want to accelerate its movement.

Flynn's approach would change current airport security procedures
from random searches of all passengers to one in which the vast majority of passengers, who have none of the characteristics consistent
with the profile of a terrorist, would be conventionally screened, and
the small portion of suspicious people would undergo more intensive search procedures. Others have noted that suspicious people may
be more efficiently identified through body language, with personnel
trained in how to read it, and circumstances (cash ticket purchase,

unusual routing, no round trip ticket, etc.) than through ethnicity (Davis, Pereira, and Bulkeley, 2002).

With regard to the larger problem of discriminatory policing, one essential has received too little attention: how the police treat people generally, and how they treat minorities in particular, appears to have a more profound impact on citizens' attitudes about the police and their willingness to cooperate than do police decisions to stop or arrest them (Tyler, 1990; Paternoster et al., 1997). Treatment of minorities by the police must begin with the understanding of the principle that people simply deserve respect.

Hiring minorities can help to generate the understanding and sensitivity needed to improve police effectiveness, especially in the highest crime rate areas. Minority police officers have been known, however, to be among the more egregiously insensitive to minority citizens (Hutchinson, 2000). To the extent that errors in policing are the product of cross-cultural misunderstanding and miscommunication, assigning minority officers to areas in which they are more familiar with the social mores and vocabularies of the residents is likely, at least up to a point, to reduce errors that interfere with the goals of both crime control and due process.

Killings by the Police

I have noted that the gravest of all due process errors occurs when the police kill an innocent person, as in the case of Amadou Diallo. The Bureau of Justice Statistics report that police in the United States killed some 370 people per year from 1976 to 1998 (Brown, Langan, and Levin, 1999).

A variety of proposals has been offered to reduce this number: more rigorous screening of officers, training that includes extensive situational role-playing and violence avoidance exercises,[35] better supervision, clearer and more thoughtfully crafted policies, internal and external systems of accountability (including civil suits, civilian review

---

[35] Fyfe (1986) has observed that an unknowable but substantial number of deadly encounters involving the police each year are preventable without an increase in crime if the police were trained in violence avoidance techniques.

boards, and the media) to ensure that the policies are followed and objectives achieved, and the use of nonlethal weapons (batons, chemical sprays, electronic devices, capture nets, and so on) instead of guns in a variety of situations calling for the use of force. These proposals are complementary; each appears to be potentially useful for reducing the use of deadly force, and they are more likely to be effective taken together than if the department is deficient in any one of them. Of particular significance here, these proposals appear capable also of strengthening the ability of the police to solve and prevent crimes.

One factor appears to be senior to all the others: leadership. Jerome Skolnick and James Fyfe have observed that nothing was as effective in fixing decades of recurring plagues of brutality and corruption in the 40,000-officer New York Police Department as was the strong leadership of Patrick V. Murphy in the early to mid-1970s. Murphy had several characteristics that helped: he was raised in a family of cops, worked his way up through the ranks in the NYPD, developed executive skills there and refined them elsewhere, as chief in Syracuse, Washington, DC, and Detroit. Skolnick and Fyfe (1993) regard the most important factor, however, to be his "genius . . . to put in place fundamental structural reforms and redundant checks on integrity and abuse in every part of the department" (p. 185). It is difficult to imagine any single factor capable of accomplishing what a leader of Murphy's caliber is capable of doing: changing the culture of the department so that police misbehavior becomes unacceptable.

Unfortunately, good leaders come and go, and since Mr. Murphy's departure the NYPD has had to deal with a few commissioners who, if a hall of fame were to be built to honor outstanding police chiefs and commissioners, would not be installed.[36] In the absence of a

---

[36] One notable exception may be William J. Bratton, appointed by Mayor Rudolph Giuliani to serve as NYPD commissioner from 1994 until Giuliani fired him two years later. Bratton is widely credited for reducing the City's homicide level from 1,997 in 1993 to fewer than 1,000 by the end of his term. Some of this reduction would likely have occurred without him, however, and the rest may have come at a cost to civil liberty. Under his "zero tolerance" policing philosophy, the number of citizen complaints jumped by about 60 percent, from 3,500 citywide in 1993 to 5,500 in 1996. (Davis and Mateu-Gelabert, 1999, p. 5) By contrast, Barrett reports a 13 percent drop in the number of shots fired by cops, from 1,193 in 1993 to 1,040 in 1997. The decline in serious crime in New York during Bratton's tenure, his innovative use of a strong

charismatic, culture-building chief or commissioner, the next best hope for a mayor or city council interested in the effective management of deadly force is the development and enforcement of sound policies. In 1985, the International Association of Chiefs of Police surveyed police departments around the country and combined from the best a set of model policies on the police use of deadly force, policies that can be imbedded in a police department's system of internal accountability and used to shape specific training programs (Matulia, 1985).[37] Some of the central features of the IACP's model policy include the clarification of fundamental distinctions among such terms as deadly force, excessive force, reasonable force, and unlawful force; an elaboration of the limited sets of conditions under which use of deadly force may be permissible; and an outline of the essential elements of training programs designed to implant the policies firmly in the minds of the officers who will be governed by them. These developments, together with community policing programs that have become popular throughout the country since the 1980s, may have helped to reduce excesses in the police use of force (Skogan, 1990; Skogan and Frydl, 2003).

Much more can be done. We stand to further reduce police killings by learning more about the problem, to provide an informed basis for taking corrective action. No federal agency currently tracks fatal and nonfatal shootings by officers on a department-by-department basis. If this were done systematically, we could then inquire into the sources of variation, to determine why some departments are better than average and others worse, to provide a basis for reducing avoidable shootings by police. The research should attempt to adjust for factors beyond the department's control. It might be reasonable, for example, to expect jurisdictions with higher homicide rates to have more unavoidable shootings.

---

accountability system, his contribution to a lifting of the morale of the NYPD, and the effects of crime reduction on the vibrancy of the city, in any case, give him standing as an exceptional leader in policing.

[37] The IACP model was published in the year of the landmark *Tennessee v. Garner* decision, in which the Supreme Court ruled that police departments could not allow officers to shoot at fleeing felons except when the person in flight poses an immediate danger of serious injury to another.

Some police departments, it turns out, really are much better and others much worse than average. A one-time survey of the 51 largest police departments, conducted by *Washington Post* reporters Craig Whitlock and David Fallis, found that during the period 1990 to 2000, some police departments were clearly more trigger happy than others. Overall, more killings occurred in larger jurisdictions, jurisdictions with more homicides, and jurisdictions with relatively few sworn officers.[38] The police departments that most exceeded the predicted number of killings based on the norms for the 51 jurisdictions and given the size of the jurisdiction and department, and homicide level for each, were Los Angeles County, Washington, DC, San Diego, Phoenix, Denver, and Prince Georges County, Maryland.[39] At the low end were Dallas, Chicago, San Antonio, New Orleans, Suffolk, New York, and Fairfax, Virginia. It would be most useful to examine these departments in depth to see whether the policies, training programs, and leadership styles of the departments at one extreme differ from those at the other.

This is a limited data set, covering just 20 percent of the population. But it suggests possibilities for the routine and much more extensive collection and analysis of pertinent data elements on use of deadly force in police departments throughout the country. This could help to substantially reduce the most serious justice error of all.

Balancing Error Management with Other Policing Goals

One of the long-standing debates in the law enforcement community and among scholars of policing has been over the goals of policing.

---

[38] The regression result is Killings $= 0.5021 + .00000394$ Population $- .00075$ Cops $+ .0161$ Homicides, with all three independent variables significant at .01 (t $= 4.87$, -3.84, and 7.30, respectively), and with $R^2 = .893$ (adjusted $R^2 = .886$; F $= 131$, significant at a level arbitrarily close to zero).

[39] Whitlock and Fallis reported Prince Georges County as highest rated, based on the number of killings per officer, under the headline, "County Officers Kill More Often Than Any in U.S." However, the county has a higher than average homicide rate and lower than average number of officers per resident population, so the number of killings per officer will be artificially high both because the number of killings in the jurisdiction are spread over a smaller base and because of the inverse regression relationship between officers and killings generally. Prince Georges County appears, in any case, to rank high under any reasonable accounting.

What precisely is the meaning of the policing mission, "to serve and protect"? Should the police aim high and wide, working to improve quality of life in the community, or should their primary goal be more focused and tangible, to reduce crime without intruding excessively on civil liberties? Should the stated goals more closely reflect shifts in policing philosophy and strategy associated with emphases on community and problem solving? Should they adopt more of a consumerist perspective, aiming primarily to improve the public's satisfaction with police service? These questions are important because they provide direction to policing. They also provide a basis for systems of accountability and performance assessment for units and individuals within the department.

Now comes yet another goal: police so as to minimize the social costs of errors of justice. How does this goal fit with more conventional goals of policing? Can it be integrated within police accountability systems?

Clearly, a focus on errors need not conflict with the serve-and-protect mission of police, although it might well conflict with the traditional crime and arrest rate measures of police performance assessment. One might argue that the police can minimize error by doing nothing, but that would ignore social costs and misread the errors of impunity side of the balance scale of justice. Minimizing the social cost of errors of crime control means intervening against crime – doing *something*, and doing it well. A focus on errors, moreover, need not conflict with the goals of policing that have become more popular in departments that embrace community policing, such as improving perceptions of the quality of community life, fear of crime, and citizen complaints. Focusing on error management could in fact contribute to quality of life and citizen satisfaction with the police to the full extent that police are able to do so.

What about the goal of crime prevention? How should the police mix their time and resources toward the goals of prevention of crime, response to crime, and error management? There are two distinct parts to the answer to this question, the first having to do with social costs and the second with the time dimension. Regarding the first, in any given period the goal of minimizing the total social cost of crime

and interventions to control crime will yield a different result from
the more conventional goal of minimizing crime subject to arbitrary
constraints on the protection of civil liberties, as the latter does not account for the social costs of crime and civil liberty. Ignoring social costs
simplifies the problem, especially when preventive activities involve
people suspected of intending to impose harms of seemingly incalculable catastrophic proportions, but doing so can produce draconian
solutions that run roughshod over either the goal of due process or
that of crime control. This approach is nonetheless the dominant one
in use today. Mayors and police chiefs have shown little stomach for
the difficult business of estimating the value of a statistical life and
other pertinent social costs, and many have shown little interest in
attempting to understand more precisely the effects of police policies
and practices on liberty and safety.

With regard to the time dimension, the goal of crime prevention
raises a different consideration: it extends the assessment beyond the
current period. The optimal allocation of police resources toward either the prevention of future crimes or the reduction of social costs
associated with future crime and interventions against crime requires
a multiperiod calculus. Policy analysts conventionally address such a
problem by assigning a discount rate to reflect the relative value of
a good or outcome now and the same good or outcome a year from
now.[40] Following this approach, the optimal allocation of resources in
the current period would be the allocation that minimizes the present
value of a stream of total social costs of crime and justice over an extended time horizon, using a standard discount rate, such as 5 percent,
or a range of discount rates that reflect alternative time preferences.

The framework proposed here requires that we attempt to confront
the twin difficulties of assessing the social costs of crime and the justice system and that of contemplating more precisely the importance
of public safety for tomorrow, in terms of appropriate discount rates.

---

[40] Frederick, Loewenstein, and O'Donoghue observe that this standard approach can be
simplistic, overlooking distinctions between time preference and uncertainty, effects
of changes in taste, and other factors that might influence intertemporal decision
making.

It requires also that we push ahead with research that attempts to understand the effects of alternative policing strategies and resource allocations on future crimes in the major settings in which crime occurs. We have a very long way to go, and will do well to move forward, if only to organize our thinking. In the meantime, there is no reason not to hold the police accountable for the errors that they are known to have been responsible for in each of the areas discussed above: witness identification, use of informants, evidence processing, and so on. They are already held accountable for lapses on the crime control side. Those systems of accountability stand to be improved, especially to the extent that they produce systematic errors of justice. It will be more than useful to consider adjustments to these systems that reduce all such errors, on *both* sides of the scale of justice.

Conclusion

The police do much to solve crimes, and they do so generally with professionalism and under extreme duress. Still, law enforcement is the engine of errors of justice. The greater the pressure to solve crimes, the more aggressive the police in attempting to do so, and the more likely that errors of due process will follow. The police can do much more to prevent crimes and solve them in a way that reduces both errors of due process and errors of impunity.

We have seen several sources of justice errors attributable to the police: flawed exercise of discretion in responding to calls for service and in reporting crimes, in identifying suspects and making arrests; improper witness identification procedures, false confessions, and improper use of informants; flawed and fraudulent evidence processing and forensic procedures; and incentive systems that induce the covering up of errors. Effective use of community and problem-oriented policing concepts and programs starting in the late 20th century may have helped to reduce some of these errors.

The police can begin to reduce errors of justice by rethinking their goals and objectives, from the aggregate department and division level to the unit and individual level, and they can adjust the

systems of accountability that grow out of these deliberations as it becomes clear that the systems produce excessive errors of justice. They
can improve their capability to "connect the dots" needed to solve
and prevent crimes by collecting and analyzing data on investigative
activities, successes and failures, and making greater use of effective,
typically computerized, decision-support technologies and civilian experts, with more reliable modus operandi files and more effective use
of them. They can reduce errors associated with rules for profiling and
screening suspects by rigorously assessing the procedures for making
stops and collecting and analyzing data on the yields associated with
current and past practices. Sound principles of error management will
be useful to deal both with crimes at the local level and with federal efforts to reduce errors in the new terrorist era of policing. Police could
reveal a genuine sense of responsibility to the public by complement-
ing efforts to reduce errors of impunity by collecting and analyzing
data on all people detained and the outcomes that follow those intrusions to develop an accounting of the costs imposed on innocent
people.

Perhaps the single most effective way for the police to manage errors of justice is to change the accountability system for detectives and
strengthen the independence of the investigative function, to trans-
form the role of the investigator from in-house advocate for crime
control to impartial scientist with greater professional autonomy. Current arrangements do not provide sufficient incentives for detectives,
especially those assigned to divisions, to weigh exculpatory evidence
objectively against incriminating evidence. Police departments can
stimulate such a transformation by first reconciling the role of the
police as the public's first line of defense against crime with their
larger responsibility for building and maintaining public support and
criminal justice legitimacy. In much the same way that in-house ac-
countants have been compromised by the interests of the companies
that pay their salaries, criminal investigators create problems for the
police and undermine criminal justice legitimacy when they operate
principally as anticrime warriors. And in much the same way that doctors employed by a hospital operate under a higher professional code
of medical ethics, professional investigators ought to operate under a

formal code of justice ethics.[41] Even patrol officers who focus first on crime prevention and control, when they act as investigators should work to minimize the costs to society associated not only with errors of failure to bring offenders to justice, but with due process errors as well. Until such a transformation occurs, we can count on an excess of errors of justice.

[41] Of course, codes of professional responsibility and ethics do not guarantee socially responsible behavior. Auditors, doctors, and other professionals are occasionally convicted of violating such codes. They do, however, provide a basis for holding professionals accountable, legally and administratively, for their decisions, policies, and practices.

CHAPTER EIGHT

Prosecution Policy and Justice Errors

The prosecutor has more control over life, liberty, and reputation than any other person in America.
— Robert H. Jackson (1940, p. 18)

Introduction

In addition to their extensive control over the lives, liberties, and reputations of violators of the law, prosecutors have substantial control over errors of justice, both the extent to which innocent people are convicted and the extent to which culpable offenders are not. They can ferret out errors made by the police by screening arrests more carefully, directing postarrest investigations to resolve conflicting sources of evidence, working more diligently with victims and witnesses to establish, precisely and accurately, pertinent events that preceded and followed the episode in question, and directing the forensic processing of key items of physical evidence to resolve ambiguities involving both incriminating and exculpatory evidence. While much of this work is initiated and managed by the police, prosecution resources are also allocated to these activities in different amounts at various stages of prosecution.

Prosecutors rarely articulate the rationale for determining how these allocations are made. It is by no means clear that the decisions in fact follow a coherent consideration of the relationships among the decisions themselves or between the policies that drive the decisions and the overarching goals of prosecution: pursuit of justice, reduction in crime, evenhandedness, efficiency, celerity, quality of life in the community, and legitimacy.

The choice of the level of evidence to be used as the standard at each stage of prosecution and the setting of plea bargaining policies are central to the control of errors. Should arrests be screened more carefully, or should more be accepted using a lower standard and then dropped later if the postarrest investigation turns up weak? Should more cases be taken on and scarce prosecution time rationed by encouraging more pleas, or should more be rejected at screening so that attention might be paid instead to preparing more cases for trial?

Traditional measures of prosecution performance – conviction rates, average case processing time, reelection success, and so on – shed little light on how these questions should be resolved, and they ignore justice errors. Research on prosecution tends also to ignore this important issue. William Landes, among the first to study prosecutors using a classical theoretical and empirical research design, theorized that prosecutors aim to maximize the weighted number of convictions, where the weights are based on offense seriousness. Landes's model made no distinction between cases in which the defendant was factually guilty or innocent, tacitly assuming that all were culpable offenders of the crime for which they had been charged.[1]

The larger social returns to a primary focus on convictions and tough sanctions have by now been revealed as extremely dubious. Reflective people who have devoted themselves professionally to assessing the criminal justice system have concluded *both* that too many people in prison and jail do not belong there, and too many culpable offenders remain at large. Aiming to convict more persons arrested for felonies and put them away for long terms of incarceration has contributed to the overincarceration of marginally harmful offenders, and may even have accelerated the release from prison of more dangerous offenders, thus diminishing our ability to control crime in the name of ending it (Blumstein, 2002). Conventional performance measures of prosecutors overlook a valid concern that the interests of the community

---

[1] Landes was not the only researcher to ignore prosecution error. His model had been criticized by Forst and Brosi (1977) for failing to consider future crimes and the crime prevention goal of prosecution, not for failing to distinguish culpable offenders from innocent defendants. Forst and Brosi's model, like Landes's, assumes tacitly and uncritically that the prosecutor always prefers a conviction to a nonconviction.

are not always served by incarcerating persons arrested for felonies. Some are in fact innocent. In capital cases, which one might expect are subject to greater due process protections than other felony cases, an astonishingly large number of persons sentenced to death have been subsequently exonerated of all charges, based largely on DNA evidence.[2] Liebman et al. (2000) report prosecutor misconduct in 16 to 19 percent of appellate reversals of capital sentences.[3] And in many noncapital cases, the costs of incarceration appear clearly to exceed the alternative costs of intermediate sanctions that would permit those offenders to contribute to the productivity of the community and well-being of their families.[4]

Managing errors of justice is a long overlooked goal of prosecution, one that warrants serious consideration as a basis for assessing case processing policies and practices. Few would argue with the proposition that the prosecutor should work to ensure that culpable offenders are brought to justice and innocent people are not convicted. Failure to do either constitutes a fundamental lapse of justice. For all cases brought to the screening room, the prosecutor is responsible for both types of error.

Prosecutorial Discretion and Errors of Justice

Prosecutors are known to exercise considerable discretion in deciding whether to prosecute individual cases and determining how much attention to assign to each case accepted. Former U.S. Attorney General

[2] See Chapter 1, Note 1. Some of these exonerations were based on procedural errors that do not necessarily imply factual innocence, and many of these may be connected to jurisdictions with serious lapses in due process controls, not typical of prosecution in most jurisdictions. Still, in most of the 80 cases forensic evidence implicated others, and in many capital cases DNA evidence is not available to exonerate the death row inmate; other death row inmates sentenced during the period may be factually innocent too. The 1.3 percent figure is, by any reckoning, alarmingly high.

[3] Liebman et al., text at Note 42. Latzer and Cauthen (2000, p. 142) point out that most appellate reversals of capital sentences leave undisturbed the guilt of the murderer. Prosecutor misconduct is documented also by Bedau and Radelet (1987, pp. 57–60); Gershman (1999); Huff et al. (1996); and Scheck, Neufeld, and Dwyer (2001, pp. 222–36).

[4] The challenge remains to distinguish more accurately the offenders who will contribute to their communities and families from those who will not. I do not wish to make light of the difficulty of making these distinctions.

and Supreme Court Justice Robert H. Jackson (see quote opening this chapter) and others have called attention repeatedly to the dangers associated with this power. Independent prosecutor Kenneth Starr's impeachment investigation of President Bill Clinton is one of the more conspicuous recent examples of prosecutors exercising discretion in such a way as to damage the lives and reputations of the accused.[5]

Prosecutors are only occasionally overruled for engaging in such excesses. In the case of *Berger v. United States*, involving a federal prosecutor who grossly overstepped the bounds of proper behavior in order to win a conviction against a defendant, Supreme Court Justice George Sutherland wrote, "While (the prosecutor) may strike hard blows, he may not strike foul ones. It is as much his duty to refrain from improper methods calculated to produce a wrongful conviction as it is to use every legitimate means to bring about a just one."[6]

Sutherland's observation has gone unheeded by many a prosecutor in the decades since. Bedau and Radelet (1987) report 35 cases of prosecutors suppressing exculpatory evidence in a sample of 350 potentially capital cases involving "wrong-person" conviction errors, and 15 other such errors attributable to "overzealous prosecution" (p. 57). Several other commentators have documented convictions of the innocent as a consequence of misconduct associated specifically with the prosecutor's withholding of exculpatory evidence from the defense (Gershman, 1997; Huff et al., 1996; Scheck et al., 2001).

Prosecutorial misbehavior is sensational, and it sometimes leads to erroneous convictions, but a basic and innocuous aspect of prosecutorial discretion may be a far more profound source of errors of justice: the power of the prosecutor to determine the extent to which the courtroom standard of evidence, proof beyond a reasonable doubt, will be relaxed at any stage of prosecution, starting with the screening

---

[5] Benjamin Wittes (2002) has offered a charitable assessment of Starr's abuse of prosecutorial discretion, attributing it to his mistaken but good-faith belief that his mission was wide-ranging, to seek the truth of any and all Presidential misconduct, rather than the conventional narrow one of investigating specific charges, in this case, the President's role in the Whitewater scandal. Starr's civil law perspective would substantially broaden the meaning of an error of justice. One might, in any case, question the ethics of the Starr team's threatening to jail Monica Lewinsky's mother for withholding information even under this more charitable view of Starr's role.

[6] 295 U.S. 78 (1935).

of arrests. In prosecutors' offices of all sizes, the exercise of discretion in screening arrests is not severely constrained by the Constitution or by case law. The decision to file an arrest in court depends on the threshold of evidence used by the prosecutor, which is largely a matter of office policy. In deciding whether to file a case in the court, the prosecutor is free to use any standard between "probable cause," the standard required for the police to make an arrest, and beyond a reasonable doubt. By lowering evidentiary standards at the pretrial stages of prosecution, the prosecutor raises the likelihood of winning convictions in cases involving innocent suspects, mostly by way of plea bargaining, and imposes potentially harmful costs on those defendants (and others) in the process. Others have noted that the controversy over plea bargaining has been misplaced: it is ostensibly a matter between pleas and trials, but more fundamentally a matter between case screening and plea bargaining (Wright and Miller, 2002).

This policy choice owes its existence to a tradition of loosely governed escalation in the legal standard of proof as felony cases proceed from arrest to indictment and adjudication in court. The level at which the chief prosecutor places the bar in the pretrial stages involves a tradeoff between the certainty and severity of applicable sanctions. Lowering screening standards and getting more convictions by way of plea negotiations and fewer by guilty verdicts in trial is likely to be associated with shorter sentences. And as sentences of probation increase, such practices can be expected to lead to reduced incapacitation effects. But it comes with the substantially increased risk of convicting more innocent people, along with some compensation in convicting a larger share of culpable offenders. This tradeoff will be considered in greater detail later in this chapter.

Improved Coordination with Police

In deciding what standard of evidence to use in screening arrests, the prosecutor makes a statement to the police. If the prosecutor uses the probable cause standard, case acceptance amounts to validating the police assessment that the evidence in the case was sufficient to make an arrest. In rejecting a case under this standard, the prosecutor ordinarily explains to the police officer either that the case was rejected "in the interest of justice," that the evidence met the probable cause standard but the nature of the case did not warrant prosecution (e.g., the arrest was needed only to prevent further harm, or the offense was trivial), or because the probable cause standard was not met, along with an explanation as to specific deficiencies in the case. If the prosecutor rejects the case using a higher standard than probable cause in screening cases, she can tell the police officer what evidence would have merited case acceptance under the higher standard. Regardless of the evidence standard used by the prosecutor at the screening stage, this explanation provides useful feedback for the police, generally given informally and recorded routinely for the prosecutor's records, although not generally a matter of open public record.

This information is routinely given to the police as a matter of record only in a minority of jurisdictions, making it virtually impossible for police executives in most places to hold their officers systematically accountable for the quality of the arrests they make. The opportunity for improved coordination and reduced errors rests generally with systems of feedback that provide routine, nonaccusatory information as to how the police can strengthen cases legitimately with stronger tangible and testimonial evidence. Such systems appear to be the exception, not the rule.

The quality of coordination in individual cases depends largely on the underlying relationship between police and prosecutor. There is some strain in the relationship in most jurisdictions, if only because the cultures of police and prosecutor tend to be quite different (McDonald, 1982; Feeley and Lazerson, 1983; Coles, Kelling, and Moore, 1998). From the perspective of the police officer, the prosecutor's position often seems a bit pristine and formal, removed from the workaday reality of the cop on the street trying to fight crime against impossible odds. From the perspective of the prosecutor, the police often appear to be excessively zealous and insensitive to the prosecutor's case backlogs and the rigorous evidentiary standards of the court. The underlying tension occasionally escalates when the prosecutor goes public with criticism of police work in a particular case or series of cases, sometimes fueled by media inquiry. In other jurisdictions, police and prosecutors enjoy a generally healthy, mutually supportive working relationship.

The quality of the police-prosecutor relationship in a jurisdiction is critical to the ability of the prosecutor to effectively monitor the problems discussed in the previous chapter: flawed lineups and other improper witness identification procedures, illicitly obtained confessions, improper use of informants, legally invalid searches, and faulty processing of physical and forensic evidence. The prosecutor cannot escape responsibility for failing to catch persistent policing problems, such as the fraudulent evidence technician. In some instances, prosecutors have been charged with conspiring with the police to make weak cases against innocent defendants appear stronger by withholding exculpatory evidence or overlooking flaws in police investigations (Scheck, Neufeld, and Dwyer, 2001, pp. 222–36). Police-prosecutor cooperation has not always been in the interest of justice.

Errors of Fact, Questions of Culpability, and Tactical Errors

Errors of due process and errors of failure to bring culpable offenders to justice are not the only kinds of errors that are influenced by the exercise of prosecutorial discretion. Prosecutors err also when they give excessive concessions to offenders who testify against low-level, less culpable collaborators, and when they play the role of adversary aiming for a high conviction rate rather than fact finder in pretrial disclosure proceedings, to such an extent that legitimacy is lost through an ends-justify-the-means approach to justice. That defense lawyers may engage in similar practices on the other side is not an acceptable justification for such practices; it is the prosecutor who bears the burden of proof for all relevant facts in a case under our system of criminal justice,[7] unlike the continental European system of criminal law. Even when prosecutors engage in such practices that do not lead directly to

---

[7] The prosecutor's responsibility for assembling and making available *all* relevant evidence, exculpatory as well as incriminating, was reinforced in a landmark 1963 ruling by the Supreme Court. Under *Brady v. Maryland*, a prosecutor's suppression of exculpatory evidence violates the defendant's right to due process. 373 U.S. 83, 83 S. Ct. 1194, 10 L.Ed.2d 215 (1963).

the sort of errors that are the focus of this chapter, the practices are unseemly. Overly aggressive prosecution tends to repel the public and subvert our system of justice.

Another important type of error can result from imprudent exercise of prosecutorial discretion: an error in the assessment of culpability. Questions about whether juveniles, or adults with serious mental impairments or emotional illness are criminally liable are questions of law and culpability rather than questions of fact. So are questions about whether a defendant acted in self-defense in a case in which he or she is charged with assault. Similarly, violations of federal RICO statutes and insider trading laws are often technically complicated and difficult to establish as criminal rather than civil matters. In all such cases, the question is not whether a defendant committed a particular act, but whether the act qualifies as criminal. Specific rulings may produce inconsistencies in the interpretation of the law or violations of ethical norms rather than errors about whether a particular person committed the act at issue. That the tools and frameworks for inquiry that are the staples of this book do not help to resolve these questions does not mean that the questions are not important.

Even among the large class of cases that qualify unambiguously as criminal rather than juvenile or civil, degrees of culpability are important to the prosecutor's decisions to accept a case and determine the level of resources to allocate to it if accepted. To the extent that the degree of harm imposed on victims and the community at large is a measure of culpability, the prosecutor should allocate more resources to cases involving greater culpability, for any margin of cases in which the strength of the evidence and dangerousness of the offender to the community are about equal. Prosecutors routinely exercise discretion in making such decisions, and occasionally use decision support tools to help guide this exercise, using such metrics as the maximum sentence associated with the charges as a measure of offense seriousness.[8]

---

[8] In the early and mid-1970s, the U.S. Attorney for the District of Columbia incorporated an offense seriousness scale developed by criminologists Marvin Wolfgang and Thorsten Sellin as the metric to assess cases at the screening stage. As a practical matter, most assistant attorneys paid little attention to the score given to each case.

Prosecutors also may miscalculate in their tactical decision making, with the result that culpable offenders go free. The notorious error of Los Angeles Assistant District Attorney Christopher Darden's having defendant O. J. Simpson try on a pair of bloody, shrunken gloves in trial may be a case in point. Such miscalculations are also beyond the scope of the present inquiry, although the prospect of empirical analysis helping to establish prosecution approaches that are more or less effective in dealing with various classes of cases cannot be ignored. One might expect that these miscalculations are no more likely to occur in cases involving culpable offenders than in cases involving innocent defendants. Nonetheless, to the extent that they reduce the conviction rate, they will increase the number of culpable offenders set free and reduce the number of innocent people convicted. As with errors of culpability, I will leave the analysis of the effect of prosecutorial tactics in individual cases on errors of justice as a topic for future inquiry.

Should the Prosecutor Emphasize Conviction Quality or Quantity?

Determining the standard of evidence to use in screening arrests involves more than a tradeoff between the certainty and severity of the eventual sanction in individual cases. It involves also a choice between the *number* of convictions and the *quality* of convictions. A prosecutor who uses a higher standard of proof in the screening room rejects arrests that would otherwise be accepted, freeing up resources to bring more cases to trial: a preference for quality of convictions over quantity. These options may have profound implications for justice errors. Emphasis on the quality of convictions includes greater attention to due process considerations and reduced risk of convicting innocent people; emphasis on the number of convictions reduces the rate at which culpable offenders are set free. Of course, higher quality of convictions need not come at the expense of the number of convictions. Additional resources can lead to a reduction of both the number of culpable offenders released and that of innocent persons convicted. For a given level of resources, however, the prosecutor often must choose among policies that tend to emphasize the minimization of one type of error or the other.

The choice between a focus on quality or quantity of convictions revolves around basic questions about the purpose of the criminal justice system, as well as consideration of the relative severity of sanctions that apply under each option. An emphasis on quality of convictions over quantity may be justified on grounds of procedural justice and due process, based on the notion that the alternative may operate to undermine the defendant's fundamental Sixth Amendment right to an impartial trial. An emphasis on the number of convictions, by contrast, may be justified on grounds of the public's right to protection against crime and disorder, to ensure domestic tranquility by minimizing the number of culpable offenders who escape criminal sanction. It may be justified as well on grounds of just deserts, the notion that offenders deserve to be sanctioned for the crimes they commit, assuming that the sanctions given to the margin of additional offenders convicted is not offset by the shorter sanctions given to offenders convicted under an emphasis on quality.

But the choice over whether to emphasize quality or quantity of convictions involves more. In using a higher standard of evidence in screening arrests, the prosecutor will be rejecting some cases at the margin that would otherwise end up as convictions by pleas of guilt. Accordingly, the prosecutor might do well to contemplate how many of those marginally acceptable cases are likely to involve true offenders and how many likely to involve innocent persons. If the prosecutor perceives that margin of cases to have a high ratio of true offenders to innocent persons, the prosecutor ought to be inclined to accept more than otherwise; if the ratio is perceived to be low, the prosecutor should reject more.

Of course, all arrestees do not fall neatly into the two categories: true offenders and innocent persons. Many cases involve arrestees who in fact committed crimes, but whose culpability is mitigated by factors such as triviality of offense, victim provocation, and a host of situational and personal factors. The social cost of pursuing convictions in such cases involving factually guilty offenders may exceed that of rejecting these cases in the screening room or dropping them (*nolle prosequi* or "nol pros") after initial filing in court. This is precisely the group of cases for which the prudent exercise of prosecutorial discretion is required.

In other cases, the choice between quality and number of convictions can involve a vexing tradeoff between the two basic types of errors of justice. The central question boils down to this: If a prosecutor were to shift from an emphasis on quantity to an emphasis on quality of convictions – that is, from a low arrest rejection rate and high ratio of pleas to trials to a high rejection rate and a low ratio of pleas to trials – what sort of shifts should one expect between the number of offenders set free and the number of innocent persons convicted? How should these expectations change as the percentage of arrests involving true offenders grows large?

Analyzing Data on Prosecution under a Range of Assumptions about Factual Guilt

Prosecutors in fact vary widely as to the standard of evidentiary proof used in the screening room, and this variation has been found to be related to the ratio of pleas to trials from one jurisdiction to the next (Boland and Forst, 1985).[9] Some prosecutors are inclined to accept only trial-worthy cases and obtain fewer convictions by plea, while others are inclined to accept marginal cases and put greater effort into the task of negotiating pleas and winning convictions in cases that would be rejected elsewhere.[10]

By incorporating available data on the court outcomes of felony arrests brought to the prosecutor in a cross-section of jurisdictions in a computer template designed to accommodate a variety of assumptions

---

[9] Wright and Miller (2002) report evidence of the tradeoff between case screening and plea bargaining decisions within a single jurisdiction (New Orleans).

[10] Examples of jurisdictions in the former camp, with higher screening standards and fewer pleas per trial in the early 1980s, included New Orleans, Portland (OR), and Washington (DC). Examples in the latter camp include Manhattan (NY), Geneva (IL), and Cobb County (GA) (Boland and Forst, 1985, p. 11). Unfortunately, the data series on which this analysis was based was discontinued a few years after the study using those data was conducted. Were data available to replicate the research reported here, the lists could well be different, although there is no compelling reason to expect that the essential findings on differences across district attorneys' offices would have changed.

about the mix of true offenders and innocent persons, we can assess the effect of a shift in strategy from quality to quantity, or vice versa, on errors of justice.[11] Two strategy scenarios are presented below, one emphasizing conviction quantity and the other emphasizing quality, both making the following assumptions: 90 percent of all arrests involve true offenders,[12] 75 percent of all trials result in guilty verdicts, and prosecutors screening cases are able to discriminate true offenders from others in such a way that produces higher case acceptance rates for true offenders than for innocent persons.[13] In Scenario A, the prosecutor opts for quantity over quality by rejecting relatively few (20 percent of all) arrests in the screening room, then engaging extensively in plea bargaining and bringing few cases to trial. In Scenario B, the prosecutor screens more selectively (rejecting 40 percent) and then accepts fewer pleas and brings more cases to trial. Under Scenario B the differential in arrest acceptance rates for true offenders and innocent people is assumed to be larger than under a policy of emphasis on quantity, a product of the additional time spent at the screening stage.[14] And, because fewer inducements to plead guilty are offered, the rate at which

[11] The scenarios presented below are based on cross-jurisdictional data on case acceptance rates, conviction and plea rates, and rates of acquittal in trial. All juvenile arrests are excluded, as are arrests accepted for prosecution and dropped later (*nolle prosequi*) following the successful completion of a treatment program (Boland and Sones, 1986; DeFrances and Steadman, 1998; Forst, 2002). *Nolle prosequis* can be regarded conceptually as a type of delayed rejection. The interests of justice may be served by filing a case and rejecting it later (e.g., because of successful completion of a drug treatment program), and a more elaborate model could be developed to account for such practices in the analysis of related issues.

[12] The reader should not infer that the assumption shown here, that 90 percent of all arrestees are culpable offenders, is in fact closer to the truth than any other number. Police and prosecutors may see it as too low, and others may see it as too high. The values assigned to this assumption ranged from 75 percent to 99 percent. Although evidence on overturned convictions does not suggest any particular number, that evidence is not inconsistent with the range used here. But even that evidence misses the point of the analysis described here: to set an arbitrary point that has plausibility on its face and see how robust the findings are to *variation* around that point.

[13] One could reasonably postulate that the screening process may in fact tend to bring cases involving innocent people to trial that look stronger than the ones involving culpable offenders. It is difficult to imagine a valid test of such a prospect.

[14] For Scenario A, cases involving true offenders were assumed to be three times more likely to be accepted than cases involving innocent arrestees; for Scenario B, the acceptance rate multiple was assumed to be four. This parameter was varied from lows of two to highs of five, subject to nonnegativity constraints for all cells and the other constraints noted.

Table 8.1a. *Prosecutor Accepts 80 Percent of Arrests, Negotiates 15 Pleas for Each Trial**

	Committed Crime	Did not Commit	Total	
Arrests rejected	**129**	71	200	
Guilty pleas	727	**23**	750	Offenders freed per innocent
Guilty verdicts	34	**4**	38	convicted: 138.1/26.1 = *5.3*
Acquittals	**10**	2	12	Percent of cases decided in
Total cases	900	100	1000	error: 164.2/1000 = *16.4%*

* Justice errors in boldface; cell entries are subject to rounding errors.

Table 8.1b. *Prosecutor Accepts 60 Percent of Arrests, Negotiates 5 Pleas for Each Trial**

	Committed Crime	Did not Commit	Total	
Arrests rejected	**316**	84	400	
Guilty pleas	495	**5**	500	Offenders freed per innocent
Guilty verdicts	68	**7**	75	convicted: 337.4/12.4 = *27.2*
Acquittals	**21**	4	25	Percent of cases decided in
Total cases	900	100	1000	error: 349.8/1000 = *35.0%*

* Justice errors in boldface; cell entries are subject to rounding errors.

innocent people plead guilty is assumed to be lower.[15] Results are shown in Tables 8.1a and 8.1b.

These two scenarios were repeated under a range of assumptions about the percentage of all felony arrests involving true offenders (from a low of 75 percent to a high of 99 percent), the likelihood ratio of the case acceptance rate for true offenders to that for innocent

[15] One might reasonably ask why an innocent person would *ever* plead guilty, especially in Scenario B, in which the prosecutor offers less incentive to do so. There are several plausible explanations. First, even when the incentives to plead are small, defendants may be inclined to take advantage of them when the evidence against them is strong. Second, some innocent defendants might plead guilty because they have gotten away with related crimes, perhaps more serious, that they fear might be unearthed if they reject the plea offer and are subjected to further investigative scrutiny. Third, judges show varying degrees of diligence to ensure that innocent people do not plead guilty. Differences in the manner in which federal judges handle the fact-finding stage of the review of a defendant's guilty plea have been documented by Jackman.

Table 8.2. *Error Ratios and Rates Under Different Prosecution Strategies and as Innocent Persons as a Percentage of Total Arrestees Increases*[*]

	Offenders Freed per Innocent Convicted			Errors as a Percent of Total Cases		
	True Offenders as a Percent of the Total			True Offenders as a Percent of the Total		
Prosecution Strategy	95%	85%	75%	95%	85%	75%
Accept 80%, 15 pleas/trial	7	4	1	20%	13%	7%
Accept 60%, 5 pleas/trial	32	23	15	39%	31%	23%

[*] Values shown are based on the midrange values of the following input parameters: True offenders are three times as likely to have their cases accepted as innocents under an emphasis on quantity and four times as likely under an emphasis on quality; 3 percent of all defendants who plead guilty are innocent under an emphasis on quantity and 1 percent are innocent under an emphasis on quality; 75 percent of all defendants tried in court are found guilty.

persons (ranging from twice as likely to be prosecuted to five times as likely), the percentage of all trials resulting in guilty verdicts (ranging from 60 percent to 90 percent), and the percentage of pleas of guilt involving innocent persons (ranging from 1 percent to 5 percent).[16] The purpose here is not to suggest the accuracy of any particular assumption or set of assumptions, but rather to examine the effect of *variation* in each assumption on justice errors, to see how sensitive the error rates and ratios are to changes in each. The true values are likely to vary from jurisdiction to jurisdiction, as do the documented values of known parameters such as case acceptance rates, plea-to-trial ratios, and conviction rates.

The findings are summarized in Table 8.2, showing how errors shift as prosecutor shifts from one strategy to the other and as the percentage of innocents arrested increases.

[16] In addition, a constraint was imposed on all scenarios: that juries were assumed to convict true offenders at a higher rate than they were innocent persons – that is, more accurately than at random. Prosecutors could conceivably bring cases involving innocent people to trial that tend to look stronger than the ones involving culpable offenders, but one would expect that the better the pretrial screening process, the more likely that trial cases involving true offenders will be stronger than ones with innocent people.

Two somewhat unexpected findings emerge consistently from these simulations. First, for all sets of assumptions tested, a shift to a prosecution strategy of more selective case screening and greater emphasis on trials increases both the number of offenders set free per innocent person convicted and the total error rate. Second, as the percentage of felony arrestees who are innocent increases, both the number of offenders set free per innocent convicted and the total error rate tend to decrease under *both* strategies, making a more selective felony case screening strategy increasingly attractive as the quality of police arrests declines, and arguably essential at some arbitrary threshold. To oversimplify a bit, as the police become more accurate in identifying true offenders, the prosecutor need not spend as much time screening cases. As the percentage of true offenders falls below 85 percent of all arrests, the less selective screening strategy causes the number of innocent persons convicted to approximate the number of offenders freed.

The increases in both the ratio of offenders freed to innocents convicted and in the total error rate for the more selective, trial-oriented strategy can be understood by comparing the scenarios cell by cell. Reductions in the case acceptance rate produce increases in the number of offenders set free at the screening stage and thus reduces the rate at which arrests end in conviction. The increase in the number of trials associated with an emphasis on quality of convictions tends also to produce an increase in the number of true offenders acquitted, but in most scenarios these increases are offset by declines in the number of innocent persons convicted by way of plea or trial. The increases in the number of offenders set free under a more selective prosecution strategy may, of course, be offset by an incapacitative effect: longer terms of incarceration for convicted offenders.[17]

These findings suggest that prosecutors can be more conscious of the effects of their case screening standards on errors of justice. They

---

[17] Any such offsets are likely to be perceived as having both utilitarian and retributive value. The accumulated evidence on deterrence and incapacitation and on the decline in criminal activity by age suggests stronger crime control effects from certainty of punishment than from long sentences (Blumstein, Cohen, and Nagin, 1978). The precise effects are likely to vary from one jurisdiction to the next.

suggest as well that prosecutors should be aware of the need to adapt their screening and plea bargaining policies to exogenous factors, such as changes in the quality of arrests brought by the police and shifts in the public's relative concerns over security and civil liberty. When the quality of arrests declines, perhaps the product of a crime wave or diversion of police resources to the press of other demands such as terrorism, more selective screening will be needed, not only to deal with the immediate need to correct the problem by checking the work of the police more carefully but also to manage the balance of errors of justice. Similarly, when crime and associated concerns for public safety subside, tougher screening standards and more focus on trials might be warranted to produce corresponding reductions in errors of due process.

Analysis by Crime Category

The results described above are limited in several respects. They are based on aggregate statistics about felony cases, and felony cases are not homogeneous. For some crime and offender categories, such as stranger rape, the social cost of an error of failure to convict a culpable offender, relative to that of convicting an innocent person, may be much higher than for others, such as shoplifting, because of the greater risk of subsequent serious crime if a dangerous offender is not incapacitated. For other categories, questions of culpability may be more important to prosecution strategy than questions of wrong-person error, as in the case of a 14- or 15-year-old who commits homicide. Prosecutors must weigh the problem of wrong-person errors with other considerations.

Another limitation lends itself to further analysis: in any given jurisdiction, the underlying rates of actual innocence, case acceptance, jury trials, guilty verdicts, and so on, are likely to vary from one offense category to another. Prosecutors should be less inclined to reject arrests for homicide than for less serious crimes, and less likely to grant concessions for guilty pleas in such cases as well, for reasons other than concerns about errors of justice. For some categories of crime the likelihood of error in arrest may be greater: stranger-to-stranger crimes that are more susceptible to erroneous witness identification, crimes for which the quality of defense counsel tends to be weak, and crimes in which the police department is under intense pressure to solve the case. Given such variation, separate analyses should be conducted for each crime category based on the known parameter values of the respective crimes.

Consider, for example, two important felony offenses: homicide and burglary. Persons arrested for homicide are much more likely to be prosecuted and convicted, and much less likely to plead rather than go to trial, than persons arrested for burglary. Data from the National Judicial Reporting Program (NJRP) for 1996 reveal that for every 100 arrests for murder, 60 people are convicted and 57 incarcerated, 55 to prison terms of at least a year (Brown, Langan, and Levin, 1999).[18] For burglary, the respective numbers are 26 convicted, 18 incarcerated, and 12 imprisoned.[19] Data from the Bureau of Justice Statistics survey of prosecutors for the 75 largest urban counties for the same year reveal that 85 percent of all murder trials end in guilty verdicts and about one defendant pleads guilty for each who chooses to be judged in trial, while only 71 percent of all burglary trials end in guilty verdicts, with about eight pleas per trial overall (Hart and Reaves, 1999, p. 24). Given these differences, how are the prosecution policy options analyzed in the preceding section likely to influence the two types of justice errors in these two very different types of cases?

---

[18] These numbers are based on estimated totals in each category occurring annually rather than the tracking of arrests over time. The Bureau of Justice Statistics discontinued case-tracking statistics documenting the arrest-to-conviction process after 1988, publishing instead numbers of convictions and incarcerations in selected years in its *Felony Defendants in Large Urban Counties* (Hart and Reaves, 1999) and *Felony Sentences in State Courts* (Brown, Langan, and Levin, 1999) series. Because many convictions reported for any given year relate to arrests made in earlier years, some distortions result, especially when the aggregates change from year to year.

[19] Conviction rates for burglary are much lower than for homicide largely for two reasons: (1) juveniles constitute a larger share of burglary arrests than they do homicide arrests, and they do not show up as convictions in either category; and (2) burglary arrests involving nonstrangers are much more likely to be dropped "in the interest of justice" than are nonstranger homicides. It would make more sense for our purposes to restrict the analysis to stranger-to-stranger (adult) crimes, but the available data do not support such an analysis.

To assess the effect of a shift in strategy from quality to quantity (or vice versa) on errors of justice, we shall use the same approach as in the previous section, but with different ranges of assumed values for each crime, based on the respective plea-to-trial ratios and conviction rates reported for these two crime categories, exclusive of juvenile cases. The mid-range assumptions for homicide used in this analysis are as follows: 90 percent of all arrests involve true offenders, 85 percent of all trials result in guilty verdicts (as reported), and the percentages of pleas involving innocent people are assumed to be 1 percent under the policy of emphasis on quantity and 0.5 percent under the policy of emphasis on quality, in which the incentives offered the defendant to plead guilty will tend to be less attractive. For burglary the corresponding mid-range assumptions used are 90 percent, 71 percent (as reported), and 3 percent and 1 percent respectively. As before, in Scenario A the prosecutor rejects relatively few arrests in the screening room (10 percent for homicides and 20 percent for burglaries),[20] then opts for quantity over quality by engaging extensively in plea bargaining and bringing few cases to trial (1.5 pleas per trial for homicide, 12 pleas per trial for burglary). In Scenario B the prosecutor uses a more selective screening strategy (rejecting 20 percent of homicides and 40 percent of burglaries), with higher rejection rates for cases involving innocents than for cases involving true offenders, and then the prosecutor accepts fewer pleas and brings more cases to trial (1 homicide plea per trial, 4 burglary pleas per trial). Results for homicide are shown in Tables 8.3a and 8.3b.

Results for burglary are shown in Tables 8.4a and 8.4b.

Given existing patterns of case acceptance, pleas per trial and conviction rates for these two crime categories, the most striking difference that emerges is that the total error rates tend to be about twice as high for burglary than for homicide under either prosecution

---

[20] Case acceptance rates are generally higher for homicides than for burglaries (Boland and Sones, 1981, 1986). For both homicides and burglaries, cases involving offenders are assumed accepted at a higher rate than cases involving innocent persons.

Table 8.3a. *Prosecutor Accepts 90 Percent of Homicide Arrests, Negotiates 1.5 Pleas per Trial**

	Committed crime	Did not commit	Total	
Arrests rejected	**32**	68	100	
Guilty pleas	535	**5**	540	Offenders freed per innocent
Guilty verdicts	284	**22**	306	convicted: 81.1 / 27.1 = *3.0*
Acquittals	**49**	5	54	Percent of cases decided in
Total cases	900	100	1000	error: 108.3 / 1000 = *10.8%*

* Justice errors in boldface; cell entries are subject to rounding errors.

Table 8.3b. *Prosecutor Accepts 80 Percent of Homicide Arrests, Negotiates 1 Plea per Trial**

	Committed crime	Did not commit	Total	
Arrests rejected	**122**	78	200	
Guilty pleas	398	**2**	400	Offenders freed per innocent
Guilty verdicts	324	**16**	340	convicted: 177.7 / 17.7 = *10.1*
Acquittals	**56**	4	60	Percent of cases decided in
Total cases	900	100	1000	error: 195.4 / 1000 = *19.5%*

* Justice errors in boldface; cell entries are subject to rounding errors.

policy, and the ratio of offenders freed per innocent person convicted is slightly higher for burglary than for homicide under either policy. The general findings of the previous section hold up under both offense categories.

One might expect the prosecutor, *a priori*, to be more inclined to choose an emphasis on quality of convictions in homicide cases than in burglary. Our results are consistent with the wisdom of such a strategy. The more selective screening strategy for homicide cases produces the smallest number of innocent persons convicted of any of the four scenarios shown above. These patterns hold for all other scenarios considered, as described earlier.

Table 8.4a. *Prosecutor Accepts 80 Percent of Burglary Arrests, Negotiates 12 Pleas per Trial**

	Committed crime	Did not commit	Total	
Arrests rejected	**129**	71	200	
Guilty pleas	716	**22**	738	Offenders freed per innocent
Guilty verdicts	40	**4**	44	convicted: 143.7 / 25.7 = **5.6**
Acquittals	**15**	3	18	Percent of cases decided in
Total cases	900	100	1000	169.4 / 1000 = **error: 16.9%**

* Justice errors in boldface; cell entries are subject to rounding errors.

Table 8.4b. *Prosecutor Accepts 60 Percent of Burglary Arrests, Negotiates 4 Pleas per Trial**

	Committed crime	Did not commit	Total	
Arrests rejected	**316**	84	400	
Guilty pleas	475	**5**	480	Offenders freed per innocent
Guilty verdicts	78	**7**	85	convicted: 346.9 / 11.9 = **29.2**
Acquittals	**31**	4	35	Percent of cases decided in
Total cases	900	100	1000	error: 358.8 / 1000 = **35.9%**

* Justice errors in boldface; cell entries are subject to rounding errors.

Conclusion

Much has been written about how prosecutors contribute to the convictions of innocent people through biased review of the evidence and breaches of ethical standards, such as failure to divulge important exculpatory evidence and fraudulent reporting of case processing practices (Scheck, Neufeld, and Dwyer, 2001; Huff, Rattner, and Sagarin, 1996; Radelet, Bedau, and Putnam, 1992). These sensational accounts are significant for calling attention to the importance of maintaining integrity in the practice of prosecution. They have probably helped substantially to deter prosecutors from engaging in such unethical practices.

This approach to reform, however, may have considerably less impact on errors of justice than prosecution policies governing the routine prosecution decisions made in some two million or so felony cases annually, policies that receive almost no attention at all. In determining whether to focus on the quality of convictions, by rejecting more cases up front and then taking more cases to trial, or on the number of convictions, by accepting more arrests and inducing more pleas and fewer trials, prosecutors appear to have a considerable impact on both the number of culpable offenders freed and the number of innocent persons convicted.

Although many of the findings reported above are robust with regard to a wide range of assumptions, such simplifying assumptions nonetheless tend to raise more questions than they answer. How do errors in the arrests brought to prosecutors *really* vary by jurisdiction and crime category? Could some of the scenarios in the real world be at rates outside the ranges considered above? What are the social cost implications of errors of justice that are the product of prosecution decisions, including the costs of sanctions that err either on the side of being too lax or too punitive? How might systems of accountability be designed to ensure that the prosecutor's responsibility for errors of justice is adequately monitored? Who should manage such systems? Are policies associated with high due process error rates and low crime control error rates more common in jurisdictions in which prosecutors are elected than in jurisdictions where they are appointed?[21]

These are matters that researchers and prosecutors would do well to come to terms with in coming years. The public is not well served by our having ready access only to media accounts of the prosecution of celebrity cases, with a paucity of data and research on what happens to the millions of felony arrests brought to prosecutors each year. Data and research on policing, sentencing, and corrections are far more

---

[21] Rainville has found systematic differences in several variables across the two settings, particularly ones related to community orientation. He concludes: "elected prosecutors appear to be more interested in the political cachet associated with community prosecution than do appointed prosecutors." He had no data on arrest screening and plea bargaining policies.

plentiful than on prosecution, despite the central role played by the prosecutor in our system of justice.[22] This is a major blind spot, one that brings with it untold inefficiencies and injustices.

[22] The National Academy of Sciences highlighted this "paucity of research on the prosecutor's function" in a report by Heymann and Petrie (2001, p. 3). Their observation echoes a 1998 survey of over 500 research projects on crime prevention, sponsored by National Institute of Justice and conducted by researchers from the University of Maryland, which found many innovative programs that were revealed to be effective, programs initiated by the police, social service agencies, schools, drug treatment specialists, housing and correctional authorities. This report found just one program focusing on the prosecutor – an experiment designed to test the effect of alternative prosecution policies in domestic violence cases. The survey was conducted and documented by Sherman et al. (1999). The prosecution experiment, documented by Ford, tested three alternative domestic violence interventions in Indianapolis.

CHAPTER NINE

The Jury

In all criminal prosecutions, the accused shall enjoy the right to a speedy and public trial, by an impartial jury of the State and district wherein the crime shall have been committed, which district shall have been previously ascertained by law, and to be informed of the nature and cause of the accusation; to be confronted with the witnesses against him; to have compulsory process for obtaining witnesses in his favor, and to have the Assistance of Counsel for his defence.

– Sixth Amendment to the U.S. Constitution

Introduction

The American public episodically shows deep concern about jury errors. This concern emerges from time to time despite the relative rarity that an offender, even if arrested, will be held accountable for his criminal act before a jury: only 5 percent of all felony arrests end up in the judgment of a jury (Brown, Langan and Levin, 1999; Hart and Reaves, 1999).[1] Public concern over jury errors is nonetheless legitimate, even if it derives principally from the handful of high-stakes jury trials that become public spectacles. These cases typically involve serious crimes; they serve as civics lessons. They shape what prospective

---

[1] The numbers vary substantially across crime categories. A person arrested for murder is almost twice as likely to go to trial (30 percent) as one arrested for rape (16 percent), about six times more likely than a robbery arrestee (5 percent), and about 15 times more likely than a person arrested for aggravated assault or burglary (2 percent) (Hart and Reaves, 1999; Brown, Langan and Levin, 1999). The denominators of the trial rates for homicide and burglary reported here include juvenile arrests, hence these rates are lower than those used in the scenarios for the previous chapter.

offenders and criminal justice officials come to expect would happen, for better or for worse, should they find themselves involved in a jury trial. Regardless of the accuracy of these perceptions, the legitimacy of our criminal justice system is undermined when it is widely believed that juries are unreliable arbiters of guilt and innocence.

The rules governing juries have developed only in part over concern about errors of jury judgments. The modern jury system has origins that are traceable to the Magna Carta, in 1215. Created by a King John under considerable duress,[2] the Magna Carta gave the public direct input into judicial decisions, quite unprecedented at the time. Concerns about jury selection and procedure continue to this day to reflect this core democratic purpose. Alexis de Tocqueville observed prominently, "The jury is therefore above all a political institution, and it is from that point of view that it must always be judged."[3] Others have expanded on Tocqueville's observations, emphasizing the jury's uniquely populist character, that its makeup as a diverse body of citizens collectively

---

[2] The king had suffered a series of battle failures in campaigns against France in the early years of the 13th century, and taxed the English barons to finance the failed efforts. In May of 1215, the angry barons revolted, capturing London. The beleaguered king consented to sign the Magna Carta at Runnymeade in June, granting broad feudal rights, including the freedom of the Church to make ecclesiastic appointments, limits on taxing authority, and the provision that freemen could be punished only within the context of common law. Article 39 of the document specifically affirmed the right to trial by jury: "No freeman shall be seized, or imprisoned, or dispossessed, or outlawed, or in any way destroyed; nor will we condemn him, nor will we commit him to prison, excepting by the legal judgment of his peers, or by the laws of the land." Article 40 added, "To no one will we sell, to no one deny or delay right or justice."

[3] Quote is from Volume 1, Chapter 8 ("What Tempers the Tyranny of the Majority in the United States: Absence of Administrative Centralization), Section entitled, "The Temper of the American Legal Profession and How It Serves to Counterbalance Democracy." Tocqueville continued, "The jury may be an aristocratic or a democratic institution, according to the class from which the jurors are selected; but there is always a republican character in it, inasmuch as it puts the real control of affairs into the hands of the ruled, or some of them, rather than into those of the rulers." Tocqueville went on to point out that English juries, unlike American ones, are drawn exclusively from the aristocratic class. He was especially enthusiastic about the benefits of ordinary citizens sitting in civil rather than criminal juries: "I think that the main reason for the practical intelligence and the political good sense of the Americans is their long experience with juries in civil cases." He concluded: "The jury is both the most effective way of establishing the people's rule and the most efficient way of teaching them how to rule." Later in the book, Tocqueville commented on the irony of juries strengthening the authority of the judge: "The jury, then, which seems to restrict the rights of the judiciary, does in reality consolidate its power; and in no country are the judges so powerful as where the people share their privileges" (Chapter 16, "Causes Which Mitigate the Tyranny of the Majority in the United States").

reflects their unique experiences and values, especially significant in deliberations over the interpretation of evidence and application of the law (Abramson, 1994).

The jury system thus presents us with a tension between two fundamentally different aspects of criminal justice legitimacy. The very existence of the right to trial by a jury of one's peers attests to the political legitimacy of the process itself, a commitment to a distinctly democratic process for protecting the rights of citizens in criminal cases. Legitimacy may be undermined under this process, however, if, along the way, serious questions are raised about the competence of jurors who are selected to pass judgment in complex cases, to decide in a manner that minimizes errors of justice.

Jury Policy, Representativeness, and Justice Errors

Critics of the jury system have raised a variety of concerns, some having little to do with errors of justice. Abramson, Gobert, and others have expressed concern about rules and procedures that interfere with the representativeness of juries and undermine the goal of ensuring that the defendant's guilt or innocence in a crime, or responsibility in a civil matter, will be decided by his or her peers. Much of the concern about jury representativeness has focused on the rules governing eligibility, with such alternatives as selection from voters lists, lists of registered drivers, tax rolls, welfare recipient files, and exemptions for occupation or hardship. No less attention has been directed to the selection of jurors by defense and prosecution from lists of eligibles, with questions about the ethics of peremptory challenges – the rejection of a set number of jurors by either side without the need to explain the reason for rejection[4] – and the goal of widening the eligibility of minorities and increasing their participation as jurors.

---

[4] Alschuler (1996) has noted that 45 percent of the 196 people summoned as jurors for the 1974 Watergate trial of John Mitchell and Maurice Stans had attended college, but only one of them ended up on the jury (p. 33). The likelihood of fewer than two persons with college educations ending up on the jury due to chance is less than .01 (calculated using the hypergeometric distribution). It might, of course, be the case that jurors with less education tend to make more accurate assessments of guilt or innocence, but most people probably would bet otherwise.

Still, concerns about jury errors remain strong. Concerns have long been expressed about whether jurors are competent to decide in complex cases.[5] Some critics have raised questions about whether rules against note-taking increase jury errors.[6] One side finds that note taking reduces error by reinforcing juror memories about what happened in trial (ForsterLee et al., 1994; Vidmar, 1989). The other side argues that notes may be in error, may divert the juror's attention away from more critical information presented in trial, may be used to bully other jurors, and are unnecessary in any case because jurors can ask for transcripts of the trial (Heuer and Penrod, 1994b).

Other critics have expressed concerns about renegade jurors, juror competency, and juror nullification of the law as prospective sources of error. Several observers of the jury have characterized juries as fallible and often unreliable arbiters,[7] easily seduced, especially in matters involving brutal crimes with unattractive defendants and victims who evoke juror sympathy (Penrod and Cutler, 1987; Scheck, Neufeld and Dwyer, 2001). In his landmark collection of case studies of wrongful convictions, Edwin Borchard commented, "Juries seem disposed more readily to credit the veracity and reliability of the victims of an outrage than any amount of contrary evidence." The jury in the O. J. Simpson murder trial, the last of several claimants to the title of Trial of the Century for the 20th century, did little to bolster support for the notion

---

[5] One noted legal scholar, following observations of numerous jury trials, wrote, "The truth is that for much of the time there are twelve wandering minds in that silent group, bodily present but mentally far away.... It is plainly said by those whose opinions command the utmost respect that the administration of the law in this land is on a lower plane than other phases of government and is unworthy of the civilization it poorly serves" (Frank, 1973, p. 124).

Rita Simon (1999), on the other hand, takes exception to this popular view of the jury "as a group of indignant, angry citizens seeking vengeance even at the cost of justice. We saw the jurors' urge to punish tempered by a sense of responsibility and socialized by the expectations which they believed were placed upon them by the judicial system" (pp. 178–9). Simon's observation followed an extensive, albeit "informal, non-quantified content analysis" of actual jury deliberations (p. 132).

[6] Several states have issued guidelines to govern note-taking by jurors, typically stipulating that the taking of notes should not be a distraction, should be used only by the individual juror to aid the memory, and should not be used to influence other jurors or outside the jury room.

[7] Kersch (2003) describes jurors as "wild cards... the enemy of rational, systematic thinking." (p. 121)

that our jury system can be trusted to produce bodies that weigh the evidence objectively and render reliable verdicts.

Jury errors may result also from a jury's failure to understand instructions from the judge and obscure legal jargon.[8] One study reports that just 5 percent of jurors understand and remember the judge's instructions on the legal standards applicable to their task (Sunstein, 2002). Jurors interviewed following a judge's repeating rather than explaining instructions have been found to be significantly less likely to understand the instructions than when the judge offered meaningful clarifications (Eisenberg and Wells, 1993; Garvey, Marcus, and Johnson, 2000). In the 2000 case of *Weeks v. Angelone*, a defendant who killed a Virginia State trooper was executed following the jury's apparent failure to understand that they were permitted to exercise an option not to vote for execution, a misunderstanding that the judge presiding in the case took no action to clarify (Berlow, 1999).

In 1999 Supreme Court Justice Sandra Day O'Connor expressed strong reservation about whether juries render informed decisions:

> Too often, jurors are allowed to do nothing but listen passively to the testimony, without any idea what the legal issues are in the case, not allowed to take notes or participate in any way, and finally to be read a virtually incomprehensible set of instructions and sent into the jury room to reach a verdict in a case they may not understand much better than they did before the trial began.

Some of the questions about jury reliability are empirically testable. Kalven and Zeisel (1966) found a rate of 78 percent of agreement between judge and jury, a finding replicated approximately by others (e.g., Heuer and Penrod, 1994a), but these studies say nothing about which of the two are in error when they disagree, nor do they suggest that even when they agree, both the judge and jury may be in error.

---

[8] In commuting the death sentences of all 156 death row inmates in 2003, Former Illinois Governor Ryan included this justification: "What are we to make of the studies that showed that more than 50 percent of Illinois jurors could not understand the confusing and obscure sentencing instructions that were being used?"

The presumption that the judge is a more reliable arbiter than the jury is implicit in much of this work, but we really do not know. One can imagine an experiment in which edited tapes or summaries of transcripts are shown to a judge and a mock jury, some validated afterward by evidence technologies not available at the time of the trial, and others invalidated, in order to permit inferences as to the relative accuracy of judges and juries, but even such a test would not provide the incontrovertible truth of such inferences, given that inferences based on DNA evidence may be flawed.

Evidence of errors of justice has already come forth implicating juries as fallible. Over 100 convictions involving death sentences have been overturned since the mid-1970s, nearly all involving jury verdicts and many involving DNA evidence. The previous chapter speculates on the errors on the other side as well, which we refer to as "errors of impunity," but the results in any jurisdiction will depend on the quality of the screening processes that precede trial and the ability of the jury to accurately assess the information presented in trial. We are not likely to learn as much about DNA evidence that turns out to be consistent with the defendant's culpability in pre-DNA-technology cases in which the defendant was acquitted as we do exculpatory DNA evidence in cases in which the defendant was convicted, largely because of the double jeopardy rule. Moreover, exculpatory DNA evidence is often more powerful for exonerating a defendant for a crime in question than is a DNA match for incriminating a defendant. A semen match with a man known to be a victim's lover is less useful in a homicide-rape case, for example, than a semen match with a stranger. DNA evidence has proven extremely useful for exonerating defendants wrongfully convicted and given death sentences in homicide-rape cases (Scheck, Neufeld, and Dwyer, 2001).

The discovery of DNA technology nonetheless provides a unique opportunity to learn more about jury errors on both sides of the coin. For a sufficiently large and representative cohort of cases decided by jury prior to the availability of DNA technology and involving blood or semen evidence, it could be useful to examine the DNA evidence to validate the accuracy of jury decisions.

How Many Jurors? Must Their Decision be Unanimous?

A good deal of attention has been given to two other matters that bear directly on errors attributable to the jury: (1) the pros and cons of alternative jury arrangements, especially the effects of different numbers of jurors – from 6 to 12 – and (2) rules regarding whether the verdict should be unanimous or by as little as a two-thirds majority (e.g, Abramson; Gobert; Saks, 1977, 1996). While the merits of the various alternatives may be argued on grounds of fairness and costs, we can assess the effects in terms of conviction probability, both under the simplifying assumption of independence (i.e., that the probability of an individual juror's voting to convict will be unaffected by any other juror's vote) and using empirically derived information about the impact of dependencies associated with intrajuror dynamics on the conviction probability and the resulting effect on the risk of errors. The eventual goal: By comparing the effects under the assumption of independence with those using empirically derived information, we can examine the degree of nonindependence and its effect on justice errors.

Under both the assumption of independence and dependence, we can address the following questions: As the underlying probability that a randomly selected juror will vote the defendant guilty grows, what happens to the probability that the entire jury will render a guilty verdict under various rules about jury size and size of majority needed to convict? How do those probabilities compare with actual conviction rates in the jurisdiction by jury size? In light of the findings of Chapter 6, what can be said about the resulting effect of the nonindependence on the likelihood of a factually erroneous decision?

Let us first consider the logical and historical precedents of the rules that govern these matters. The presumption-of-innocence feature of our system of justice is reflected in the common requirement that a guilty verdict is not binding unless jurors are unanimous in their assessments that the defendant is guilty beyond a reasonable doubt. The presumption of innocence is also strengthened by this requirement. Under the unanimity rule, if a single juror is not satisfied that the evidence in a case meets the beyond-a-reasonable-doubt threshold, the defendant will not be convicted, even if all the other jurors are certain of the defendant's guilt.[9] As the size of the jury grows, so does the likelihood that at least one juror will show up with a dissenting vote.[10]

Juries have consisted traditionally of 12 members, although the origins of that precedent are unclear. In the 1970 case of *Williams v. Florida*,[11] the Supreme Court observed that the Constitution does not stipulate that juries should be any particular size, that the 12-member jury convention is "a historical accident, unnecessary to effect the purposes of the jury system and wholly without significance 'except to mystics'" (p. 102, with quote to *Duncan v. Louisiana*, 391 U.S. 145 (1968), at 182).[12] The Court concluded that a jury should:

> be large enough to promote group deliberation, free from outside attempts at intimidation, and to provide a fair possibility for obtaining a representative cross-section of the community. But we find little reason to think that these goals are in any meaningful sense less likely to be achieved when the jury numbers six, than when it numbers 12 – particularly if the requirement of unanimity is retained. And, certainly the reliability of the jury as a factfinder hardly seems likely to be a function of its size. (pp. 100–1)

Following the *Williams* decision, six states allow juries of fewer than 12 people to render verdicts in felony cases, in which imprisonment may be imposed for terms of more than one year: Florida, Louisiana, Oregon, South Carolina, Texas, and Utah. Several more states permit juries of fewer than 12 to decide in misdemeanor cases, involving jail

---

[9] It is, of course, also true that without unanimity for acquittal, there will be no verdict, a "hung jury." Still, in order to secure a conviction in most settings, the state must get all jurors to vote to convict. Although a hung jury is legally and substantively quite different from an acquittal, the practical consequence of a hung jury can be the same: a freed defendant.

[10] It is no coincidence that no state allows a capital case to be tried by a jury of fewer than 12 people and with less than a unanimous verdict. All the states recognize the need to set the highest standards for such cases, despite the occasional errors that show up even under these standards.

[11] 399 U.S. 78 (1970). See also *Colgrove v. Battin*, 413 U.S. 149 (1973), in which the Court held that juries of six members did not violate the Seventh Amendment right to a jury trial.

[12] Proffatt (1877) attributed the number 12 to an Eighth century king of Wales, Morgan of Gla-Morgan, who derived the number from Apostolic Law: "As Christ and his twelve apostles were finally to judge the world, so human tribunals should be composed of the king and twelve wise men" (Note 2).

terms of up to a year: Alaska, Georgia, Iowa, Kentucky, Mississippi, and Oklahoma. A few states even allow misdemeanor verdicts without right to trial by jury: Arkansas, Maine, New Hampshire, and Virginia. The Constitution protects the right to trial by jury primarily in felony cases.

In reaching its conclusion in *Williams*, the Court reviewed several real-world experiments and psychological studies, concluding, "In short, neither currently available evidence nor theory suggest that the 12-man jury is necessarily more advantageous to the defendant than a jury composed of fewer members" (p. 101–2). The Court's use of the modifier "necessarily" may suggest that those in the majority in *Williams* were not terribly interested in studies that suggested otherwise.[13]

It is useful, in any case, to consider how such empirical evidence is derived: through the analysis of data obtained either from real-world juries or from experimentation. The advantage of research based on data from actual jury deliberations is that it is not biased by contrived, unrealistic conditions. There are, however, two basic disadvantages: first, data on erroneous decisions are virtually nonexistent, except for the relative handful of cases in which wrongfully convicted defendants are exonerated following the revelation of exculpatory evidence, and second, even the more abundant data on conviction outcomes masks the basic input variables of interest here, including the initial assessments of the individual jurors, the factors describing what happened in trial, and the dynamics of jury deliberations. Experiments on the effect of jury size on outcomes typically involve students who decide after witnessing a videotape of a trial, with outcomes consisting of whether the finding is guilty or innocent rather than jury error.[14] Studies of the effect of jury size on outcome focus also on whether the defendant was convicted or acquitted rather than errors.

An alternative approach is to focus on the effect of jury size and decision rules on conviction rates – and, in turn, on error rates, following the logic of Chapter 6 – under a range of assumptions about the

---

[13] Zeisel (1971); Zeisel and Diamond (1974); Buckhout et al. (1977); and Saks (1977) have lent credence to this proposition, concluding that the Court's review of the relevant research in *Williams* was driven primarily by ideology rather than interest in objective, rigorous assessment.

[14] For example, Davis et al. (1975), compared 6- and 12-person mock juries of college students, in which the students viewed a 45-mm tape recording of a rape case and were instructed to deliberate for a minimum of thirty minutes.

underlying probability that an individual juror will vote to convict and the extent of nonindependence of the assessments of individual jurors, and then test the independence assumption against available data. The assumption of independence is more convenient and easier to work with – it is impossible to exhaust the various sources of the dependencies that might exist – although the assumption may bear little resemblance to reality. The dynamics of jury decision making is a subject rich in speculation and intrigue – regarding questions about leadership and peer pressure, coalitions and negotiations among jurors, and so on – with little consensus as to how it works generally and how it varies from setting to setting and under different circumstances.[15] We shall take this up in greater detail in the next section.

Under the conventional 12-person, unanimous consent jury rule, the likelihood that the entire jury will vote to convict drops sharply under the condition of independence as the probability that individual jurors vote to convict departs from 100 percent. As the probability declines from 99 percent to 95 percent for the individual jurors, the probability that the entire jury will convict drops from 89 percent to 54 percent. When the probability for an individual juror drops from 90 percent to 80 percent, the probability for the entire jury declines from 28 percent to 7 percent. The corresponding effects on the number of offenders freed per innocent defendant convicted and the overall error rate are shown in Table 9.1.

The most interesting variation occurs when an individual juror's probability of convicting is above 90 percent. Below that level, the number of offenders freed per innocent defendant convicted and overall error rates become arbitrarily large. For the 12-person jury, the declines from 99 percent to 95 percent and from 95 percent to a

---

[15] Kalven and Zeisel (1966) conducted a landmark study into the workings of the jury. Their study was extraordinary, among other things, for the way it overcame limitations of most other research on the jury: they bugged a jury room in Wichita to obtain candid information about the dynamics of jury deliberations in a civil proceeding, following a controversial approval by the presiding judge. Kalvin and Zeisel also surveyed the judges who presided over some 4,000 trials. In 78 percent of the trials, the presiding judges said they would have ruled the same way as the juries, had the decision been theirs to make. A more recent econometric analysis by Helland and Tabarrok produced similar concordance between judges and juries. One can, of course, speculate as to whether the judges truly had a more accurate sense of the truth in each case than the juries. See also Hastie, Penrod, and Pennington.

Table 9.1. *Error Ratios and Rates Under 12-Person Jury, Unanimous Rule, Under Assumption of Independence Among Jurors*

Conviction Rate per Juror	Conviction Probability, Entire Jury	95% of All Convicted Committed Crime		99% of All Convicted Committed Crime	
		Offenders Freed per Innocent Convicted	% of Cases Erroneously Decided	Offenders Freed per Innocent Convicted	% of Cases Erroneously Decided
50%	0.0%	*	90%	*	90%
60%	0.2%	*	90%	*	90%
70%	1.4%	*	89%	*	89%
80%	6.9%	242	84%	*	83%
90%	28.2%	45	65%	220	62%
95%	54.0%	14	41%	68	37%
99%	88.6%	1.3	10%	2.6	3%

Assumption: 90% of cases involve true offender.
* Number larger than 1,000.

90 percent conviction probability for the individual jurors have dramatic impacts on the likelihood that the entire jury will convict and, in turn, on the number of offenders freed per innocent convicted and overall error rate.

How do these results compare for the 6-person unanimous and 9-person jury with two-thirds majority rules,[16] assuming that the probabilities for individual jurors remain unchanged? The findings are shown in Tables 9.2 and 9.3.

Not surprisingly, we see higher jury conviction rates for the 6-person jury than for the 12-person jury. Holding all other factors constant, it is more difficult to get 12 jurors to agree unanimously than for 6 to do so. These results are consistent with prior empirical evidence (Saks, 1977).

For the nine-person jury with two-thirds majority rule, and again holding all other factors constant, the jury conviction rates are higher still. This produces generally lower numbers of offenders set free per innocent person convicted and lower total error rates. Note under this system the unlikely prospect of jury conviction rates of 99 percent for instances in which conviction probabilities for individual jurors exceed 90 percent.

Jury Dynamics

The assumptions of the preceding section may bear little resemblance to a variety of real-world settings and circumstances, as I have noted. For one thing, the probability that an individual juror will vote to convict might change as the number of jurors and jury rules change. Research has found that verdicts tend to be rendered more quickly, presumably with less deliberation, when the juries are smaller (Tamm, 1962) and when subject to majority rather than unanimous verdict rules (Hastie et al., 1983; Davis et al., 1975). Less deliberation is likely to mean that in a smaller jury a juror would be less likely to change his or her vote. And, although we cannot be certain of it, we might reasonably expect the revised vote to be more accurate than the original.

---

[16] In *Ballew v. Georgia* (1978, 435 U.S. 23), the United States Supreme Court ruled that six-person juries are permissible. The Court upheld a 9 out of 12 majority in *Johnson v. Louisiana* (1972, 406 U.S. 356). Several states allow verdicts of 9 or 10 of 12 including Louisana, Montana, Oklahoma, Oregon, and Texas.

Table 9.2. *Error Ratios and Rates Under 6-Person Jury, Unanimous Rule*

Conviction Rate per Juror	Conviction Probability, Entire Jury	95% of All Convicted Committed Crime		99% of All Convicted Committed Crime	
		Offenders Freed per Innocent Convicted	% of Cases Erroneously Decided	Offenders Freed per Innocent Convicted	% of Cases Erroneously Decided
50%	1.6%	*	89%	*	88%
60%	4.7%	364	86%	*	85%
70%	11.8%	134	79%	664	78%
80%	26.2%	50	66%	245	64%
90%	53.1%	15	42%	71	38%
95%	73.5%	5.5	24%	23	18%
99%	94.1%	**	**	**	**

* Number larger than 1,000.
** Assumptions: 90% of cases involve true offender, number convicted will not exceed number of true offenders.

Table 9.3. *Error Ratios and Rates Under 9-Person Jury, 2/3 Majority Rule*

Conviction Rate per Juror	Conviction Probability, Entire Jury	95% of All Convicted Committed Crime		99% of All Convicted Committed Crime	
		Offenders Freed per Innocent Convicted	% of Cases Erroneously Decided	Offenders Freed per Innocent Convicted	% of Cases Erroneously Decided
50%	25.4%	52	67%	256	65%
60%	48.3%	18	47%	88	43%
70%	73.0%	5.7	24%	24	19%
80%	91.4%	*	*	*	*
90%	99.2%	*	*	*	*
95+%	99.9%	*	*	*	*

* Assumptions: 90% of cases involve true offender, number convicted will not exceed number of true offenders.

A more basic factor is that the reality of jury dynamics – the effects of psychological and social influences, including peer pressure, emergence and decline of leaders, formation and collapse of coalitions, negotiations among jurors, and so on – renders the assumption of independence among jurors unrealistic. The appropriate question is not whether the assumption of independence is unrealistic, but to what extent is there dependence among the assessments of individual jurors under various circumstances. We could infer this from real-world jury decisions for juries of any size if we knew the individual juror assessments at the outset, but except for one landmark jury study,[17] it is extremely difficult to conduct post mortem surveys that are capable of unearthing them validly. We could infer the direction and extent of dependence from juries of different sizes if all relevant factors other than jury size were held constant, but they are not. This leaves mock juries as the lesser of evils, the most viable option for learning about the effect of jury rules on jury dynamics and outcomes.

Suppose that a controlled experiment of mock juries revealed that for a given case shown on videotape, 90 percent of mock 6-person juries voted unanimously to convict. If the individual juror assessments were independent and equal, 81 percent of mock 12-person would vote to convict.[18] If for a particular type of case and setting the conviction rates for 6- and 12-person juries were 90 percent and 75 percent, respectively, we could infer that the dynamics of the larger jury for that situation work to reduce the likelihood of a guilty finding conviction. If the conviction rates were 90 percent and 85 percent, respectively, we could infer that the dynamics work to increase the individual assessments toward a guilty finding, although the probability of conviction for a 12-person jury is likely to be smaller than for a jury of 6, under most circumstances. As noted earlier, this is consistent with prior empirical findings on actual jury decisions.

[17] Kalven and Zeisel (1966) found, based on an analysis of data from interviews with some 2,500 jurors who sat in real cases Chicago and Brooklyn, that first ballot majorities tend to become unanimous verdicts: "With very few exceptions the first ballot decides the outcome of the verdict" (p. 488).

[18] Under independence and equal probabilities among the jurors, a 90 percent conviction rate for a 6-person jury implies that individual jurors vote to convict at a rate of 98.26 percent ($.9826^6 = .90$) and at an 81% conviction rate for a 12-person jury ($.9826^{12} = .81$).

Regardless of whether the dependency tends to move individual jurors toward guilt or innocence, it is in order to interview the jurors to learn more about the relationships between the elements of the jury dynamics and the resulting departures from independence. Such research would at best be indicative of real-world jury dynamics. Knowing these effects could nonetheless help to shape the instructions judges give to jurors, possibly with different instructions for juries of different sizes and voting rules. And while the relationship between conviction rates and error rates discussed in Chapter 6 should not be altered by dependencies among the probabilities generally, specific rules governing jury dynamics – for example, discouraging or encouraging nullification – could have a profound impact on jury errors.

Conclusion

One can imagine taking this sort of inquiry in other directions as well. I have noted the prospect of learning more about jury errors on both sides of the scale of justice by examining DNA evidence to validate jury decisions made prior to the availability of DNA technology for a large, representative sample of cases that provide such opportunity. Another potentially fruitful avenue of inquiry would be an examination of rules pertaining to jury nullification. In states in which judges are permitted to discuss jury nullification with jurors, do the proportions of acquittals and hung juries differ from those in other states? If so, what is the resulting impact on conviction rates and errors in adjudication?

Much remains to be done by way of empirical examination of this array of issues, through the analysis of data both from actual jury decisions and from mock trials and surveys. Such work may shed more light on the effect of jury rules and arrangements on conviction rates and errors. It may ultimately help to bolster from the inside what Tocqueville saw so clearly from the outside, that a sound jury system can serve to strengthen democracy.

CHAPTER TEN

Sentencing and Corrections

> Punishments may be too small or too great; and there are reasons for not making them too small, as well as not making them too great. The terms minimum and maximum may serve to mark the two extremes of this question, which require equal attention.
>
> – Jeremy Bentham[1]

Introduction

Errors of justice can be made after a defendant is convicted, even when the offender committed the crime as charged. Bentham elaborates on these errors in an earlier work (1789), first by observing where sanctions are "profitable,"[2] then by identifying circumstances under

---

[1] Bentham, *The Rationale of Punishment* (1830), Book I – General Principles, Chapter 6 – Measure of Punishment.

[2] Bentham identifies in *An Introduction to the Principles of Morals and Legislation* (Chapter 13, Section I, Paragraph 2, Note 1) most of the ends that are characterized in the contemporary literature on the goals of sentencing: incapacitation, general deterrence, reformation (individual deterrence and rehabilitation), and retribution:

> The immediate principal end of punishment is to control action. This action is either that of the offender, or of others: that of the offender it controls by its influence, either on his will, in which case it is said to operate in the way of reformation; or on his physical power, in which case it is said to operate by disablement: that of others it can influence otherwise than by its influence over their wills, in which ease it is said to operate in the way of example. A kind of collateral end, which it has a natural tendency to answer, is that of affording a pleasure or satisfaction to the party injured, where there is one, and, in general, to parties whose ill-will whether on a self-regarding account, or on the account of sympathy or antipathy, has been excited by the offense.

which they are excessive.[3] As Bentham suggests, we may be able to reduce errors by assessing sanctions in terms of the extent to which they fall within reasonable boundaries between insufficient (in terms of his goal of controlling the actions of offenders) and excessive. Contemporary treatments of sentencing policy echo Bentham's justifications for sanctions – retribution, general and individual deterrence, incapacitation, and rehabilitation – and add victim and community restoration as legitimate purposes.

The extraordinary tripling of prison and jail populations in the United States from 1980 to 2000, from 1.3 million to 4.6 million, a period that also saw an astonishing decline in the homicide rate, from 23,000 to 15,000, certainly suggests a substantial shift toward systematic errors of overincarceration.[4] The challenge we confront is to see whether Bentham's principles can be used as a departure point for finding a basis for making a more definitive assessment.

In this chapter, we shall go about this task by considering the following questions: How do the various goals of sentencing policy listed above relate to one another? What is the meaning of "error" under any particular sentencing framework? How does each framework deal with the assessment of alternative sanctions: jail or prison, fines, community-based correctional alternatives, community service, and so on? Are the answers to these questions dependent on time, place, and situation? How do the sentences suggested by these principles

---

[3] At Section I, Paragraph 3, Bentham observes (with emphasis in the original): "It is plain, therefore, that in the following cases punishment ought not to be inflicted:

- Where it is *groundless*: where there is no mischief for it to prevent; the act not being mischievous upon the whole.
- Where it must be *inefficacious*: where it cannot act so as to prevent the mischief.
- Where it is *unprofitable*, or too expensive: where the mischief it would produce would be greater than what it prevented.
- Where it is *needless*: where the mischief may be prevented, or cease of itself, without it: that is, at a cheaper rate.

[4] Some see these numbers as prima facie evidence of overincarceration, while conservatives may be more inclined to see them as evidence of the effectiveness of the deterrent and incapacitative effectiveness of incarceration. A third position is that regardless of how far the current incarceration rate departs from the socially optimal rate, current sentencing policies and practices *guarantee* that many persons currently in prison or jail do not belong there while other persons currently on probation belong behind bars.

compare with sentencing practices in the real world? To the extent that they differ, how might we reconcile the differences? To what extent should sentencing be left to the discretion of practitioners, and to what extent should it be codified as uniform policy? To the extent that sentencing policy is codified and uniform, how complex should it be? Why bother with lofty abstractions about the principles of sentencing and elusive social costs of sentencing errors if those who shape sentencing policy and administer it do not take them seriously? What is the nature and sources of errors in corrections? How can systems of accountability help to reduce errors?

Optimum Sanctions under Alternative Frameworks

The idea that sanctions can be either too lax or too harsh presupposes the notion of an optimal sanction, one that is just right, or nearly so. The determination of a just-right sanction, in turn, depends on the purpose of sanctioning. Two fundamentally different philosophical perspectives provide departure points for establishing such sanctions.

The Utilitarian Framework

Under the first of the two, the *utilitarian* framework, an optimal sentence is one that minimizes the discounted present value of the social costs of crime and sanctions. The logic of this framework, described in Chapter 5, is at the core of a well-established branch of normative ethics, rooted largely in the late 18th and early 19th century work of Cesare Beccaria and Jeremy Bentham.[5] When sanctions are too severe, further increases in punishment will produce additional intervention costs that exceed the amount of decline in costs associated with the marginal reduction in crime. When sanctions are too lenient,

---

[5] The central idea of Beccaria's moral philosophy of punishment is that sanctions should be certain and uniform, to minimize crime at a minimum of misery inflicted on the offender. Bentham extended this notion by developing a complex catalogue of crimes and punishments based on the central notion that punishments should be sufficient to prevent crime and no more, that excessive punishments might indeed be counterproductive. It is noteworthy that both Beccaria and Bentham opposed the death penalty, and did so at a time when such a position was widely opposed and often ridiculed.

additional increases in punishment will produce declines in the costs associated with crime that exceed the additional intervention costs.

The utilitarian framework embraces any and all functions of sentencing that reduce crime or restore victims of crime: general deterrence (the notion that a sanction given to one person causes others to commit less crime), specific or individual deterrence (the notion that an offender will commit less crime in the future upon experiencing directly the undesirability of a sanction), incapacitation (the notion that the community will be protected from the crimes otherwise committed by an offender while the offender is incarcerated), rehabilitation or treatment (the notion that an offender will commit less crime in the future after receiving job skills, drug treatment, or other therapy that gives the offender tools to discontinue criminal behaviors), victim restoration (direct compensation from offender to victim in cash, kind or services, to return the victim to a prior status), and community service (to repay the community for crimes that harm the community at large).

The utilitarian model encompasses these various avenues of reducing crime and its costs. It does so by focusing on the offense, offender, the effects of alternative sanctions for a particular type of case on further crime by the person being sentenced and by others, and the social costs of crimes and sanctions. As a practical matter, it may be sufficient to know the effects of the sanction on future crime among various classes of individuals without distinguishing deterrent, incapacitative, and rehabilitative effects. It will be interesting and more useful nonetheless to be able to make these distinctions, both for the sake of understanding human nature and for policy purposes.

Rehabilitation

Throughout most of the 20th century, sentencing policy was dominated by rehabilitation, an aspect of the utilitarian framework as noted above, but no less a manifestation of a widely held commitment to belief in the behavioral repair of individuals who have strayed from legitimate behavior. Rehabilitation was an important facet of the Reform movement of the late 19th and early 20th centuries. Prisons had been called "penitentiaries" in the 19th century, reflecting the dominant retributive ethos of the time, and eventually became more widely known as "reformatories" and "correctional institutions" in the early and mid-20th century, following the emergence of a liberal and secular sense that the concept of repentance was neither as humane or effective as the idea that people were fundamentally good and could be restored to that natural state following an appropriate treatment. The writings of psychiatrist Karl Menninger and reform advocate Jessica Mitford provided much of the intellectual sustenance and political support for the mid-1900s theory of rehabilitation and the idea that sentences should be less harsh. Rehabilitative strategies relied on interventions designed to alter the offender's behaviors, and the attitudes beneath those behaviors, or to provide the inmate with therapies or job skills that would reduce criminality after a flexible term of incarceration. By the 1960s, the indeterminate sentence became the standard sanction, with parole boards assigned the responsibility for determining precisely when an offender had been rehabilitated and was ready to be released safely from prison.

The advocates of rehabilitation were able to provide little empirical validation of its effectiveness, beyond the occasional uplifting success story of the ex-convict who found the light and turned his life around, perhaps to become a successful minister or prison trainer and inspiration for the reform of other offenders. Support for the rehabilitative goal began to erode with the rapid escalation of crime in the 1960s, and the erosion accelerated in the 1970s, first with a deadly riot at the Attica Prison in 1971 that revealed wide disparities associated with indeterminate sentencing as a cause of the riot, and then a devastating critique of rehabilitation programs in 1974 by Robert Martinson – headlined in the popular media as the study that found that "nothing works." In 1979, the National Academy of Sciences issued a report on rehabilitation echoing Martinson's critique:

> The one positive conclusion is discouraging: the research methodology that has been brought to bear on the problem of finding ways to rehabilitate criminal offenders has been generally so inadequate that only a relatively few studies warrant any unequivocal interpretations. The entire body of research appears to justify only the conclusion that we do not now know of any program or method

of rehabilitation that could be guaranteed to reduce the criminal activity of released offenders. Although a generous reviewer of the literature might discern some glimmers of hope, those glimmers are so few, so scattered, and so inconsistent that they do not serve as a basis for any recommendation other than continued research. (Sechrest, 1979, p. 3)

Empirical validation of the theory of rehabilitation relies principally on observed reductions in recidivism (i.e., subsequent criminal behavior, usually measured as subsequent arrests or convictions) as the test of effective behavioral transformation, with secondary interest in such indicators as increased rates of employment, reduced rates of drug use, and other manifestations of successful reintegration into the family and community. Reduced recidivism in an individual could, of course, reflect individual deterrence rather than rehabilitation, so studies of rehabilitation generally attempt to follow an experimental or quasi-experimental approach, along the following lines: examine whether a specific therapeutic intervention administered to a panel of inmates is followed by a lower rate of arrests for the panel than for a control group of similar inmates who did not receive the intervention. These studies typically are plagued by the absence of randomized assignment of offenders to the experimental and control groups, resulting in selection biases of either or both of two types: the program agents' selection of individuals who appear to be more susceptible to rehabilitation ("skimming the cream"), or self-selection by the individuals themselves, with volunteers more committed to personal improvement and hence less likely to recidivate at the outset than nonvolunteers (Rhodes et al., 2000).

Many liberal-minded practitioners, and even ordinarily skeptical scholars, have not given up on the rehabilitative ideal. People of good will generally prefer to believe that people *are* fundamentally good, that our failure to find rehabilitative programs that work reflects primarily our not yet having searched thoroughly enough. If true, the challenge is for us to find that formula that will allow those who have strayed from the path of lawful behavior to discover their core decency and become responsible citizens and productive members of the community. We may simply not yet have tailored treatment programs that can be made to work in response to the unique needs of the individuals we wish to reform.

A less promising but not altogether hopeless prospect is that people do tend eventually to stop committing crime as a natural part of the aging process. The natural decline in crime associated with maturation, in any event, provides a baseline against which rehabilitation programs can be assessed; any systematic reductions in criminal activity ahead of Mother Nature's schedule are the benefits of such programs. One authority offers this justification for continuing the search for programs that may offer such benefits: "In the current context, I suggest that whatever humanity the practice of rehabilitation brings to the correctional enterprise is much needed. And if reaffirming rehabilitation makes corrections a bit more paternalistic and kindhearted, I am all for it" (Cullen, 2002, p. 289).

What, then, can we say about the effect of rehabilitation policy on errors of justice among sentenced offenders? First, that rehabilitative programs may have benefits that fall outside of crime, so they cannot be assessed solely in terms of the social costs of crime and sanctions. We may be willing to incur the costs of rehabilitation programs beyond any positive effects they may have to reduce crime, and perhaps even if they have no such effects at all. Second, failure to have found positive effects thus far may only reflect our not yet having tested enough prospects or made sufficiently useful distinctions among the various classes of offenders to permit a tailoring of the programs to the unique needs of the program candidates. Errors may, indeed, have been made in the determination of who should receive what sort of treatment. Finally, rehabilitation policy may be largely independent of the incapacitative purpose of sentencing and may conflict with retributive and deterrent objectives, but we should explore ways in which rehabilitation may interact positively with other aspects of sentencing policy. Opportunities for rehabilitation may be greater, for example, when considered in conjunction with restitution (transformation may result when restitution instills a sense of responsibility) and incapacitation (while protecting others through separation, the offender may receive potentially useful job skills and treatment as an alternative to serving time idly), which we take up next.

Incapacitation

Perhaps the least controversial purpose of incarceration is its use to separate criminally active offenders from society. Some controversy will be inevitable at the margins, in terms of both frequency of offending and the seriousness of the offenses, but for offenders who have revealed themselves to be clearly dangerous to the community or incapable of restraining themselves from participation in crime, prison serves the community's need to restrain the active offender and perhaps quarantine him from other prospective offenders in the community. The incarceration of offenders who have recently revealed a criminal propensity is likely to produce a *general* or *collective incapacitation* effect, that is, an effect of reducing their opportunities to commit crime while incarcerated, an effect that is not based on the singling out of any particular offender as being more crime-prone than others (Cohen, 1978; Greenberg, 1975; Blumstein et al., 1986).

The incapacitative purpose of sentencing received convincing empirical support in the early 1970s with the publication of a landmark study that found, among a cohort of 9,945 boys born in Philadelphia in 1945, that a handful of 627, just 6.3 percent of the cohort, were arrested at least five times before their 18th birthday, accounting for 82 percent of the robberies, 71 percent of the homicides, and 64 percent of the aggravated assaults committed by the entire cohort (Wolfgang, Figlio, and Sellin, 1972). These findings were replicated in Philadelphia 13 years later, and in research conducted in California, Washington, DC, England, and elsewhere (Wolfgang, Thornberry, and Figlio, 1972; Peterson and Braiker, 1980; Chaiken and Chaiken, 1982; Williams, 1979; Farrington and West, 1981). To the extent that arrests reflect true criminal activity – we know that some offenders are more skillful at avoiding arrest than others, and at the other extreme, some arrestees are factually innocent of the alleged crimes – it is evident that a policy of reserving scarce prison and jail space for the more criminally active offenders is capable of producing a larger reduction in crime than a policy of sentencing that ignores criminal activity. How much larger depends on a variety of factors, including the competing goals of sentencing currently in use, the correlation between the severity of the current offense and the seriousness and number of other crimes committed if freed, and the accuracy of our ability to identify the convicted offender as one who is criminally active and who commits crimes that are costly to the community based on factors unrelated to the seriousness of the current offense. The problem of unmeasured crime may be especially great among white collar offenders, raising questions of fundamental fairness of an incapacitative sentence.

The incapacitative purpose of sentencing becomes controversial not just at the margins of criminal frequency and seriousness and on questions of fundamental fairness. It becomes especially controversial under a policy of *selective incapacitation,* in which certain offenders are singled out for more certain and longer terms of incarceration based on predictions that they are likely to be more criminally active (Cohen, 1978; Greenberg, 1975; Blumstein et al., 1986). It is one thing to identify a pool of criminally active offenders after the fact, as in the Philadelphia birth cohort study, and quite another to predict future criminal activity of a pool of convicted offenders up for sentencing. The limits in our ability to predict subsequent criminality – we cannot even be sure that our *ex post* identifications of offenders in the cohort studies are correct – should make us humble about using prediction tools as a part of sentencing policy. I will speak more directly to this question of the ethics of prediction in sentencing later in this chapter.

General Deterrence

The theory of general deterrence was a centerpiece of Beccaria and Bentham's utilitarian philosophies. The deterrence theory had not been abandoned with the emergence of the goal of rehabilitation and the practice of indeterminate sentencing throughout most of the 20th century, but it was clearly deemphasized. In the 1960s two significant developments reversed these priorities, on two fronts of engagement: The crime explosion provided a strong *political* stimulus for deterrence and against rehabilitation, and a seminal 1968 article by economist Gary Becker revived *academic* interest in the deterrence theory.

Becker's theory of general deterrence descended from the 18th century Age of Enlightenment emphasis on rationality, making more explicit than had Beccaria and Bentham the specifics of prospective offenders responding to incentives: that they choose consciously to allocate their time and energy between legitimate and illegitimate activities, that their decisions to participate in each domain are based on the prospective gains and losses associated with participation in each domain, and that those gains and losses are based in turn on their prior investments in education and external factors such as the unemployment rate. Becker observed that fines may be a more efficient sanction than imprisonment for many crimes, especially those for which incapacitative effects are small, because they impose lower costs on both the general public and the offender. He offered a limited empirical test of the theory based on a simple analysis of the seven index offenses for 1960, finding that more serious crimes received larger expected punishments, with higher probabilities of conviction and longer sentences. But his work was significant principally for developing a theory that opened the door for a new generation of economists to conduct much more extensive empirical testing of the response of prospective offenders to changes in sanction levels. Becker's article spawned an outpouring of such research on the economics of crime, based on analyses of variation in crime, sanctions, and other key variables over time and across geographical entities.

The work made an impression on some noneconomists as well. James Q. Wilson, in his landmark essay, "Thinking About Crime,"[6] observed that when the national crime commissions of the 1960s turned to criminologists trained in sociology for advice on how to deal with the crime explosion, people the commissioners presumed to be experts on crime, "they could not respond with suggestions derived from and supported by their scholarly work" (1975, p. 42). Wilson added, "Now, to an increasing extent, that inquiry is being furthered by economists rather than sociologists" (p. 50).

Many criminologists are justifiably skeptical of the economist's rather narrow approach to analyzing crime, regarding it not so much incorrect as reductionist and incomplete. They see the problems

---

[6] The essay, originally titled, "Crime and the Criminologists," appeared in the July 1974 issue of *Commentary* (pp. 47–53). It became the central chapter, "Thinking About Crime," of a famous book of the same name published the following year.

of crime, justice, and justice policy as infinitely more complex and nuanced in important ways than the narrow economic models recognize. They find the economic approach limited and inaccurate for its assuming unrealistically that the tastes of prospective offenders, victims, and other participants are fixed, that psychological and sociological factors do not matter, and that offenders are accurate in their assessments of the risks involved and rational in their calculations of the pertinent factors. They argue that while the deterrence theory may apply to some people and for a range of settings, it is especially limited as a policy tool against others, such as violent crimes committed impulsively, often as expressions of anger and ego rather than as instruments designed to gain cash or property. Many take strong moral exception to the idea that one person should receive the full brunt of a punishment in order that others receive the benefit of general deterrence (Hegel, 1821; Duff, 2000; von Hirsch, 1992; Zimring, 1971).[7]

Proponents of deterrence theory respond that the power of the theory lies not so much in the realism of its assumptions as in the accuracy of its predictions, as well as its parsimony and generalizability, its ability to predict accurately and simply across a wide array of circumstances, following a well-established tradition of neoclassical economics (Friedman, 1953). Levitt (2002) observes, for example, that "many criminologists mistakenly believe that criminals must be 'rational' for deterrence to exist" (p. 435). He goes on to explain that the theory of deterrence does not require any such rigid requirement; it needs only to be correct *on average* to be valid (p. 438). And it is, he concludes, at least with respect to increases in police, the number of prisoners, sentence lengths, and victim precaution (p. 450). He

---

[7] Zimring (1971) puts it simply: "Why should his (the punished) grief pay for their (the public's) moral education?" (p. 23) Bentham's concern for the welfare of the punished under general deterrence was conspicuous:

> Every particle of real punishment that is produced more than what is necessary for the production of the requisite quantity of apparent punishment, is just so much misery run to waste. Hence the real punishment ought to be as small and the apparent punishment as great as possible. If hanging a man in effigy would produce the same salutary impression of terror upon the minds of the people, it would be folly or cruelty ever to hang a man in person. (*The Rationale of Punishment*, Book I – General Principles, Chapter V – Expense of Punishment)

notes that other factors matter too, including family, community, and demographics, but that does not invalidate the deterrence theory.

Which side of the debate is more strongly supported by the empirical evidence? It turns out that the dissensus over belief in the deterrence theory is mirrored by variability of statistical findings produced by tests of the theory. This is due largely to difficulties in conducting statistical tests and interpreting the results. To begin with, the data are flawed, with errors both in the number of reported crimes from jurisdiction to jurisdiction and over time, and in the factors that explain crime. About half of all felony offenses are not reported to the police, and those that are known to be occasionally misreported as to the offenses that occurred, the number of offenders and victims who were involved, questions of victim provocation, involvement of drugs or alcohol, weapon involvement, and so on.[8]

Second, to the extent that the evidence indicates a systematic negative relationship between a sanction level and a crime rate, we cannot be certain how much of it is attributable to deterrence and how much to incapacitation. We can attempt to "net out" the incapacitation effects from estimates of a combined effect based on prior estimates of incapacitation, but estimates of the incapacitation effects vary substantially (Blumstein, Cohen, and Nagin, 1978; Gottfredson and Hirschi, 1986; Horney and Marshall, 1991).

Third, threats to validity raise questions about the evidence available to date. Experimentation is the gold standard of empirical research on cause-effect relationships, and experimentation on general deterrence is infeasible.[9] In the absence of randomized experiments, correlations between sanction levels and crime rates serve as the standard test of the deterrence theory, based on natural variation in crime rates, sanction levels, and, to minimize the prospect of finding spurious relationships between the two, other factors that precede both crime rates

[8] Much of this introduces statistical "noise" to the analysis, random errors that tend to bias the findings away from a finding of deterrent effects. Other errors may contribute to a false finding of deterrence, as with errors in the number of crimes, which is typically both the numerator of the dependent variable and the denominator of the sanction variable in deterrence research.

[9] Sherman and others have conducted controlled experiments on the individual deterrent effect of arrests for domestic violence, but these ignore any general deterrent effects.

and sanction levels.[10] The validity of these tests is threatened also by feedback effects: any observed relationship between crime rates and sanctions will reflect not only deterrence and incapacitation effects, but reverse effects of crime rates on sanction levels as well. In the short term, when criminal justice resources are overwhelmed by occasional bursts in crime, arrest rates decline; in the long term, increases in crime tend to increase the demand for spending on criminal justice resources and higher sanction levels. Statistical methods for disentangling these reverse effects from the effect of sanctions on crime rates, through proper identification of the separate relationships, are complex and often produce disparate findings (Lynch and Sabol, 2000; Levitt, 2002; Nagin, 1998).[11]

The accumulated evidence on deterrence to date is generally consistent with the theory, and despite the problems noted above, even skeptics acknowledge considerable gains in our understanding of deterrence and convergence in the estimates,[12] but much more work is needed. One of the substantial gaps in our knowledge of deterrence is the absence of evidence to permit an understanding of the relationships between actual sanction levels and the levels as they are perceived by prospective offenders, and in turn the effects of those perceptions on crime rates. Information on these separate links in the deterrence chain could provide useful insights for reducing errors of impunity by combining strategies for setting sanction levels with strategies for communicating more effectively the prices of participation in illegitimate activities to prospective offenders.[13]

---

[10] Sociodemographic variables such as education, income, wealth, ethnicity, and age are examples of variables that precede both crime rates and sanction levels. Even these variables cannot be fully reflected in the available data, and other variables matter as well. This is confirmed in study after study finding that much of the variation in crime rates is unexplained by available data.

[11] Progress has been made on this problem through the use of sophisticated models that incorporate lags in relevant variables to help disentangle relationships running simultaneously in opposite directions.

[12] Daniel Nagin (1998), in the second of two scholarly assessments of research on deterrence over a 20-year period, concludes, "Evidence for a substantial deterrent effect is much firmer than it was two decades ago" (p. 1).

[13] In the tradition of effective strategic Madison Avenue marketing, effective strategic communication of these prices does not necessarily imply more accurate and honest communication. It might be in the best interest of society not to advertise accurately the rates of arrest for those categories of crime for which the rates are low. See Bentham's distinction between real and apparent levels of punishment, Note 7, *supra*.

Questions remain also about long- and short-term deterrent effects, deterrent effects for specific situations, and the deterrent effects of nonincarceration alternatives.

Individual Deterrence

Sentencing could satisfy the utilitarian goal of reduced recidivism if it leaves the offender with an unpleasant experience he or she wishes not to repeat, an effect known as "individual deterrence" or "special deterrence." This effect is not readily inferrable from data on crimes following release from correctional authority, for several reasons. First, subsequent arrests and convictions are imperfect measures of subsequent criminality, sometimes overstating and sometimes understating true criminal activity. Second, even if accurately measured, a reduction in recidivism could be attributable to a complex mix of positive and negative experiences – and combined further with maturation, the natural tendency of individuals to commit less crime as they grow older – making it difficult to disentangle individual deterrent effects from other stimuli to reduced crime.

There is a moral hazard associated with individual deterrence as well: if it works, correctional authorities may have inducements to making the correctional experience even more unpleasant than it already is, risking violations of the Eighth Amendment protection against cruel and unusual punishment.

The Retributive Framework

The standard alternative to utilitarian sentencing comes from another branch of moral philosophy: the *desert-based* or *retributive* framework. Under this system, a sentence should be commensurate in severity with the seriousness of the crime committed. The more serious the crime, the more deserving is the offender of a harsher punishment. The logic of retribution is rooted in primitive traditions of justice: an eye for an eye,[14] a pound of flesh,[15] and *lex talionis* (law of retaliation). But it is

---

[14] "And if any mischief follow, then thou shalt give life for life, eye for eye, tooth for tooth, hand for hand, foot for foot, burning for burning, wound for wound, stripe for stripe" (Exodus 21:23–5). The eye-for-eye metaphor is also found in the Code of Hammurabi, dating to 1780 BC. Hammurabi ruled Babylonia, a kingdom of Mesopotamia, from 1792 to 1750 BC.

[15] From Shakespeare's *Merchant of Venice*, Act I (1598).

consistent with higher level abstractions on retributive ethics in law and punishment, offered most prominently by Immanuel Kant and Georg Hegel. Kant (1790) set much of the philosophical foundation for retributive sentencing in emphasizing the importance of fair dealings among free and responsible individuals, observing that failure to adhere to reciprocity creates disequilibrium and warrants discipline, not so much for the sake of deterrence as on simple grounds of deservedness. Hegel (1821) amplified Kant's notion of responsibility by emphasizing the state's imperative to punish the offender as a consequence for violating an ethical responsibility to refrain from criminal activity.[16]

Retributive sentences are consistent as well with utilitarian Cesare Beccaria's maxim that punishment must be "proportionate to the crimes, dictated by the laws."[17] Beccaria aimed to make sentencing more coherent, but no less significantly, to make it more humane. The Bill of Rights echoed Beccaria's moving the notion of deservedness away from archaic notions of vengeance and in the direction of humane but just sanctions, in establishing the Eighth Amendment protection against cruel and unusual punishments.

Constitutional reforms to civilize the criminal law have been carried forward to the present day by legal philosophers, criminologists, and enlightened practitioners, with the objective of removing the remnants of cruelty from the concept of sentencing based on culpability and deservedness and translating principles into something more tangible. H. L. A. Hart (1968) provided much of the modern intellectual respectability to this movement, advancing Kant's deontological ethics by emphasizing the individual's personal responsibility in the matter,

---

[16] In his *Philosophy of Right* (1821), Hegel asserts: "Punishment is the right of the criminal. It is an act of his own will. The violation of right has been proclaimed by the criminal as his own right. His crime is the negation of right. Punishment is the negation of this negation, and, consequently an affirmation of right, solicited and forced upon the criminal by himself" (pp. 70–1).

[17] The full quote, which Beccaria uses to conclude his brief but monumental *On Crimes and Punishments* (1764), is as follows: "In order for punishment not to be in every instance an act of violence of one or many against a private citizen, it must be essentially public, prompt, necessary, the least possible in the given circumstances, proportionate to the crimes, dictated by the laws" (p. 99). Beccaria appreciated the need for proportionality, but he was more fundamentally a utilitarian ("It is better to prevent crimes than to punish them" [p. 93].) And, in emphasizing moderation in sentencing, he revealed himself as a humanitarian.

the notion that we have a duty to behave morally or be subject to censure. Hart was clearly interested not just in advancing the philosophy of punishment, but in relating his high level abstractions to a palpable system of sentencing: "The guiding principle is that of a proportion within a system of penalties between those imposed for different offences where these have a distinct place in a commonsense scale of gravity" (p. 25).

Andrew von Hirsch's *Doing Justice*, the 1976 book version of the report of the Committee for the Study of Incarceration, then advanced Hart's proportionality idea a few steps further. The centerpiece of von Hirsch's sentencing framework was his "principle of commensurate deserts," which he defined with stark simplicity: "Severity of punishment should be commensurate with the seriousness of the wrong."[18] Von Hirsch attempted to operationalize this principle by developing a scale of penalties arrayed on a scale, with the creation of a "presumptive sentence ... prescribed for each gradation of seriousness – with limited discretionary authority to raise or lower it for aggravating or mitigating circumstances" (p. 132). He envisioned a two-dimensional input scale, with one dimension for seriousness of the offense and the other for the extent and seriousness of the prior record of the convicted person.[19] The primary goals of von Hirsch's sentencing system were to make sentencing policy more coherent, make sentences more uniform, and reduce sentence severity across the board, while ensuring that offenders serve their full, albeit shortened, terms (pp. 139–40).

Von Hirsch's desert-based sentencing system became the core of the first major sentencing guideline system in the United States, the Minnesota Sentencing Guidelines, which took effect in 1980. Von Hirsch continued working to refine the relationship between the scales

---

[18] Von Hirsch took care to distinguish his principle from that of "proportionality" and "just deserts" (p. 66), and distanced it more significantly from the idea of retribution (pp. 45–6), and farther still from all utilitarian principles: "We want to argue that departures from the (commensurability) principle – even when they would serve utilitarian ends – inevitably sacrifice justice" (p. 69).

[19] Von Hirsch does not attempt to justify the second scale, although he suggests that allowance should be made for utilitarian considerations: "If the magnitude selected leads to a substantial rise in overall crime rates, an upward adjustment can be made (within the upper bounds of commensurate deserts)" (p. 135).

of offense seriousness or culpability and sentencing schedules, including not only terms of incarceration, but nonincarcerative sanctions as well (Kleinig, 1974; von Hirsch, 1992).

A basic limitation with the use of this framework is that it does not suggest a unique optimum sentence for any particular offense, since the endpoints of the sentencing scale and the scales themselves are arbitrary. Proponents of the system must simply agree on which offenses will qualify for no incarceration at all and which will qualify for a life sentence, and on some calibration system that preserves ordinal consistency or transitivity between the two scales, to ensure that more serious crimes will receive longer sentences. Nothing in the logic of retribution is capable of establishing nonarbitrary equivalences between trivial offenses and light punishments, or between serious offenses and long sentences, or for that matter establishing whether the scales are linear or nonlinear. As Morris and Tonry (1990) put it, "mortal minds do not possess moral calipers that can tell us exactly how much punishment any wrongdoer deserves" (p. 84). Equivalences between crime and punishment under this system can be achieved only by way of agreement among sentencing authorities.[20]

Reconciling the Utilitarian and Desert-Based Frameworks
The utilitarian and desert-based logics have little in common, yet they may suggest sentences that are similar, at least to the extent that both are based on the seriousness of the offense. The desert-based sentence is driven principally by offense seriousness, and the utilitarian term of incarceration is based largely on the demands of deterrence, which sets a higher price on more serious crimes in order to produce a stronger disincentive for prospective offenders to commit such offenses. I have noted that Cesare Beccaria, a founding father of utilitarianism, emphasized that sanctions should be "proportionate to the crime," an idea that is at the heart of the principle of just desert.

The two systems are compatible as well to the extent that retributive sentences can be viewed through a utilitarian lens as satisfying a public

---

[20] Norval Morris (1974) proposes a theory of "limiting retributivism," in which arbitrary upper limits are placed on just deserts sentences based on notions of uniformity and "parsimony" (p. 75).

desire for "closure," the response to a collective demand for justice with punishment.[21] If we cannot ignore the loss of utility to the person who receives a sentence that aims to satisfy this demand, neither should we be quick to dismiss the gain of utility to others who experience the sentence as justice, a substantive official public denunciation of a wrong following an illicit transfer from victim or community to the offender. Just as the transfer associated with a crime generally produces a net loss of utility, so is there likely to be a net public loss associated with a retributive sentence, even when restitution or community service is imposed; the victims and community are usually not as well off as before the crime. Still, the general public may derive a psychic benefit from a sentence even beyond any crime control benefits that may accrue from it.[22]

However, to the extent that the desert-based philosophy looks backward and the utilitarian logic looks forward, the two might indeed produce quite different sentences for certain classes of offenders. In the case of homicide by an aggrieved lover with no criminal history, for example, one can imagine a more severe desert-based sentence than would ordinarily be suggested under a utilitarian framework. In the case of a 19-year-old burglar with a serious record of violent crime, by contrast, we might imagine a considerably longer sentence based on the utilitarian logic than one based on just deserts.[23] To the extent that the utilitarian logic focuses on the characteristics of the offender as well as the offense, in order to provide a basis for predicting the incapacitative effects of a sanction, utilitarian sentences will be longer for those who have characteristics that are associated with people who

---

[21] Bentham recognized this as well. See Note 2, *supra*.

[22] There is a danger that a sentence will not satisfy the demand for retribution by victims or others in the community, even under a retributive sentencing policy, thus creating a demand for private retaliation, or "curbside" justice by the police; or that an overly harsh sentence may create a residual demand for retaliation from the person sentenced or his allies against the victim or others who contributed to the sentence. It is not clear, in any case, that any such perceived injustices and the associated crime costs will be either greater or less under a sentencing policy that is explicitly retributive.

[23] It is noteworthy that for offenders with serious criminal histories, the forward-looking utilitarian system calls for a longer sentence, while such a sentence is expressly forbidden under the retrospectively oriented double jeopardy rule, holding constant the current offense.

commit more crime. This raises ethical questions that we will consider in a later section of this chapter (Should Sanctions Be Based on Predictions?).

Each of the two primary sentencing frameworks, utilitarian and retributive, has its own fatal flaw. The flaw in the utilitarian system is exemplified by a term of life without parole for a person who has been found guilty of committing a trivial criminal infraction but who is perceived to be a significant crime risk to the community, and the flaw in the retributive system is exemplified by a sentencing system in which all offenders receive sentences that are much too harsh. The flaws can be stated more generally. A utilitarian system will be unjust if it assigns either a very harsh sentence to an individual who has been found guilty of having committed an arbitrarily trivial criminal infraction but who is assessed as dangerous, or an arbitrarily lenient sentence (perhaps none at all), based on an assessment of low risk of future dangerousness, to a person who has committed a grave offense.[24] Moreover, utilitarian sentencing may fail even to achieve its own objectives if the factors on which it bases its sentencing calculus are seriously in error. And a retributive system that ignores either the costs of future crimes to the community or the costs of sanctions on the persons sentenced and their dependents will be unacceptably insensitive to the interests of at least one significant segment of society, and it may be unacceptably inefficient for the community as a whole. Retributive sentences that lay claim to justice could thus easily be less just than utilitarian ones in the manner by which they shift the burdens of crime on the public.

That each system has a fatal flaw, however, does not imply the need to reject both. The failure of each to deal with the importance of the other suggests the need for a hybrid system. The alternative of sanctions that have no coherent supporting logic at all is far worse. Architects of sentencing systems on the ground generally do justify them both in the language of retribution and using utilitarian considerations such

---

[24] An even greater injustice is created when such a sanction is given to a person who has not been convicted, such as in the case of fatal episodes of police brutality and cases in which persons are held indefinitely as threats to the community without having had criminal charges filed against them.

as deterrence and incapacitation, often after much deliberation, as do judges in explaining the sentences they administer in individual cases. The flaws of each system do not eliminate prospects for determining optimal sentences and assessing whether the sentences given in individual cases are either excessively harsh or lenient. The major blind spot in a retributive system can be remedied, and in the real world they are, with sentences that have a dimension associated with the dangerousness of the offender. Presumptive sentencing systems that are rooted primarily in notions of deservedness have, in fact, incorporated such a dimension from the start.[25] The blind spot in the utilitarian system can be remedied by setting desert-based maximum and minimum limits on the sentence given to a person convicted of any particular offense. The deficiencies in the existing estimates of the pertinent parameters in the relationships between sanctions and crimes under a utilitarian framework, and the relevant costs, are serious but not fatal; they can be dealt with by improving the estimates and the data from which they are derived. Sanctions borne of the capricious alternative have contributed to unwarranted disparity in sentencing.[26] They undermine basic principles of justice and the legitimacy of our courts. The primary question is how, not whether, to mix the utilitarian and just deserts frameworks.

Alternatives to Incarceration

One way to reduce tensions between utilitarian and just deserts goals is to consider sentencing options that can accommodate both frameworks simultaneously and serve each more effectively. Until the end of the 20th century, just two sentencing options were dominant for persons convicted of felony crimes: prison or probation. In the late 1980s and early 1990s an array of intermediate sanctions between

---

[25] Frase (1997) observes that the Minnesota Sentencing Guidelines, in incorporating a dimension for the prior record of the person convicted, started with an eye toward utilitarian considerations, and the system became even more utilitarian in the years following (p. 388).

[26] Blumstein et al. (1983), in a review of the literature on the determinants of sentencing, report that some two thirds of the variation in sentencing is unexplained; the other third is associated with factors related to the offense and offender (pp. 72–87).

prison and probation emerged, largely because of two developments: a growing awareness that a sharp discontinuity in the in-or-out sentencing option was incompatible with a virtual continuity of the scale of seriousness of the cases eligible for sentencing – "as if the only cure for a head pain was either an aspirin or a lobotomy" (Morris, 1993, p. 307) – and a growth of interest in restorative justice.

Awareness of the need for intermediate sanctions to fill the void in the in-out polarity was stimulated largely by an influential 1990 book by Norval Morris and Michael Tonry, *Between Prison and Probation: Intermediate Punishments in a Rational Sentencing System*. Morris and Tonry argued that both prison and probation were used excessively: "Our plea is for neither increased leniency nor increased severity; our program, if implemented, would tend toward increased reliance on punishments more sever than probation and less severe than protracted imprisonment" (p. 3). They proposed a variety of alternative sanctions to smooth the discontinuity in sanctions: fines, community service, house arrest, intensive probation (involving more attention and more frequent visits and calls by probation officers with smaller caseloads), closely supervised treatment programs for drugs, alcohol and mental illness, and electronic monitoring of movement.[27] Their call for a "humane, well-run, fairly administered" (p. 241) program of such an array of alternatives within a few years appears to have contributed to serious reform in some jurisdictions, but the funding for such programs has not followed calls for their expansion. Joan Petersilia (1999) estimated that some 10 years after the initiation of intermediate sanction programs, only about 10 percent of all adult probationers and parolees were participating in them. She concludes in another work (2002) that cost reduction, rather than humanistic or reintegrative appeal, is the prime political motivator for the adoption of such programs.

The emergence of restorative justice has been the other major stimulus to the creation of an alternative to the prison-or-probation

---

[27] Other options have been proposed and tried as well, including boot camps, drug courts, and day reporting centers. The evidence on the effectiveness of these alternatives has been mixed, with drug courts faring somewhat better than boot camps, and little by way of empirical evaluations of day reporting centers (Boyum and Kleiman, 2002; Cullen, 2002).

dichotomy. Restorative justice is an old idea, with origins in the civil justice system and the idea of restitution. It has been renovated as a program that can simultaneously compensate the victim for her crime losses and reform the offender. The popularity of restorative justice programs has been stimulated largely by victim rights advocates who have complained that under our common law system of criminal justice the victim often gets harmed twice, first by the offender and then by a callous criminal justice system that regards the victim officially as no more than a witness who can help the state to bring justice to an amorphous abstraction: the "people." Restorative justice programs assume a variety of forms, most having certain features in common: the offender is held accountable for bringing the victim as close as possible back to the precrime state; the victim or family of the victim has a say in the crafting of the terms of restoration; retribution and rehabilitation of the offender may serve as residual benefits, often by moving from a formal justice model to one in which the offender is induced to see victims as people with whom they share a permanent personal relationship (Eglash, 1977; Van Ness and Strong, 1997).

The development of alternative sanctions does not lead automatically to socially optimal sentences. Just as incarceration may be overused or underused, so might fines, intensive supervision, community service, and even victim restoration (e.g., if it were to create an open-ended type of enslavement or an incentive to be victimized). In any particular case, the bottom-line question is this: What mix of sanctions minimizes the total social costs of crime and justice?[28] Some sanctions will be substitutes for one another and others complements. One can imagine that one case involving a dangerous offender might call for incarceration to achieve incapacitation, while another calls for alternatives to incarceration to reduce costs while serving the goals of general and individual deterrence, and justice. A restorative sanction may be a more efficient way of achieving the goals of reducing

---

[28] A more complex version of this question incorporates the socially desirable tradeoff between costs incurred in the present and future: What mix of sanctions minimizes the discounted present value of the total social costs of crime and justice? See Chapter 5 for a discussion of analysis of the time dimension.

recidivism (through individual deterrence or rehabilitation, or both) and achieving justice for certain classes of offenses and offenders; a fine may be more efficient in cases without identifiable victims; community service for similar cases in which the offender cannot pay the fine; and so on. There are, of course, questions of equity associated with different offenders having different abilities to pay fines and restitution. If such a question were to become a public issue following media coverage of a celebrity case, it could conceivably be resolved through a popular vote in the jurisdiction. Tailoring a package of sanctions for a particular offender following input from the victims regarding their interests and in consideration of special needs of the dependents of the offender would seem, in any case, to produce less costly sanctions without a loss of justice, than the rigid and limited set of sentencing alternatives that have been traditionally used.

Sources of Excessive Social Costs in Sentencing

The determination of whether a sentence is either excessively harsh or lenient must begin with the notion of an optimal sentence, to provide a basis for establishing whether it departs excessively from an established norm. The utilitarian framework provides such a norm, at least in principle, and while the just deserts framework may not provide the means for determining a unique optimal sentence, it does offer the basis for producing a ranking of severity of the offense and sanction, as has been done in the development of uniform "presumptive" sentencing guideline systems. Even a guideline system based purely on consensus, constructed without the benefit of a coherent logic, could provide a basis for assessing sentences as either excessively harsh or lenient, outside some norm of mutual agreement. One might imagine, for example, that such a norm could arise from the recent history of average sentences for particular crimes in a jurisdiction, regardless of how illogical, incoherent, or disparate the sentences on which those norms are based may be.

It was noted in Chapter 5 that one of the basic questions in the calculus of an optimal sanction is whether the offender's utility function should be included in the determination of the sentence.[29] This is an ethical question. A retributivist might argue that the offender relinquishes the right to such consideration in violating others. An advocate of rehabilitation would be more inclined to include the offender's utility function either out of humanitarian concerns or utilitarian ones, to reduce alienation and speed the offender's reintegration into the community. Amitai Etzioni (2001) finesses the issue by giving the offender sentencing options that may all be acceptable to the community at large.[30] Of course, many criminal convictions may not present such an option, but the lesson that we might be able to lower social costs and satisfy a public demand for justice at the same time by finding more creative sentencing options that consider the offender's interests should not be forgotten.

Who Might Cause Sentences to be Outside the Norm?

Inappropriate sanctions can result from the actions of officials in any of the three branches of government. It is worthwhile to consider these roles and the incentives that induce the actors who fill them to act as they do, so that we can explore opportunities to bring the incentive systems that shape those actions and decisions into closer alignment with the public's welfare.

---

[29] It is occasionally asserted that the utilitarian position excludes the utility of the offender in the social calculus (e.g., Duff, 1996, at p. 1: "Consequentialist accounts, however sophisticated, remain open to some version of the general objection that they fail to respect the moral standing of those who are punished or threatened with punishment.") A utilitarian may choose to take such a position on moral grounds, but there is nothing inherent in the utilitarian logic that supports it. Jeremy Bentham, father of utilitarianism, is explicit in his opposition to exclusion: "The profit of punishments has reference to the interests of two parties – the public, and the party injured. The expense of the punishment adds to this number a third interest, that of the delinquent . . . the delinquent is a member of the community, as well as any other individual – as well as the party injured himself; and that there is just as much reason for consulting his interest as that of any other" (*The Rationale of Punishment*, Book I – General Principles, Chapter V – Expense of Punishment).

[30] Etzioni praises a Eau Claire, Wisconsin, judge for letting a woman convicted of welfare fraud choose to be jailed rather than wear a sign admitting, "I stole food from poor people." The offender in this case ended up choosing the more socially costly option of jail over public humiliation, but the lesson of providing sentencing options that provide opportunities to consider the offender's utility along with the community's retributive goals need not be lost by this outcome.

Legislators may enact sentencing laws that impose mandatory minimum sanctions that are excessive, beyond socially optimal levels, thus imposing needless costs both on offenders and on the taxpayers who must cover the costs of overincarceration. They could conceivably make sentences too lenient, but real-world forces tend to move legislation in the opposite direction. Scheck, Neufeld and Dwyer (2001) put it this way: "No greater terror exists than the accusation that a politician coddles criminals" (p. 234). Tough sentencing laws that appeal to politicians and a fearful public have been especially popular since around 1990. Prominent examples include draconian drug laws and three-strikes laws (Skolnick, 1994; Jacobs and Potter, 1998; Greenwood et al., 1994). This turn in political thinking appears to have been profoundly influenced by the presidential election of 1988, in which candidate Michael Dukakis's prospects spiraled steeply downward when he responded feebly to accusations by the Bush campaign that Dukakis was responsible for Willie Horton's rape while on furlough from prison and, when asked in a Presidential debate what penalty would be in order for a hypothetical man who raped and murdered Dukakis's wife, responded blandly about his opposition to the death penalty.

Probation officers also influence sentencing decisions, in preparing presentence investigation reports that provide a primary source of information to sentencing judges. In many jurisdictions, the report ends with a recommended sentence. As with legislators, probation officers have strong incentives to prepare reports that overstate rather than understate the dangerousness of the person convicted. They are more likely to be held accountable for a freed offender who commits subsequent harm against an identifiable victim than for a report that leads to an overly lengthy term of incarceration. The burdens of this excess fall disproportionately on the offender and his family, and taxpayers in most jurisdictions have not been averse to paying for more prisons and jails to house these offenders. Probation officers responsible for such errors have remained well below the horizon of accountability.

The *judge*, in turn, may or may not follow the recommendations of the presentence investigation, but may sentence the person to a term that is either too light, imposing excessive crime costs on the community, or too harsh, imposing excessive and avoidable costs on both the person convicted and the taxpayers who bear the costs of incarceration.

Prison *parole authorities* may then keep the person in prison for either too long or too short a term, thus imposing higher than optimal costs on society. Parole authorities operate under incentive systems akin to those that shape the probation officer's recommendations, and they too are likely to lean toward erring on the side of overly long terms of incarceration.

It is tempting to think that the errors on one side are neutralized by the errors on the other side, but they are not. Society pays *both* for convicted persons who receive sentences that are too lenient and for those who receive sentences that are too harsh. The simultaneous existence of some lenient sentencing judges and actors who impose overly tough sentences may bring the average sentence closer to an optimal level, but suboptimal sentencing may be more clearly revealed by levels of sentencing disparity than by the average sentence level.

A governor, president, or other *chief executive* officer of a jurisdiction can pardon a convicted offender, grant clemency, or commute a sentence previously handed out by a judge. Any such action may either serve to correct a prior error of due process or impose an error of impunity, with associated social costs. These errors tend to be rarer than others, but they tend also to be more spectacular.

The magnitude of excessive cost associated with sanctions that are either to light or too heavy depends on the extent to which the actual decisions depart from optimal decisions, based ideally on valid estimates of the probabilities of recidivism and the costs of the harms imposed on the community and person sentenced. (See Chapter 5, Assessing the Cost of Justice Errors.) Even under the alternative "pure justice" or desert-based model, terms of incarceration may be mutually inconsistent, with a less serious offense receiving a harsher sentence than a more serious one, or they may overshoot or undershoot sentences that correspond to a broad consensus about the appropriate sentence for a particular offense. Consideration of such errors should be crime-specific, making use of estimates of the costs of crimes, costs of sanctions, and the effect of changes in sanction levels on crime rates at various margins.

Should Sanctions be Based on Predictions?

One of the problems with the utilitarian system of sentencing is that, in aiming to minimize the discounted present value of the stream of social costs associated with crime and justice, it must predict the amount of crime that will be prevented by the offender's incarceration. To do so, it must incorporate, along with elements of the crime, information that may be unrelated to the crime for which the offender was convicted, including information about the characteristics of the offender and prior behavior. Even if this were to produce sentences that minimize social costs in the aggregate, it will nonetheless assign a longer than optimal sentence to about half of the individuals who share that profile, those who would in fact turn out to be less recidivistic than their profile predicts, due to unmeasured factors and unaccounted for interactions among variables and nonlinearities that make for less-than-perfect predictions. There will be little consolation to such an individual that this random error will be offset by other offenders with similar profiles who would have recidivated at rates that exceed the prediction. Is this ethically and legally justifiable?

Even retributive sentencing systems on the ground include a dimension for the prior record of the offender, as noted earlier. This is done, clearly, with an eye toward the future, otherwise the use of such information would violate Constitutional protections against double jeopardy. A National Academy of Sciences panel on sentencing found the offender's prior record to emerge consistently as the second strongest predictor of sentence, after the seriousness of the current charge (Blumstein et al., 1983, p. 83). Prediction is bound to be a part of sentencing even if not officially acknowledged; the question is not so much whether it will be done as how. Prior record alone is a blunt, often poor prediction tool. The age and employment status of the offender, together with prior record, make for much stronger predictions of future criminal activity. A 19-year-old offender with five prior arrests is likely to be more criminally active than a

50-year-old one with 10 priors, all committed many years earlier. And people with jobs tend to be less criminally active than people who are unemployed.

It is often claimed that it is wrong to incorporate statistical predictions in criminal justice policy because they inevitably involve false positives, people who are predicted to be recidivists but who in fact would not commit subsequent crimes if released. The ethical argument for sentences based on statistical predictions is that the alternative is to impose even higher costs on society – victims, persons sentenced, and taxpayers. Punitive nonutilitarian sentences may satisfy a primal human instinct, but they come at the expense of prisons and jails occupied by people who are less likely to impose further crime costs on the community than more dangerous offenders who are released, and they may introduce a brutalizing effect along the way that creates further crime. Moreover, statistical predictions are often criticized for producing both false positive errors and false negative errors, but subjective predictions by sentencing authorities, the conventional alternative, have been found repeatedly to produce both false positive and false negative errors at an even higher rate than statistical ones (Monahan, 1981; Steadman and Cocozza, 1978; Meehl, 1954). Sanctions based on predictions have not been found unconstitutional, and sanctions that are systematically related to ethnicity have similarly been upheld as constitutional.[31]

Utilitarian sentences would be ethically and legally flawed, however, if they allowed for long terms of incarceration for trivial criminal infractions, on grounds of dangerousness – say, as in the case of

---

[31] In *McCleskey v. Kemp* [481 U.S. 279, 283 (1987)], the Supreme Court ruled that a 1986 statistical study by David Baldus et al., finding systematic racial effects in capital sentencing determinations does not render a sentence handed down to a particular individual as discriminatory under the Fourteenth Amendment, or irrational, arbitrary, or capriciousness under the Eighth Amendment. The Court explicitly assumed that the findings of the Baldus statistical study were valid, and based its decision on the absence of any revealed discrimination in the specific case at issue. The language of the Court was interesting: "Our assumption that the Baldus study is statistically valid does not include the assumption that the study shows that racial considerations actually enter into any sentencing decisions in Georgia. Even a sophisticated multiple-regression analysis such as the Baldus study can only demonstrate a risk that the factor of race entered into some capital sentencing decisions and a necessarily lesser risk that race entered into any particular sentencing decision" (Note 7).

a 19-year-old turnstile jumper with a juvenile felony record and no warrants outstanding.[32] Utilitarian sentences could also be called into question if the statistical basis for the predictions were substantively flawed, either because the data on which the predictions were based are unreliable or because the prediction tool is inappropriate, producing significant inaccuracy. Statutory limits based on the conviction charges might be useful for imposing practical constraints on flawed or unreasonable predictions.

Errors in Corrections

Even when sentences are neither excessively lenient nor harsh, errors can occur afterward. The judge or other sentencing authority decides only whether the offender will be imprisoned and the term of punishment; what follows is determined by correctional officials. In the United States, over six million people are under correctional authority, with about two million in prison or jail, the rest on probation. Errors can occur with both the incarcerated and probationer populations. Probation officers routinely decide on whether terms of probation or parole have been violated and whether probation or parole revocation hearings should be held, and parole authorities similarly make routine decisions about whether an inmate is ready for release from prison. Prisons and jails that allow inmates to escape by imposing inadequate security provisions produce systematic errors that compromise the public's safety.

As with prediction errors in sentencing, prediction errors can occur either in determining whether to incarcerate a probationer or reincarcerate a parolee, or whether to release an inmate eligible for parole. Empirically derived parole guidelines often help to reduce the latter type of errors. The decision to incarcerate a probationer or parolee can be more difficult, both because it is more often based on subjective

---

[32] The problem is more complicated when the danger is immeasurably great, as with a person with established terrorist associations convicted for a visa violation. It is difficult to establish a sanction that is ethically and legally warranted for such a person, but the judgment will be based on a subjective rather than a statistical prediction, since there is an insufficient empirical basis for prediction in such cases.

assessments and because the decision to incarcerate may conflict with the reintegration and treatment objectives of probation and parole departments.

Charles Logan (1993) has observed that prison authorities are capable of committing other errors as well:

> We ask an awful lot of our prisons. We ask them to correct the incorrigible, rehabilitate the wretched, deter the determined, restrain the dangerous, and punish the wicked. We ask them to take over where other institutions of society have failed and to reinforce norms that have been violated and rejected. We ask them to pursue so many different and often incompatible goals that they seem virtually doomed to fail. Moreover, when we lay upon prisons the utilitarian goals of rehabilitation, deterrence, and incapacitation, we ask them to achieve results primarily outside of prison, rather than inside. By focusing on external measures, we set prisons up to be judged on matters well beyond their direct sphere of influence. (pp. 23–4)

Logan's solution to these multiple dilemmas is the "confinement" model, under which "the mission of a prison is to keep prisoners – to keep them in, keep them safe, keep them in line, keep them healthy, and keep them busy – and to do it with fairness, without undue suffering, and as efficiently as possible" (p. 25). Logan goes on to offer a set of specific prison performance measures in each of eight corresponding areas: security, safety, order, care, activity, justice, conditions, and management. The social costs associated with errors in each of these domains are not clear, and attempts to estimate them could serve to prioritize them. In the meantime, Logan's system provides potentially useful standards for identifying and managing errors in corrections.

Joan Petersilia (1993) has offered a parallel system of performance measurement for the larger pool of nonincarcerated persons under correctional authority. She identifies the following as the primary goals of community corrections:

1. Assess offender's suitability for placement
2. Enforce court-ordered sanctions
3. Protect the community

4. Assist offenders to change
5. Restore crime victims

As with Logan's prison goals, a system such as Petersilia's could provide a basis for error management in the supervision of probationers and parolees in the community. And as with the refinement of a prison model in terms of the effects on crime and social costs, it will be in order to do the same for persons under correctional authority in the community.

The Critical Role of Incentives and Systems of Accountability

We need not wait for precise estimates of all the pertinent social costs of sentences that are unduly harsh or lenient, and more precise estimates of the relationships between sanction levels and types and crime and recidivism rates. To the extent that some sentences are obviously too harsh or lenient under any reasonable standard – some of the more draconian three-strikes laws and mandatory drug statutes surely qualify as viable candidates (Lithwick, 2002) – we may be able to bring them into line by focusing on the incentive systems that cause the excesses in the first place.

Lawmakers who enact sentencing statutes that impose overly long sentences might be dissuaded from doing so if the sort of attention that has been given to scary stories about crime were given as well to the extraordinary waste borne by taxpayers associated with prison and jail costs and the burdens on families of offenders, especially offenders who pose little or no danger to the public. The public deserves to know roughly how much it pays, per citizen, for these excesses.

Probation officers should be evaluated, at least for purposes of promotion, based on the accuracy and comprehensiveness of their presentence investigations, with disincentives against shaping the information in a manner that biases the sentencing decision to follow.

To induce judges to better manage sentencing errors, the first challenge is to find incentive and accountability systems that balance the need for thoughtful consideration of the most pertinent factors in a case with the need to avoid unwarranted disparities in sentencing that tend to accompany the vagaries of judicial thoughtfulness. For a sentencing decision in any particular case, the idea of an optimal sentence – a standard for identifying errors – implies the management of variation. In their exercise of discretion in sentencing prior to guidelines, judges were found to introduce unwarranted disparity because they disagreed with one another about the fundamental goals of sentencing or about the relative social harm associated with particular offenses, because they were internally inconsistent in their decisions, or from a combination of these sources of disparity.[33] Sentencing guideline systems have been devised that attempt to account for the details that matter, but more detail has brought with it complexity and confusion, especially at the federal level (Tonry, 1996; Stith and Cabranes, 1998). Guidelines are clearly capable of simultaneously reducing unwarranted disparity in sentencing, a problem of equitability, and helping to minimize random errors of justice, a problem of lost social welfare, but they must be instituted and administered in a manner that deals more effectively with the politics of sentencing than many of the guideline systems have to date, to ensure against guidelines that serve to institutionalize systematic sentencing errors.[34] In jurisdictions that permit broader exercise of sentencing discretion by judges, the appellate review process can be made more mindful of errors of justice, and judges can be persuaded to work more diligently to ensure that they are in fact effectively managed.

Judges can also be shielded from the political pressures that interfere with balanced sentencing policy by moving from appointment by election, common in Texas and elsewhere, to appointment by the executive branch and tenure following a probationary period.

---

[33] See Hogarth (1971); Diamond and Zeisel (1975); and Forst and Wellford (1981). The National Academy of Sciences Panel on Sentencing Research offered this summary assessment: "Despite the number and diversity of factors investigated as determinants of sentences, two-thirds or more of the variance in sentence outcomes remains unexplained." Blumstein et al. (1983), p. 10.

[34] This suggests the need to assess the relative costs of systematic and random errors of justice, an overlooked and important empirical question. It calls as well for the development of a theory of the optimal control of discretion. We should always work to identify systematic errors and move them toward zero. If the average social costs of random justice errors are greater than the average social costs of systematic justice errors, it will be more important to deal with the problem of abuse of discretion than to adjust sentences downward or upward.

Incentive and accountability systems can also be introduced to ensure that parole authorities are more conscious of the need to manage errors of justice. As with judges, guideline systems have been introduced to reduce unwarranted disparity in parole release decision making. And as with sentencing guidelines, parole release guidelines can also be shaped with an eye toward the management of errors.

Conclusion

Sentencing has long been the most basic and controversial area of criminal justice policy. While sentencing and corrections conclude the formal criminal justice process, they also shape virtually everything that happens beforehand in a case, starting with the prospective offender's decision to commit a crime. The controversy has been framed traditionally as one between conservatives interested in tougher sentences that aim to serve the welfare of victims and liberals interested in more humane sanctions that will speed the reintegration of defendants back into the community. I have attempted here to deal with the issue in a manner that may be more productive, by considering the goals of sentencing, alternative sanctions for achieving those goals, relationships between sanctions and crime, and the costs associated with crime and sanctions. This may seem a bit Quixotic, but the shouting-match alternative world in which we live has been both divisive and unproductive. While the shouting continues, we should try to see if we can move to a process that is more effective and just, and less costly. Democracy in the 20th century produced some dubious, fear-driven sentencing policy, and we would do well to see if enlightened notions from 18th-century enlightenment can be reintroduced into the 21st century.

It is standard practice to conclude with a recommendation that more research is needed. The conclusion here will depart from that convention slightly by adding that much better data are needed first, to improve the reliability of the findings that come out of any research that aims to support sentencing, and make sentencing more rational, and lower the social costs of crime and sanctions. It has been well over 200 years now since Jeremy Bentham gave us his visionary system for sanctioning criminal offenders. We have made some progress at the margins, especially in creating intermediate sanctions between prison and probation, and have moved well along the path to understanding relationships between sanctions and crimes, but we are still a long way from realizing the rational and humane sort of sentencing system that Bentham envisioned. The barriers at this point appear to be more political than technological.

CHAPTER ELEVEN

Homicide

Our capital system is haunted by the demon of error: error in determining guilt, and error in determining who among the guilty
deserves to die. Because of all of these reasons today I am commuting the sentences of all death row inmates.
> – Illinois Governor George H. Ryan (2003)

Criminologists should not... belittle the lived experiences of the
Klaas family and others that, like my own, have suffered the murder
of a loved one at the hands of a released repeat criminal.
> – John DiIulio (1994)

Introduction

The case for managing errors of justice is most strikingly made for
the crime of homicide. This is the most serious of all offenses, and we
have better data on homicides than on any other major category of
crime. Errors that involve the arrest and conviction of a wrong person
are especially critical in cases in which defendants found guilty are
eligible for the death penalty; an error of justice could conceivably
result in the taking of the life of an innocent person. It was noted
in Chapter 1 that over 100 death row inmates were found innocent
and released from prison in the United States from 1976 to 2002. As
the second of the two quotes that open this chapter makes clear, however, some people find it no less tragic when innocent people are bru-
tally murdered by a prematurely released offender, a phenomenon
that the documented evidence suggests has been more common

at least over the past 50 years than has the execution of innocent defendants.[1]

This chapter reviews the crime of homicide and how it is handled, in an attempt to compare conventional treatments of the subject with the error management perspective taken throughout this book. The crime of homicide will also serve as a vehicle to revisit and apply elements of the framework described in the preceding chapters.

Basics about Homicide: Opportunities for Error in Classification

Homicide is very similar to one other crime, aggravated assault – differing only with respect to whether the victim died of the wounds sustained. Although the death of the victim is often the objective of the offender in homicide cases,[2] homicide frequently follows an attempt to commit another crime, such as rape, robbery, assault, or burglary. Accordingly, it tends to have characteristics in common with the crimes that give rise to it. It can involve one or more offenders, and one or more victims; it entails offender-victim relationships involving strangers and nonstrangers alike; and it includes offenders who are both repeaters and first-timers. It encompasses offenders and victims of every major sociodemographic category, but falls disproportionately among young African-American males.[3] Because

---

[1] The documented evidence is likely to understate both types of errors. Although none has been documented, it is not inconceivable that one or two of the 749 people executed in the United States from 1976 through 2001 were actually innocent of the crimes for which they were executed. Officials are understandably reluctant to inquire into the prospect that such errors have occurred in their jurisdictions, especially on their watch. It is no less plausible that some unsolved homicides were committed by persons with histories of serious criminal violence, and that those homicides were facilitated by prior lapses in law enforcement, lenient sentences by judges, or early releases at the discretion of parole authorities.

[2] Offenders err, too, sometimes killing a person they intended only to incapacitate, at other times failing to kill a person when they had intended to do so. There are likely to be some interesting theoretical implications for criminal justice policy in focusing on the offender's decision calculus. I will limit this discussion to a brief note, however, to restrict opportunities for prospective offenders with scholarly inclinations to benefit from instruction in error management.

[3] The young and minorities are disproportionately represented among both victims and offenders of homicide. According to the Centers for Disease Control for 1997,

it can emanate from so many different motives, it generates an unusually diverse variety of crime scenes, investigative approaches, and sanctioning alternatives. This complexity contributes to the exercise of considerable discretion by the police, prosecutors, and when sentencing is not tightly controlled by statute or rigid guideline systems, judges. Greater opportunities for the exercise of discretion suggests larger variation in the interpretations of justice and standards of evidence by practitioners and greater opportunities for random errors of justice.

Errors of justice in cases of homicide begin with the requirement that the police establish the existence of homicide, and then that they determine the legal class to which a particular homicide case belongs. Deaths that appear at first to be the product of criminal activity sometimes turn out to be something else: suicide, an accident, death from natural causes, or occasionally, justifiable or excusable homicide. *Justifiable homicide* consists of the intentional, yet lawful, killing of another, such as when the state executes a capital offender, when a security guard kills a robber, or when a police officer kills an offender in self-defense. *Excusable homicide* involves one's killing another by accident, without negligence and without an intent to injure. Examples include hunting accidents, one child killing another while playing with a gun kept in a usually locked cabinet, and a traffic fatality in one car resulting from a collision caused by a tire blowout in another.

Errors in classifying these cases may occur when offenders kill persons intentionally and then rearrange the evidence to make the killings appear as though they were accidents. They may occur because of erroneous information provided by witnesses, or by mistaken inferences of investigating officers. Or they may occur when assessments of the cause of death by the medical examiner or forensic pathologist are made by less than competent professionals or by technicians who may feel pressured to find one way rather than another. The sources of

the victimization rates were highest in the 18- to 24-year-old group, with 20 homicides per 100,000 people, and according to the Uniform Crime Reports for the same year, the arrest rates for homicide were also highest for that group, with 33 homicide arrests per 100,000 people. African Americans represented 48 percent of all victims in 1997 and 56 percent of all persons arrested. The highest victimization rate in 1997 was for African American males in the 18- to 24-year-old group: 143 per 100,000 in 1997.

errors as to whether a homicide occurred and whether it was a crime are, in short, nearly as varied as homicide itself.

Many homicides are at the margin of criminality, both legally and socially. The courts routinely decide whether a homicide offender was criminally responsible for the act – common examples include 16-year-old offenders, emotionally disturbed offenders, and others who commit homicide while in states of diminished capacity due to circumstances largely beyond their control – and an element of arbitrariness inevitably plays a central role in determining whether the case shall be treated as a criminal matter. The criminal justice system and other institutions in the community, public and private, may be able to do much to prevent such homicides, and our best solution may be to focus on prevention. When such deaths occur, we may minimize social costs by treating them as serious health problems or accidents rather than as criminal homicides. The arbitrariness involved in drawing boundaries of criminality in such matters must be acknowledged, in any case.

When it is clear that a criminal homicide did occur, errors can be made afterward in establishing the degree of seriousness of the crime. Criminal homicide includes several varieties of murder and manslaughter. *First degree murder* is the most serious, involving premeditation (a degree of planning to kill) and "malice aforethought" (the deliberate intention to kill rather than injure or incapacitate). Under the felony murder rule, first degree murder includes killings carried out in the course of committing an inherently dangerous felony such as rape, robbery, or arson, and in most states, burglary. *Second degree murder* involves criminal intent, like first degree murder, but without premeditation. In most jurisdictions second degree murder is the consequence of committing an act like domestic violence or larceny, rather than a planned act aimed principally at the death of the victim. Common examples of second degree murder are the spouse who finds his wife and lover in the bedroom and kills both in a fit of rage, or a fatal stabbing in a bar brawl.

There is no bright line that allows us to establish after the fact whether the murder was premeditated, that is, whether a first or second-degree murder. Clearly, all domestic homicides are not the consequence of an assaulter who simply gets carried away in a violent act. In some domestic homicides, the offender planned to kill the victim. Such errors may often occur in nondomestic homicides as well. It is often difficult to establish premeditation and malice aforethought when the facts are ambiguous, and ambiguity inevitably increases the risk of error. Detectives, prosecutors, and judges may conclude second degree murder when murder was in fact the primary motive, or they may conclude first degree murder when murder was not the primary motive. The evidence standard of proof beyond a reasonable doubt should lead to a preponderance of the former type of error over the latter, but there really is no way of knowing definitively about primary motive. DNA evidence will ordinarily be of little help here.

Errors can occur in establishing lower levels of homicide as well. *Manslaughter* is one such broad category of homicide, less serious than murder in that it does not involve an intent to kill, or even to commit serious injury in some cases. Examples include killings by a first-time drunk driver and hunting accidents involving negligence. Manslaughter may in fact be more serious than murder in terms of the number of deaths, but it lacks the element of premeditation to cause grave harm to another that is associated with both first and second degree murder.

Manslaughter is in turn divided into two principal categories: voluntary and involuntary. *Voluntary manslaughter* involves the killing of another on an impulse, typically following provocation and under an impairment because of an abnormality of mind, as in cases of an excessive response in self-defense and in instances of infanticide following attempts to quiet a crying baby. This is a lower level of homicide than second degree murder because it lacks both premeditation and malice aforethought. Errors may occur in such cases when an offender wishes to make his intention to kill someone appear as though it had been unintentional; one cannot be sure of the extent to which voluntary manslaughter cases are actually misclassified cases of murder in the first degree. Determining whether an offender committed the killing while still in the heat of passion or after a brief cooling-off period is not always straightforward. Errors may occur as well in the less serious crime of *involuntary manslaughter*, involving the taking of another's life through a reckless but accidental act, such as a death due to drunk driving, or a killing that results from playing with a loaded gun, or the killing of a neighbor's child by a vicious and uncontrolled dog. Even this relatively low level of homicide is a felony offense, subject to a sentence of a year or more in prison.

Legal procedure is designed to clarify relevant elements of a crime and minimize the error of classifying a noncriminal act as a crime or vice versa. In criminal homicide, as in other felonies, the collection of facts needed to indict a suspect, known as the "*corpus delicti*," must establish the commission of a crime rather than an accident, a suicide, or death by natural causes.[4] This determination is made typically by a forensic pathologist. The facts must also establish the responsibility of some person or persons, as determined by the investigator.

All of these assessments are subject to errors, from the determination of whether a crime has been committed to the classification of category of homicide. The errors may be random, the product of circumstances or varying levels of competence of the officials involved in these determinations. Or they may be systematic, the product of poorly crafted laws, questionable policies and procedures, and institutional pressures to draw a particular conclusion, pressures that may be especially strong in urban settings with high homicide rates. One potential source of systematic errors was noted in Chapter 7: investigators are accountable primarily to the police department rather than the court, so their incentives may be biased toward finding evidence that supports arrest and conviction, leading to systematic errors that favor incriminating evidence over exculpatory evidence.

In all such questions of classification error, it is important for our purposes to ask: What are the social costs of a misclassification? From a retributive perspective, it may matter whether the offender committed a voluntary manslaughter, while still in the heat of passion, or whether the killing occurred after enough time for the offender to decide to kill with malice aforethought. But should it matter from a utilitarian perspective? Sanctions designed to deter may have more impact on

---

[4] The term *corpus delicti* is sometimes equated erroneously with "corpse." There is, in fact, no meaningful relation between the two.

people inclined to commit crimes following a plan, but people who
have difficulty managing their anger may in fact be more likely to
commit future crimes than others. Errors that occur because the offender rearranged the evidence to make the act appear spontaneous, a
manslaughter, rather than intentional and premeditated, a first degree
murder, are more serious in that they represent attempts to deceive
the justice system, and society should wish to deter such acts of decep-
tion separately with additional punishment. Premeditated homicide
acts warrant a harsher punishment to the extent that they are more
deterrable than spontaneous homicide, and it is in the interest of the
justice system to provide further disincentives against attempts to escape the incremental portion of a sanction associated with deterrence,
but only up to the point at which an additional increment of punishment adds an increment of cost that begins to exceed the value of
the reduced crime. The case for a more severe sanction in cases of
evidence tampering can be made on retributive grounds as well: it is
simply wrong to attempt to deceive our system of justice.

Failures to Bring Homicide Offenders to Justice

Chapter 1 referred to murder victims who gained tragic prominence:
Megan Kanka in New Jersey in 1994, Polly Klaas in California in 1993,
and Stephanie Roper in Maryland in 1982. Each of these cases, involving brutal offenders who killed their victims after being released from
custody following prior acts of violence, was sufficiently heinous to
be immortalized by legislative proposals for tougher sanctions, in the
victim's name – in each case a young girl, one of the more sympathy-
arousing categories of victims. In none of these cases, however, had
the offender been previously charged with a murder. Each of these
murders might have been prevented by tougher sanctions in earlier
cases, but it is easier to make these assessments in hindsight, after a
murder, than before.

   Lapses in bringing homicide offenders to justice are more rigorously indicated by data on reported homicide offenses and their
outcomes. Each year some 15,000 to 20,000 homicides are typically

reported to the police in the United States,[5] and about 65 to 70 percent of those are cleared by arrest. Some 60 to 65 percent of those arrests are resolved in the courts as convictions (about 60 percent by guilty pleas, 40 percent by trial verdicts), so the vast majority of homicide offenders are not held formally accountable for their crimes. Because many of the homicides involve multiple offenders, however, in a year in which 18,000 victims are murdered, some 10,000 offenders are typically incarcerated, most for long periods of time. Most people who commit murder typically end up getting incarcerated eventually, although often for a different crime. Still, most murders do not result directly in incarceration. This lapse in justice tends to occur disproportionately in big cities, where police must confront the barriers associated with social disorganization, large crime loads per unit of resources, and often unresponsive bureaucracies.

Homicide offenders are, nonetheless, less likely to escape arrest and punishment than are those who commit an offense in any other broad category of crime.[6] Lapses in bringing offenders to justice typically begin with failure to report crimes and arrest the offender, and the rates of reporting and clearance by arrest are considerably higher for homicide than for any other felony offense. Except for classification errors of the sort discussed in the previous section, virtually all homicides are reported to the police.[7] The reporting rates for felonies in the aggregate are under 50 percent, ranging from about 30 percent for larceny to about 80 percent for auto theft. And for all reported crimes, the police clear homicides by arrest at a substantially higher rate than they do any other crime category. Each year about 65 percent of all homicides in the United States result in arrest (Federal Bureau of Investigation, 2000). Although this rate is substantially lower

---

[5] The number of homicides in the United States ranged from 15,000 to 23,000 annually from 1971 through 1997, and dipped below 15,000 from 1998 through the early 2000s.

[6] This assertion is contingent on the assumption that due process errors are not substantially more likely in homicide cases than in other cases. If this assumption were incorrect, we would not be able to use convictions for homicide as a valid reflection of homicide offenders having been brought to justice.

[7] Reporting rates for other crimes are derived from the National Crime Victimization Survey (NCVS), administered by the Bureau of Justice Statistics and fielded by the U.S. Census Bureau. Reporting rates are not available from the NCVS for homicide, as the NCVS data are derived from interviews with victims.

than in earlier times, primarily because of increases in stranger-to-stranger and drug-related homicides,[8] it remains substantially higher than the rates of clearance by arrest for other crimes. The clearance rate for rape was below 50 percent throughout the 1990s, with rates of 25 percent for robbery, 13 percent for burglary and 14 percent for auto theft. Not surprisingly, rates of clearance by arrest in homicide cases have been found to be lower when they occur as a consequence of stranger-to-stranger or drug crimes (Mouzos and Muller, 2001).

High rates of clearance by arrest for homicide are attributable primarily to two factors. First, most homicides are committed by offenders who know (and were known by) their victims, and such cases are inherently easier to solve. The identity of the offender is usually immediately apparent, and the motive is typically not difficult to establish, often following an argument or series of disputes, frequently committed in a state of drunkenness, and generally done with an abundance of incriminating evidence. Criminologist Richard Block has reported that an investigator from the Chicago Police Department once referred to these cases as "smoking gun" homicides when the offender is at the crime scene when the police arrive, and as "known but flown" homicides when the evidence points unambiguously to a person who has fled the scene of the crime.[9] Second, homicides command and usually receive a significantly larger share of investigative time, effort, and resource commitment than less serious crimes, and this higher priority attention raises solution rates.

The Skillful Offender

A third category of Block's informal system of classifying homicides, "mysteries," are attributable largely to the skillful offender. We considered in Chapter 3 the problem of the skillful offender as one source of lapses in bringing offenders to justice, and some homicide offenders meet this standard. Deranged but cagy homicide offenders are able occasionally to inflict substantial damage before being captured or

---

[8] The rate at which reported homicides are cleared by arrest declined from 94 percent in 1961 to about 65 percent in 1992, and it remained at that level throughout the 1990s.
[9] Oral communication, November 16, 2002.

killed, especially mass murderers, who kill several victims within a few minutes or hours, spree killers, who do so over a matter of a week or so, typically on the run, and serial murderers, who kill several victims over longer periods of time. These distinctions are useful to the extent that they help in profiling the offender and solving the crimes more quickly. Timothy McVeigh's 1995 bombing of the Murrah Federal Building in Oklahoma City and the 1999 Columbine High School killings are mass murders that received considerable media attention, as did the crimes of spree killers John Allen Muhammed and John Lee Malvo, and serial killers Ted Bundy, John Wayne Gacy, Wayne Williams, Theodore Kaczynski, and a host of others. These offenders all managed to inflict extraordinary damage because their acts were carefully planned and skillfully executed. They are, however, exceptional cases, and they receive attention that is disproportionate to that given to the vastly larger pool of homicides that occur more routinely each year.

Mass murders typically occur in densely populated areas. They may be most effectively countered through prevention, including the use of more defensible architectural designs, road barriers, and improved surveillance and security systems (Clarke, 1997). Spree and serial killings occur in a wider range of settings, from urban to rural. They are difficult to prevent, and are ended usually through a combination of skillful detective work and offender miscalculation.

Law Enforcement
Skillful policing, however, does not appear to be in equal abundance from one police department to the next. Police departments in more affluent jurisdictions tend to have larger budgets, and less well-endowed police departments are often saddled with a lethal mix of unusually high homicide rates, lower than average salaries and officer retention rates, tired equipment, and obsolete crime-solving technology. In 1990 the District of Columbia became notorious for having one of highest homicide rates and lowest homicide clearance rates in the United States, and the Washington Metropolitan Police Department only worsened the problem in relaxing new recruit screening standards to hire more police officers to deal with the problem. As homicide rates started declining in other cities in the early 1990s, they

remained high in Washington until the mid-1990s, and homicide clearance rates remained low, as the MPD became burdened with a cohort of disproportionately incompetent, corrupt and brutal police officers.

The rates at which the police are able to clear homicides by arrest, more generally, are lowest in cities having populations of over one million people, with clearance rates running about 10 percentage points below that for the United States as a whole (Federal Bureau of Investigation, 2000). This is largely the product of a higher incidence of drug-related and stranger-to-stranger homicides in large cities, but it is due as well to high rates of other crimes in large cities. The number of serious crimes per officer, prosecutor, and judge tend to be much higher in urban settings, and overloaded resources surely have much to do with these lower rates of clearance by arrest and convictions afterward.

In a study of 798 homicides committed in 1994 and 1995 in four large U.S. cities,[10] Wellford and Cronin (2000) found that the clearance rates were influenced by the nature of the homicide itself (especially, high clearance rates for domestic homicides and low rates for drug-related homicides), but also by the actions of the investigating officer. They found that the probability of clearance increases significantly when the first officer on the scene quickly notifies the homicide unit, the medical examiners, and the crime lab and attempts to locate witnesses, secure the area, and identify potential witnesses in the neighborhood and obtain essential information while it is fresh (p. 6; also Isaacs, 1967; Folk, 1971; Ward, 1971). They also found that clearance was significantly more likely as the number of detectives assigned to the case increased, especially in the early stages of investigation, and when the detectives made computerized record checks of victims, suspects, witnesses, and guns.

Variation in the competence of investigators varies both between police departments and among individual officers within given police

---

[10] The cases were selected so that the proportion of open and closed homicide cases in the sample matched that of the entire homicide caseload for each city in the years studied. This resulted in a total of 589 (74 percent) solved cases in the sample; 50 percent were solved within one week, and 93 percent within one year. The identities of the four cities studied were not revealed.

departments. Research has found that what the first officer arriving at the scene of a homicide does immediately can weigh heavily not only in the department's success in clearing the case by arrest, but also in bringing cases to the prosecutor with stronger evidence, more likely to end in conviction (Forst et al., 1977; Forst et al., 1982). As noted in Chapter 7, variation in investigative success within a police department is attributable also to the detective's workload (Ward, 1971) and to the department's organizational structure and procedures (Elliot, 1978; Bloch and Bell, 1976; Schwartz and Clarren, 1977). Some variation in abilities across individuals and departments is inevitable, but an aggregate U.S. homicide clearance rate as low as 65 percent may be remediable. Lapses are common even in the better police departments. We will address prospects for raising homicide clearance rates later in this chapter.

Prosecution, Adjudication, Corrections
What happens after the arrest of a homicide offender? It is common to hear the police complain of prosecutors and judges "letting offenders off the hook," as though the vast majority of the people they detain and arrest really committed the crimes for which they are suspected. In many instances, the police are likely to be correct in this assessment, evidently more so in some jurisdictions than others.[11] The standard of proof for conviction – evidence sufficient to justify a trial verdict of proof beyond a reasonable doubt – is, after all, well above that for an arrest (probable cause), and a potentially large group of true offenders is bound to pass through this difference in standards.

---

[11] Variation in errors across jurisdictions is suggested by the sharp contrast in rates at which arrests for homicide ended in conviction in two major cities in 1977–78: 23 percent in New Orleans and 70 percent in Los Angeles. (Forst et al., 1982, p. 13) Assuming few wrong-person convictions in both sites, either many more wrong persons are arrested in New Orleans or more culpable offenders are getting let off the hook, because of some combination of police failures to collect sufficient evidence, tougher prosecutor screening practices, and higher evidentiary standards for conviction in court. It is virtually impossible to know the relative contribution of each of these prospects. A plausible explanation is that more offenders did get away with murder in New Orleans, and the police contributed to the problem by failing to find the offenders in the first place and failing to bring good evidence to the court in homicide arrests made.

Persons arrested for homicide are in fact *less* likely to be let off the hook in most jurisdictions than are other arrestees. Prosecutors generally obtain higher rates of conviction for homicide arrests than for arrests in most other categories of crime.[12] Still, even in the jurisdictions with the highest rates at which homicide arrests end in conviction, 30 percent of the arrestees are not convicted. We are left to wonder what proportion of the thousands of arrests for homicide that wash out of the courts each year involve true offenders. Under prevailing systems of accountability, neither the police nor the prosecutor is responsible for those cases, which could help to explain why there are so many and why we know so little about them. This hole between adjacent systems of accountability may offer substantial opportunities to reduce, simultaneously, errors of impunity and errors of due process in homicide cases.

Incarceration rates and terms of incarceration also tend to be much higher for homicide than for other offenses, which should come as no surprise, given that homicide is the most serious of all felony crimes.[13] The rates and terms of incarceration tend to be higher and harsher also for first degree murder than for second degree murder, and higher for second degree murder than for manslaughter. Longer terms of incarceration for all crimes have become especially pronounced since the growth of mandatory sentencing and truth-in-sentencing laws and the replacement of parole release with statutory guidelines in most states and in the federal system during the 1980s and 1990s (Tonry, 1996).

A final source of errors of impunity, homicide offenders who escape from prison, are sufficiently rare as to be ignored. The few who do escape capture the headlines locally and sometimes nationally, but the commercial entertainment value of these cases surely exceeds the crime costs that these extremely rare cases impose on society.

---

[12] Forst et al. (1982), pp. 11–13. The rate at which homicide arrests ended in conviction was above 60 percent for four of the seven jurisdictions studied – Los Angeles, Washington (DC), Indianapolis, and Cobb County (GA) – generally well above the rates for other felonies in those jurisdictions, based on analysis of data for 1977–8. (Sixty percent will seem low to those who are used to hearing about conviction rates of 90 percent; prosecutors do not ordinarily calculate their conviction rates with arrests as the denominator.) For the other three jurisdictions, the rates were 50 percent for Manhattan, 40 percent for Salt Lake, and an astonishing 23 percent for New Orleans.

[13] Forst and Lynch, 1997, pp. 105–7.

Excessive Intrusions in Homicide Cases

In comparing victimizations and reported offenses with convictions we can draw plausible conclusions about failures to bring culpable offenders to justice. It is more difficult to draw similarly plausible conclusions about the extent to which innocent people are detained, arrested and convicted, and the extent to which excessive intrusions are imposed on culpable offenders. This is true for homicide, and for every other crime category as well.

This problem begins with a dearth of information about police stops, detentions, interrogations, and arrests, especially of suspects or "persons of interest" in stranger-to-stranger homicide cases. In 1977–8, an extraordinary 77 percent of the 396 arrests for homicide in New Orleans did not end in conviction (Forst et al., 1982). What do we know about the costs imposed by police on those 305 defendants? Some may have been real homicide offenders, but surely many were not. Was the New Orleans Police Department simply trying to record high rates of clearance by arrest for reported homicide cases? Costs may have been imposed also on homicide suspects interrogated intensively but not arrested. How many of those were there, and what was the extent of those intrusions? The absence of any systematic attempt by the police to document known errors in detaining and arresting suspects makes it difficult to establish estimates of the rates at which these errors occur with degrees of validity and reliability that satisfy conventional standards of empirical research. The unknown errors are likely to be much larger, to vary substantially from police department to department, and for the most part to be matters of pure speculation. In homicides involving solo offenders, the police frequently detain (and occasionally arrest) more than one person, although not ordinarily at the same time. In such cases excessive costs (and possibly wrongful arrests) are incurred by at least one person. At the very least, it would be useful for the police to maintain and analyze data on all people detained for homicide (and other crimes as well), and the outcomes of those detentions.

A rare exception to the absence of systematic data on due process problems by the police is the existence of data on felony arrest rejections and case dismissals by prosecutors, and the reasons given for the washouts. These data indicate, in jurisdiction after jurisdiction, that due process protections are vastly more likely to produce case rejections and dismissals for drug offenders than for homicide defendants.[14]

Prosecutors, however, tend to maintain better data on due process errors by the police than they do on such errors for which they may be responsible. Convictions are occasionally overturned based on evidence brought to the court after the conviction, revealing a wrong-person error, which may suggest a need for more thorough screening of arrests. Prosecutors could, in any case, do more to document and analyze such cases and learn from them as they occur.

Due process errors fall on a spectrum from inadvertent to venal, as was noted in Chapter 2, and this diversity of errors appears to have been better documented for homicide than for any other crime, largely because of media interest in such errors. Persons are occasionally convicted for homicide mistakenly due to sheer bad luck: being at the wrong place at the wrong time and having characteristics in common with the offender, with a positive witness identification in spite of effective police precautions to prevent such mistakes (Huff et al., 1996; Scheck et al., 2001, pp. 53–8). The homicide convictions that have been overturned following DNA evidence exonerating the defendant suggest that wrongful homicide convictions occur more commonly because of institutional pressures on police to solve important cases and prosecutors to win convictions, with accountability systems that provide weak incentives to give equal weight to exonerating evidence (Connors et al., 1996; Huff et al., 1996; Scheck et al., 2001).

The rate at which due process errors attributable to false confessions occur may well be *higher* for homicides than for other crimes. It was

---

[14] These data were reported by the Bureau of Justice Statistics from 1979 until 1992. See Chapter 8, Note 6. They reveal, generally, that arrests rejected at the screening stage or dismissed afterward because of police violations of Fourth or Fifth Amendment rights almost never occur in homicide cases. About 5 percent of all felony arrests rejected by prosecutors are refused because of due process violations, and the vast majority of those occur in drug cases (Forst, Lucianovic, and Cox, 1977; Brosi, 1979; Boland, Mahanna, and Sones, 1992).

noted earlier that homicides are more diverse than other crimes in that they can emanate from a wider variety of motives, generating a more diverse variety of crime scenes, investigative approaches, and opportunities for considerable discretion by the police, prosecutors, and judges, and in turn, greater opportunity for random errors of justice.

What may be the most pervasive source of errors of due process in homicide cases is beyond the reach of the court: informal rewards and formal incentive systems that often put the police under undue pressure to solve high-profile cases. The pressure has led, clearly, to the arrest of many a leading suspect who has turned out to be innocent. In their zeal to justify an identification of the person arrested as the true offender, police often persuade themselves of the correctness of the decision. A variety of errors have followed: witness inquiries and lineup procedures that produce false identifications, use of untrustworthy snitches, overlooking (and occasionally suppressing) exonerating evidence, inducements to false confessions; and shopping for laboratory technicians who are more inclined to find incriminating evidence against the suspect (Connors et al., 1996; Huff et al., 1996; Scheck et al., 2001).

The Death Penalty

The ultimate error of justice is the sanctioned taking of an innocent person's life in the name of justice. There have been no documented cases of an innocent person executed in the United States for several decades, but many sentenced to death since 1977 (the year executions resumed in the United States) have had their convictions overturned on appeal. And while not a death penalty case, the killing of Amidou Diallo by New York Police Department officers, discussed in Chapter 7, did much to undermine the legitimacy of both the police and the courts that exonerated them. It did so even under the most charitable assessment of the episode, that the killing was a grievous error, an excusable homicide rather than an intentional act.

The prospect of error in the use of the death penalty has only recently come into prominence. For decades the death penalty fight had been waged principally on other fronts, especially ethical questions such as whether it is cruel and unusual (from the left) or whether lesser punishments are unjust to the victims of murder and their survivors (from the right), and empirical questions as to whether it deters or brutalizes and whether it is applied in a discriminatory manner, especially with regard to the races of the defendant and the victim.[15] Then in 1987, Hugo Bedau and Michael Radelet published a landmark study documenting of 350 cases involving defendants convicted of capital crimes in the United States between 1900 and 1985 and who were later found to be innocent.[16] In the decade following the publication of that study, scores of additional death row inmates were discovered to have been falsely convicted, largely through the emergence of DNA evidence. The prospect of an error in the use of the death penalty thus emerged to transcend all other challenges to the use of this absolute sanction.[17] As a consequence, some are now arguing that the standard of proof for capital cases should be higher than beyond a reasonable doubt, that the standard should be beyond *any* doubt (Liebman et al., 2002).[18] Such a standard might be so high as to preclude any convictions, but we should be able to find a standard of evidence higher than that currently used in death penalty cases that would reduce the risk of executing innocent people while permitting the execution of offenders who have clearly committed horrific crimes,

[15] These various aspects of the debate are taken up in a single volume by Bedau (1982). The Supreme Court has weighed in on several of these matters. In *Furman v. Georgia* (408 U.S. 238, 1972) the Court ruled, by five-to-four majority, that the death penalty as then applied violated the cruel-and-unusual provision of the Eighth Amendment. Four years later, in *Gregg v. Georgia* (428 U.S. 153, 1976), the Court reversed its 1972 ruling, by a seven-to-two majority, ruling that the death penalty was not per se unconstitutional. Then, in *McCleskey v. Kemp* (481 U.S. 279, 1987), the Court ruled that a racially disproportionate system of administering the death penalty is not unconstitutional if the decision in any particular case has not been shown to have been influenced by race.

[16] Bedau had earlier (1964) published findings that some 85 defendants had been wrongly convicted of capital crimes from 1893 through 1964, which served as a precursor to the more extensive 1987 survey of wrongful convictions in capital cases.

[17] See Chapter 1, supra, Note 1.

[18] Governor George Ryan's commutation of the death sentences of all 156 Illinois death row inmates in 2003 was accompanied by a statement that gave essentially the same reasoning: "If the system was making so many errors in determining whether someone was guilty in the first place, how fairly and accurately was it determining which guilty defendants deserved to live and which deserved to die?"

often repeatedly, sometimes using torture, or aimed at hindering the justice system (Turow, 2003, p. 47).

One might expect judges and juries to be inclined already to use a higher standard of evidentiary proof for homicide cases than for less serious ones, because of the harsher sentences associated with these cases, and a higher standard still for cases that qualify for capital punishment in a given state. After all, few people would care to live with the worry that they contributed to the execution of an innocent person. Moreover, these cases tend to receive disproportionate amounts of courtroom time and attention than other cases.

It is plausible, however, that the opposite may be closer to the truth: wrongful convictions may be more common in homicide convictions, even in death penalty cases. Judges and juries in murder cases may care as much or more about subsequent victims of the offender in question if they vote to acquit or give a lenient sentence than they do about the defendant if they decide in such a way that contributes to a long term of incarceration, which is the norm for the vast majority of murder convictions. And in the approximately two percent of all murder cases that are death penalty cases, the jurors are typically screened to ensure that they are not opposed to the death penalty, a practice that was held Constitutional by the Supreme Court under *Witherspoon v. Illinois*.[19] Juries made up of exclusively of folks who support capital punishment may be more inclined to find the defendant guilty than are the juries in other felony cases. Moreover, the police and prosecutors put considerably more time and energy into gathering incriminating evidence in these cases than in others, while the typical defense lawyer in these cases is appointed by the court and often unable to put a great deal more time into these cases than others and, in any case, unable to give as much time as other defense lawyers do in such cases.

Still, over 100 death row inmates were released from prison from the time the Supreme Court reinstated the death penalty in 1976 until 2002 – 1.3 percent of all inmates sentenced to death during the period – their convictions overturned by flawed procedure and, in

[19] 391 U.S. 510 (1968).

some cases, strong evidence of total innocence.[20] Several teams have thoroughly dissected the anatomies of these and earlier wrongful convictions in capital cases (Bedau and Radelet, 1987; Huff et al., 1996; Bedau, 1997; Liebman et al., 2000; Scheck et al., 2001; Death Penalty Information Center, 2002). The pathologies uncovered by these investigations include one or more of the following in a given case: misidentification by witnesses, often induced by flawed identification procedures used by the police, use of an opportunistically dishonest jailhouse snitch, suppression of exculpatory evidence or other professional misconduct by police and sometimes by prosecutors, fraudulent laboratory work by a forensic technician, incompetent defense lawyer, a judge who biased the proceedings in the instructions given to juries and in decisions to sustain or overrule objections, and jury selection procedures that produced a biased jury. The convictions in these cases were overturned through none of these original sources of wrongful conviction. Rather, the sources of the reversals were typically DNA evidence or confessions by true offenders, often years later.[21]

In a second study by James Liebman and his associates at the Columbia University Law School (2002), the team identified 5,826 death penalty convictions during the period 1973 to 1995 (p. 36). Their finding of 2,349 of those cases reversed and sent back to trial revealed both a higher incidence and higher rate of reversals in jurisdictions that were more likely to sanction persons convicted of murder to the death penalty.[22] They reported also that reversals were more common in the least aggravated of capital cases. They posited a plausible

[20] Berlow reported at least 80 death row inmates found innocent from 1976 to 1999. See also Ho (2000), Leahy (1999), and Liebman et al. (2000).

[21] Although not a death penalty case, both DNA evidence and a confession 13 years later by the true offender contributed to the overturning of the conviction of five Harlem teenagers in 2002 in the notorious "wilding" rape of a 28-year-old investment banker jogging in Central Park in 1989 (Saulny, 2002).

[22] The Liebman team's categorization system failed to distinguish between legal-procedural errors and wrong-person errors in the cases studied. Some unreported number of the original convictions in the 2,349 reversals documented were upheld following reconsideration. Other writers have argued that even the overturned convictions may have been motived at least in part by appellate judges opposed to the death penalty, and more fundamentally that among the many thousands of cases studied the Liebman team was unable to identify a single instance of the execution of an innocent person (Cassell, 2000; Wilson, 2000).

explanation for the findings: as the death penalty is more widely used, the proportion of death-penalty-worthy cases declines, and its use may be more prone to error in jurisdictions that use it less selectively (Liebman et al., 2002).

Two additional findings from the Liebman (2002) report are particularly interesting and relevant to our inquiry: reversal rates are higher in states with low rates of apprehension, conviction and imprisonment, and higher in states in which judges are elected. The first of these suggests the need to monitor more carefully the work of police by prosecutors – and the work of both by judges – in jurisdictions with low clearance rates, where the pressures to arrest and convict may be more intense. The second raises new questions as to the wisdom of selecting judges through elections, and possibly as to whether it is prudent to select prosecutors that way as well.

The death penalty is very much a moral issue. We may not be able to resolve the death penalty question on utilitarian grounds, but we should pay especially close attention to the effects of the use of the death penalty on errors of justice, not only to minimize the risk that innocent people will be killed, but to reduce allied social costs, including those associated with the demagoguery that often accompanies this most sensational of sanctions.

Remedies and Impediments to the Management of Errors in Homicide Cases

In "A Cold Case," a *New Yorker* essay turned into a book of the same name, Philip Gourevitch (2001) documents the true story of an about-to-retire chief investigator for the Manhattan District Attorney's office, Andy Rosenzweig. In his nearly 30 years with the NYPD, Rosenzweig had worked on hundreds of cases and supervised the work of detectives in several thousand more. One case, involving the murder of two old friends in 1970, had nagged at him throughout his career. The case was closed in 1992, with the last line in the file concluding matter-of-factly that the only viable suspect "is dead." The story chronicles Rosenzweig's meticulous tracing of tedious telephone records of the suspect's family members in 1997, which eventually turned up the killer under a different identity in the San Francisco area. Gourevitch observes that Rosenzweig was given permission by his supervisor to put the extraordinary time into the case largely because the homicide caseload in New York, when Rosenzweig worked so painstakingly on the case, had declined to less than half the level of 1991, just six years earlier. Workload, in short, can be a critical variable in the ability of detectives to solve cases, a point that had been made more systematically in earlier research.[23]

Other factors may be even more critical. One of the most insidious sources of wrongful arrests and convictions in homicide cases is the pull of incentive systems, formal and informal, that induce the police to weigh incriminating evidence more heavily than exonerating evidence. Police are rewarded for making arrests regardless of the outcome of the case in court, and the pressure to clear homicide cases is especially strong. An officer's prospects for promotion are unlikely to be hindered, by contrast, if he or she brings arrests to the prosecutor that end in conviction at unusually low rates. Police departments tend not to know even who these officers are, since feedback about how arrests are resolved in court is not routinely provided to the police in most jurisdictions (Forst et al., 1976; Forst et al., 1982).

While complaints are common that our police are hamstrung by constitutional protections that are weighted too heavily in favor of offenders, one rarely hears the complaint that police incentive systems are biased toward arrests without convictions. Perhaps we should not be quite so surprised of the extent to which witness identifications turn out to be erroneous in homicide cases, that information provided by untrustworthy snitches is used as often as it is as a primary basis for

[23] In Richard Ward's 1971 doctoral dissertation, a study of detective operations in 21 police departments, Ward concluded: " . . . there is little time for investigation, at least the kind of investigation that might produce greater results. The implications of these findings are far reaching, for they tend to indicate that detectives are physically unable to handle the number of cases assigned to them." Of course, one compelling anecdote (Gourevitch's) and a single study (Ward's) do not settle the issue, despite the fact that they conform to common sense. Peter Greenwood (1970) studied operations of the New York Police department at about the time of Ward's research and concluded that caseload had no effect on investigative performance, and Parkinson's Law (i.e., work expands so as to fill the time available for its completion) suggests that performance is independent of workload. Decades later, this clearly remains a vastly understudied matter, an area ripe for deeper empirical inquiry.

arrest in murder cases, that DNA evidence has revealed murder confessions induced by police to have been false, that exonerating evidence is often overlooked in these cases. While it may be impossible to eliminate the pressures that lead to these systematic errors of justice in murder cases, it may be possible to reduce the errors substantially. This could begin by subjecting homicide detectives to different systems of accountability and giving them greater professional autonomy within police departments, perhaps with certification standards and degree requirements in a relevant scientific discipline (e.g., chemistry, biology, forensic science) that induce them to operate primarily as objective scientists rather than advocates for crime control. This transformation of the role of the police investigator could be complemented by an expansion in the use of professional investigators responsible primarily to the courts rather than to the chief of police. Such persons could serve as officers of the court, to review the investigative work of police investigators on a random or routine basis, to be available in selected cases, as determined by the judge, or to review the evidence routinely or selectively in cases before appellate courts. Their primary role would be to provide an element of investigative balance where and when it is needed.

Other systematic errors of due process in homicide cases have been dealt with effectively through landmark court rulings. A prime example is the 1985 Supreme Court decision in *Tennessee v. Garner*,[24] which found that a police department policy permitting an officer to shoot a fleeing felon was unconstitutional, except when there is probable cause to believe that the person fleeing poses a serious and immediate danger to the officer or the community. The Garner case involved a Memphis police officer's 1974 killing of an unarmed 15-year-old who had stolen $10 and a purse from an unoccupied house. The killing was considered a justifiable homicide under a Tennessee statute that read, "If after notice of the intention to arrest the defendant, he either flees or forcibly resists, the officer may use all the necessary means to effect the arrest."[25] Such statutes, and police department policies that

[24] 105 S. Ct. 1694 (1985).
[25] Section 40-7-108 (1982).

derived from them, had been lawful prior to the Supreme Court's ruling in this case. In Garner the Court determined that the consequences associated with a failure to capture a felon were generally less grave than those associated with the killing of a fleeing person, who often committed a crime no more serious than larceny or burglary, involving no physical harm to a victim. The six-juror majority of the Court put it simply: "It is not better that all felony suspects die than they escape."

Several other avenues are promising as well: the expanded use of available forensic and information technology, and the continuing development of styles of policing that induce public support. Each of these deserves close attention. Advances in forensic science and information technologies have vastly improved our ability to link offenders to their crimes by processing unimaginably large data bases involving complex pattern-matching algorithms. Technologies for improved surveillance and security are being installed as well to solve crimes, and to prevent them as well. Reduced opportunities to commit crimes in the first place also reduce opportunities for prospective offenders to evade arrest and punishment.

Unfortunately, however, applications of sophisticated technologies for crime prevention have not always found their way to the places where they are most needed. The most crime-infested places tend to have smaller per capita tax bases, and hence are generally less able to make substantial investments in such technologies. More affluent suburban areas are able to make such investments, both publicly and privately, and they do so. Homicide clearance rates tend to be lower in high-crime areas, due in large part to greater caseloads per detective (Ward) and higher rates of stranger-to-stranger and drug-related homicides, crimes that have inherently lower clearance rates (Wellford and Cronin, 2000).

Most jurisdictions, rich and poor alike, can use more sophistication in the collection and maintenance of reliable data – especially greater care in maintaining accurate, up-to-date modus operandi files – and more intelligent use of such data for solving and preventing crimes. Even in the most well-endowed municipal police departments, few homicide detectives have the levels of education and training in the analysis and use of information that is common in other settings in which professionals are responsible for analyzing complex data: medical specialists, engineers and architects, financial portfolio analysts, and so on.

In the sniper attacks that paralyzed the Washington, DC, metropolitan area in the fall of 2002, one of the offenders was identified through fingerprints taken a month earlier from an unsolved murder at a liquor store in Montgomery, Alabama. The Montgomery police simply had not processed the prints through the FBI's automated fingerprint identification system until the events in Washington led to the linking of the two cases, making the liquor store murder suddenly much more important. It is conceivable that some or all of the 10 killings that followed could have been spared had this readily available technology been used to solve the earlier case (Serafin, 2002).

Failure to use available crime-solving technology is not a problem unique to local police departments. The FBI, an especially well-endowed law enforcement agency that established itself as a pioneer in applying advanced forensic technology to solve crimes in the early and mid-20th century, earned the dubious distinction of being at the conservative, take-no-chances end of the technology innovation spectrum by the end of the century, especially with regard to the computerized processing of massive amounts of data. In a case far more serious than the Washington sniper case, the FBI was charged with failure to "connect the dots" to prevent some 3,000 deaths in the terrorist attack of September 11, 2001 – especially, backwardness in the use of available computer technology (Kessler, 2002; Wilke, 2002) – a problem that had been sufficiently well-documented prior to the attack to give the charge more than mere hindsight wisdom. The attack came just 12 weeks after a Senate Judiciary Committee hearing, "Oversight: Restoring Confidence in the FBI," chaired by Patrick J. Leahy (2001), who cited mistakes in the handling of numerous high-profile cases and concluded that the agency's "much vaunted independence has transformed, for some, into an image of insular arrogance." A classified 576-page report issued two years earlier by the Office of the Inspector General had cited problems in the use and maintenance of the FBI's computer database systems (Fine, 2001). One account of the FBI's primitiveness in computerization, just one month before the attack, documented instances of "vast delays in investigations and lost information" (Bendavid, 2001).

Los Angeles Times reporters Lichtblau and Piller (2002) offered a postmortem of the FBI's failures in this area that included accounts of information that, properly used, would have prevented a border crossing by known murderer Maturino Resendiz, who went on to kill four more people in the United States in a cross-country railroad trek; lapses in catching spy Robert Hanssen; and failure to find more than 4,000 pages of documents and properly turn them over to Timothy J. McVeigh's attorneys following the Oklahoma City bombing case. Under the Homeland Security initiative, the federal government has begun to take measures designed to substantially improve its ability to collect, screen, maintain, process, link, and analyze data to help prevent and quickly solve terrorist acts. This under-one-roof approach could conceivably make it more difficult for offenders to get away with murder, assuming that these capabilities will be made available for the investigation of local crimes.

Errors, both random and nonrandom, surely could be reduced if the police and prosecutors had more valid empirical information about the returns associated with alternative allocations of their time and other resources to investigative and prosecutorial activities, for each major category of cases. Which activities available to the police officer who is first to arrive at the scene are most likely to lead to arrest when an apparent homicide victim is found in her or his own home? When found indoors elsewhere? When found on the street? Once an initial homicide investigation has been completed under a basic class of unsolved homicide case (by victim characteristics, apparent cause of death, and crime scene evidence and location), what sort of leads, if pursued, are most likely to result in arrest and conviction? Useful answers to these questions could be obtained once data on the actual allocations of investigative resources and the outcomes that followed are accurately recorded and analyzed for each major category of homicide. When the returns to these allocations are known, in terms of their effects on the likelihood of arrest and conviction, it might then be possible to combine those results with estimates of the effects of arrest and conviction on future crimes, so that alternative allocations of investigative resources could be assessed in terms of their expected effects on future crimes, weighted by the social costs of each type of crime.

With similar data on the effects of alternative allocations of prosecution resources on case outcomes in court, parallel analysis could be done to examine the effects of different prosecution strategies on expected sentence lengths and future crimes.[26] This sort of analysis could well have greater implications for felony crimes other than homicide, especially to the extent that there is greater variation in sanctions for other felonies.

Data to support this sort of analysis have existed for some time. Under the Time Utilization Record-Keeping system, the work of all Federal Bureau of Investigation agents is routinely recorded in 15-minute intervals, to monitor agent activity and provide a basis for interoffice resource allocations, along the lines of billing and accountability systems routinely used in private law firms. Similar systems have been in use to account for the time and work of federal prosecutors in all of the 94 U.S. Attorney Offices throughout the country. These systems are costly to maintain, may be abused, and can sap the morale of independent-minded agents, hence they may be more effectively done periodically with representative samples of investigators rather than universally. The essential point for our purposes is that this sort of information is not outside the realm of feasibility, at least on an occasional, as-needed basis. We know too little about the returns to crime-solving associated with alternative time allocations, and much of the data needed to address this important matter appear to be already available.

Further advances in our ability to solve homicides may be possible through advancements in the professionalization of investigation and use of "no-technology" human skills that have come to be associated

---

[26] Landes (1971) has theorized that prosecutors, aiming to maximize expected convictions weighted by case seriousness, will allocate more resources to serious cases and cases in which the allocation of resources produces larger increases in the probability of conviction. Forst and Brosi (1977) amended Landes's model by incorporating a component to reflect the prosecutor's interest in allocating additional resources to cases that are more likely, if not convicted, to produce more future crime in the community.

with new styles of policing, especially those that fall under the rubric of community policing and its sibling, problem-oriented policing. Effective use of these policing concepts and programs starting in the late 20th century may have helped to reduce errors of justice associated with the police by creating stronger ties to agents in the community who can act both to prevent crimes and provide greater support to the police in solving crimes that are not prevented.[27] Hard evidence on the effectiveness of community policing has lagged substantially behind the rhetoric supporting the idea, and specific interventions associated with the concept often defy replication from one jurisdiction to the next in a manner that permits such empirical support,[28] but the indirect evidence is nonetheless encouraging (Skogan, 1990; Skogan and Frydl, 2003). One distinguishing aspect of community policing is conspicuous: the test of success of any community policing initiative is the degree to which it reduces crime and delinquency by building social capital in an area (Taylor, 2001; Akerlof and Yellen, 1994). Improvements in our ability to work more diligently to understand the relationships among specific policing interventions, social capital and crime could go a long way to reduce the low homicide clearance rates that plague many of our most crime-ridden neighborhoods.

Conclusion

Errors of justice in cases of homicide have, from time to time, dominated the public consciousness. The 1995 criminal exoneration of O. J. Simpson in "the trial of the century" (one of several)[29] left much

---

[27] John Eck and William Spelman (1987) report success in preventing domestic homicides in Newport News, Virginia, through the use of a problem-oriented policing strategy.

[28] One problem with community policing is its vagueness and ubiquitousness, often to the point of incoherence. Virtually every police department claims to be doing it, in part because the flow of several billions of federal dollars to police departments since 1990 – $9 billion under the Violent Crime Control and Law Enforcement Act of 1994 alone – has been contingent on such claims.

[29] The Sacco and Vanzetti (1921), Leopold and Loeb (1924), Lindbergh baby murder (1935), Scopes "Monkey" (1925), Nuremberg (1945–9), Rosenberg (1951), and the Chicago Seven (1969–70) trials – not all homicide cases – were also called "trials of the century." Questions about miscarriage of justice were not fully resolved in any of these trials.

of the public with a sense that a serious lapse in justice had been done. Marquee attention has also been given to questions about errors in capital executions under federal and state death penalty statutes, as DNA evidence began to contribute to the exoneration of dozens of death row inmates in the 1990s. We will never be able to eliminate doubt in homicide cases that find themselves on the cusp of reasonable doubt in trial, but we may be able to accurately resolve many of those cases before they reach the trial stage, by reassessing policies in place that may contribute excessively to errors of justice. A few prospects have been raised here and in previous chapters: improving witness identification procedures; expanding the use of effective crime-solving logic and technology and employment of civilian technicians by police departments; introducing new systems of accountability to the criminal investigative function that incorporate standards of professional responsibility and ethics, paralleling the medical profession's Hippocratic oath; continuing the expansion of approaches to policing that induce greater public cooperation and support; and considering the social costs of alternative prosecution, sentencing, and correctional strategies for dealing with homicide offenders, to balance more consciously the errors of failing to bring culpable offenders to justice with those of wrongful convictions. Procedures and policies that reduce errors of justice in homicide cases are likely to reduce them in other cases as well.

CHAPTER TWELVE

A Matter of Legitimacy

What happens when we no longer respect the courts?
— Jeffrey Rosen (2001)

Introduction

In a well-working system of justice, both basic types of criminal justice error will be small: culpable offenders will be convicted and innocent people will remain free and minimally encumbered by criminal justice agents. In such a system, procedures designed to protect the innocent function as intended and agents of public safety operate effectively. Moreover, when the public perceives those errors to be small, they will be more inclined to support the criminal justice system and trust the police, prosecutors, defense counsel, judges and juries. When they perceive otherwise, the criminal justice system loses public support and crude informal mechanisms for achieving justice tend to fill the void, mechanisms that have been known to violate basic principles of ethics and efficiency. So we have more than ample reason to ensure that criminal justice policies and procedures work effectively to reduce justice errors; doing so is likely to increase both the actual and perceived quality of justice. This is a matter of *legitimacy*.

In this chapter we shall look at errors of justice as a central aspect of legitimacy in greater detail. The notions of due process legitimacy and crime control legitimacy, discussed in Chapters 2 and 3, are revisited and considered against other important aspects of legitimacy ignored by the inferential and normative framework described in this book. The book closes with a discussion of other limitations of this framework for criminal justice policy assessment and the key implications of the findings documented in prior chapters for criminal justice policy and future research.

What is Legitimacy?

The concept of legitimacy is basic to political theory, regarding questions about the source and limits of the authority of government: What are the proper aims for which government has a right to exercise authority to coerce individuals to comply with the common good, to regulate their behavior? What are the limits of that authority? To what extent should people have rights under that authority? Under what sort of collective choice procedure do the governed give consent to such authority? General principles about these questions have been set forth by Locke, Hume, Hobbes, Rawls, and others.

These principles provide a foundation for the criminal justice system, an essential component of government. As it is widely applied to criminal justice, "legitimacy" is used as if to do primarily with the public's *perception* that the system is just and effective. But public perceptions about such matters are often seriously flawed. The public perceived crime to be on the rise through much of the 1990s when, in fact, the rate of serious crimes dropped each year from 1991 to 2000. The public has also widely perceived draconian sanctions as effective for reducing crime: drug kingpin statutes were a centerpiece of the politically popular 1980s war on drugs, and in the 1990s "three strikes and you're out" laws were all the rage. The popularity of these schemes is often betrayed by an absence of systematic empirical support of their effectiveness in reducing crime, and much evidence has come forth revealing their wastefulness (Tonry, 1996; Zimring, 2001; Greenwood et al., 1994). Such misperceptions nonetheless profoundly influence political strategy, just as they may serve to undermine criminal justice legitimacy by contributing to systematic errors of justice. Legislators, governors and mayors, district attorneys, and other elected officials who shape criminal justice policy tend to be quite sensitive to public opinion, irrespective of the inaccuracies on which those opinions are based and the injustices and inefficiencies they produce.

Mark Moore (1997) has noted that "(t)he loss of popular legitimacy for the criminal justice system produces disastrous consequences for the system's performance" (p. 55) and that it has abstract value as well, "an ideal to be achieved" (p. 56). The consequences of loss of legitimacy are likely to transcend criminal justice performance. To the extent that those consequences include the expansion of private security alternatives and communities walled off to outsiders, they tend to separate and divide society. The result is to factionalize legitimacy in the eyes of the public, with one group (typically the affluent) seeing the justice system as legitimate while the other (minorities and the poor) sees the same system as lacking in legitimacy.

Legitimacy, indeed, extends far beyond public perception. It embodies abstractions that are not directly perceptible to the public, but that may nonetheless enter the public's awareness in ways that are difficult to discern. Legitimacy surely is enhanced, whether the public is aware of it or not, under processes designed to ensure that errors of justice are managed, if not held to a minimum. Moore, for one, acknowledges that legitimacy requires that the criminal justice system not diverge substantially from an elusive equilibrium that underlies these errors:

> It falls to the Nation's criminal justice agencies to teach two of the hardest lessons that citizens in democracies must learn. The first lesson is the most obvious: It is wrong to give offense to other citizens, that one has to be restrained and respect other people's lives and properties. The second lesson is far less obvious but potentially as important: Namely, it is wrong to take offense too easily or to respond to offense disproportionately. The second lesson requires of us that we be tolerant. In many ways it is much more difficult to be tolerant than to be offended when we are attacked. (p. 63)

Criminal justice legitimacy is, of course, a matter of more than justice errors alone. Even if there were no errors of justice, the system could be regarded as lacking in legitimacy if the laws were unjust, or if enforcement lacked evenhandedness. Legitimacy depends also on distributive and racial justice, access to justice for suspects and victims (to assure that the process is fair, regardless of outcome, including the assurance that people who cannot afford high quality defense or who do not have social status or political influence will receive just treatment as a victim, or will be adequately represented), and celerity ("Justice delayed is justice denied"). Legitimacy also connotes political obligation, accountability, normative (ethical) justice, the extension of the legitimate authority of the state, the existence of a system without corruption and public malfeasance, and so on.

Legitimacy is a concept, in short, that has considerable depth and breadth. It is related to other big themes in justice: the role of discretion, questions of basic justice, the goals of criminal justice agencies and their respective systems of accountability, the role of community, and informal (private) versus formal (legal, public) systems of social control. It extends beneath and beyond errors of justice. Yet, excessive errors, by any reckoning, reflect a lapse in legitimacy and serve to diminish it further by undermining the public's support of the criminal justice system.

Operationalizing the Notion of Legitimacy

It was noted at the outset of this book that the assessment of criminal justice policy has focused primarily on matters other than errors of justice: crime rates, recidivism, fear of crime, evenhandedness, costs, and a host of other measures. A critical aspect of criminal justice effectiveness has gotten lost under these conventional standards: legitimacy. This omission is undoubtedly due largely to the absence of attempts to operationalize a concept as abstract and elusive as legitimacy and use it as a systematic basis for policy assessment.

We can attempt to operationalize this critical aspect of legitimacy – the minimization of justice errors – more specifically, following Herbert Packer's nomenclature (1968, p. 175): Policies and practices that increase the rate at which innocent people are convicted can be regarded as threats to *due process legitimacy*, and policies and practices that reduce the rate at which culpable offenders receive less than socially optimal sanctions can be regarded as threats to *crime control legitimacy*.

Due process legitimacy is enhanced by processes that protect the innocent against coercion by the state. Errors that threaten due process may be inadvertent, such as those associated with mistaken eyewitness testimony or innocent defendants who match an unusual constellation of incriminating facts due purely to chance, or with incompetent or unenthusiastic defense lawyers or ill-conceived legislation, or with more deeply sinister motives such as police or lab technicians tampering with or fabricating evidence to satisfy a community passion or discriminatory inclination. Prosecutors are not immune from these pressures, as in cases in which exculpatory evidence is withheld from the defense, or when police misconduct is ignored, or when prosecutors strike off on "frolics" – cases against unpopular figures without adequate evidence to support a conviction (Easterbrook, 1983, pp. 300–1). All such cases threaten the integrity of the justice system by revealing a government that overreaches its authority and strips citizens of basic rights. This type of error concerns all who cherish justice and the fundamental right of individuals to be free from tyranny.[1]

The criminal justice system loses crime control legitimacy, by contrast, as the number of culpable offenders released prematurely, or who remain free, increases, compromising public safety and quality of life and inducing citizens to become more concerned about injustices to victims. The integrity of the justice system thus becomes threatened by ineffectualness. Lapses that threaten crime control legitimacy can run through the entire justice system, from policing and prosecution to sentencing and corrections (as in the case when an inmate escapes). They may be attributable to skillful offenders; failures in police operations attributable to insufficient resources, inadequate screening, training and supervision, ineffective techniques for securing and processing physical evidence, interviewing witnesses, and interrogating suspects; lack of community cooperation, sometimes leading to crimes reported as accidents, suicides or missing persons; insufficient prosecutorial resources and inefficient use of existing

---

[1] Errors of this type are vexing for another basic reason: they often threaten *both* due process and the ability to control crime. If one person is wrongfully convicted and sentenced for a crime he did not commit, the real offender may not be brought to justice. It is, of course, virtually impossible to establish the proportion of errors of due process that also involve lapses in crime control. In some unknown proportion of cases involving the conviction of innocent defendants, the defendants are convicted for crimes that were not in fact committed by anyone.

resources; insufficient court resources, flawed judicial decision making and jury processes (juror selection, number of jurors, majority requirements, opportunities for "nullification," and so on); and faulty parole release decision-making processes.

Conclusion

Regardless of where one stands on the importance of other aspects of criminal justice legitimacy, errors of justice harm us all. The work documented here aims to stimulate more systematic inquiry into the management of justice errors, toward the reduction of the harms associated with those errors. A serious practical issue is at stake: I have noted that we have a coherent and effective framework for managing errors in statistical inference, but no such framework for managing parallel errors in the criminal justice system. At the least, we should extend the cataloguing of the nature and sources of errors on both sides of the scale of justice and consider how they are likely to be affected by changes in rules and laws, policies and procedures. Errors of justice are surely no less important than errors in statistical estimation and testing.

The presence of a framework for managing errors of statistical inference but not errors of justice represents an extraordinary imbalance of priorities, but there may be an explanation. When it comes to influencing public policy, it has been noted that anecdotes frequently trump data (Brennan, 2001; Paulos, 1995). Criminal justice policy may be especially sensitive to the power of the sensational anecdote – the Willie Horton and Polly Klaas episodes have no parallels in health care, education, or any other public policy domain that comes to mind. Recognizing that our system of justice warranted insulation from the often perverse influences of an unenlightened public, our founders shielded the courts from the public to a considerably greater degree than they did the legislative and executive branches of government.[2] Errors of

---

[2] For example, Article III, Section 1 of the Constitution grants lifetime tenure to Supreme Court justices, power not granted to top officials in the legislative and executive branches of government.

justice, in any case, impose too great a threat to the public's trust in our system of justice to permit this drift from reason to continue. They are largely a product of what has been called "the distressingly subjective nature of the law" (Bronner, 2001). They force us to confront legal commentator Jeffrey Rosen's question that opens this chapter: "What happens when we no longer respect the courts?"

Lest we forget, the executive branch is part of the criminal justice system too. So we must ask, "What happens when we no longer respect the *police?*" Support for the law enforcement arm of criminal justice is harmed by the perception of ineptness, as when a police department is criticized for an unusually low homicide clearance rate – the Metropolitan Police Department of the District of Columbia in the mid-1990s serves as a prominent example. But such a problem pales when compared to the destruction of the legitimacy of a law enforcement agency that comes inevitably with patterns of corruption, brutality, and deceit, whether or not such practices lead to errors of justice. Managing errors of justice should not be regarded as the primary goal of the justice system. They are generally a manifestation of deeper problems. Their discovery should stimulate inquiry into their systemic causes.

Tensions between errors of due process and impunity have been raised to a new level in the era of terrorism. Should we aim to protect people's civil liberty when doing so raises appreciably the risk of a terrorist act that could jeopardize the lives of hundreds of thousands of innocent people?[3] Should we restrict civil liberty, in the interest of preventing acts of terrorism, if doing so makes life unbearable for large numbers of innocent people? Finding a balance between these two deeply unpleasant extremes will surely be done using conventional political processes, without the benefit of a decision calculus based explicitly on the minimization of social costs. Assessments of the relationship between alternatives and their consequences are likely to be based not so much on empirical estimates as

---

[3] In his dissent to the majority opinion in the 1949 case of *Terminiello v. Chicago* (334 U.S. 1), Supreme Court Justice Robert Jackson famously wrote, "There is the danger that, if the court does not temper its doctrinaire logic with a little practical wisdom, it will convert the constitutional Bill of Rights into a suicide pact."

on common sense, taking into account the relevant social costs and probabilities.[4]

In the meantime, the problem is certain to grow increasingly more difficult as technology permits weapons of mass destruction in brief-cases or knapsacks to come into the hands of individuals with dark intentions. These are crimes in the extreme. We often agree that it is better to prevent crimes in the first place than to have to solve them and sanction offenders afterward. We can move beyond rhetoric on this matter and act to prevent catastrophes that make our modern crime waves appear trivial, and there are surely ways of doing so that do not compromise our rights and freedoms, by building bridges inter-nationally to communities that produce disproportionate numbers of people inclined to commit acts of terrorism through the strengthening of common interests, education, and mutual understanding through dialogue and cultural exchange. Surely the best way to reduce errors of justice is to prevent the circumstances that give rise to them.

Although it cannot resolve such issues, the inquiry documented here aims to bring more coherence to the problem of dealing with conventional crimes, a more manageable matter. This is a modest be-ginning. It will be important for subsequent work to focus more deeply on the criminal justice issues raised above and their logical extensions – specific policing, prosecution and legal defense practices, judicial and jury rules and decision processes – to assess the effects of a wider range of policies and procedures on errors of justice than have been consid-ered here. In the process, we may be able to enhance the legitimacy of the criminal justice system and make it more difficult for the anecdote to trump coherent analysis. We might even find ways to reduce justice errors.

---

[4] Federal judge Richard A. Posner (2001) puts it this way:

> Concretely, the scope of these rights has been determined, through an interac-tion of constitutional text and subsequent judicial interpretation, by a weighing of competing interest. I'll call them the public-safety interest and the liberty interest. Neither, in my view, has priority. They are both important, and their relative importance changes from time to time and from situation to situation. The safer the nation feels, the more weight judges will be willing to give to the liberty interest. The greater the threat that an activity poses to the nation's safety, the stronger will the grounds seem for seeking to repress that activity, even at some cost to liberty. This fluid approach is only common sense. (p. 46)

Bibliography

Jeffrey Abramson, *We, the Jury: The Jury System and the Ideal of Democracy* (New York: Basic Books, 1994).

Stephan J. Adler, *The Jury: Trial and Error in the American Courtroom* (New York: Times Books, 1994).

Peter B. Ainsworth, *Offender Profiling and Crime Analysis* (Portland, OR: Willan, 2001).

George Akerlof and Janet L. Yellen, "Gang Behavior, Law Enforcement, and Community Values," in *Values and Public Policy*, Henry J. Aaron, Thomas E. Mann, and Timothy Taylor, editors (Washington, DC: Brookings, 1994).

Ellen Alderman and Caroline Kennedy, *In Our Defense: The Bill of Rights in Action* (New York: Morrow, 1991).

Geoffrey Alpert and Mark H. Moore, "Measuring Police Performance in the New Paradigm of Policing," in *Performance Measures for the Criminal Justice System* (Washington, DC: Bureau of Justice Statistics, 1993), pp. 109–42.

Albert W. Alschuler, "Our Faltering Jury," *The Public Interest*, Number 122 (Winter 1996), pp. 28–38.

Jonathan Alter, "Actually, the Database Is God," *Newsweek* (November 4, 2002), p. 39.

American Civil Liberties Freedom Network, "'Driving While Black' Is Not a Crime . . . So Why Are Incidents Like These Occurring Across the Country?" *Arrest the Racism: Racial Profiling in America* (2003), <http://archive.aclu.org/profiling/tales/>.

American Civil Liberties Union, "Is Jim Crow Justice Alive and Well in America Today?" *Arrest the Racism: Racial Profiling in America* (2002), <http://archive.aclu.org/profiling/>.

American Heritage Dictionary of the English Language, 4th edition (New York: Houghton Mifflin, 2000).

Amnesty International, *Equatorial Guinea: An Opportunity to Put an End to Impunity* (London: Amnesty International, 1997).

David A. Anderson, "The Aggregate Burden of Crime," *Journal of Law and Economics*, Volume 42 (1999), p. 611–42.

David C. Anderson, "Crime Control by the Numbers," *Ford Foundation Report* (Winter 2001) Associated Press, "DNA Helps Exonerate Prisoner After 17 Years," *Washington Post* (August 27, 2002), p. A2.

Associated Press, "Airlines Accused of Discrimination" (June 10, 2002), <http://www.rockthevote.org/issues_civilrights.asp>.

Attorney General Benjamin Civiletti, "U.S. Attorney General's Guidelines on Criminal Investigations and Use of Informers," *Criminal Law Reporter*, Volume 28 (January 7, 1981), p. 3032.

Kris Axtman, "US Milestone: 100th Death-row Inmate Exonerated," *Christian Science Monitor* (April 12, 2002).

Earl Babbie, *The Practice of Social Research*, 7th edition (Belmont, CA: Wadsworth, 1995).

Francis Bacon, "Aphorisms Concerning the Interpretation of Nature and the Kingdom of Man," *Novum Organum* (1620).

Alan D. Baddeley, N. Thompson, and M. Buchanan, "Word Length and the Structure of Memory," *Journal of Verbal Learning and Verbal Behaviour*, Volume 1 (1975), pp. 575–89.

David Baldus, George Woodworth, and Charles A. Pulaski, Jr., "Arbitrariness and Discrimination in the Administration of the Death Penalty: A Challenge to State Supreme Courts," 15 *Stetson Law Review*, Volume 15 (1986), pp. 133–262.

Jerry Banks, *Principles of Quality Control* (New York: John Wiley and Sons, 1989).

Wayne Barrett, "White Pols and Press Tread Lightly on Rudy Role in Cop Brutality: Ducking Diallo," *The Village Voice* (March 3, 1999).

Cesare Beccaria, *On Crimes and Punishments*, 6th edition, translated by Henry Paolucci (Indianapolis: Bobbs-Merrill, 1963). Original edition, *Dei delletti e delle pene* (1764).

Gary Becker, "Crime and Punishment: An Economic Approach," *Journal of Political Economy*, Volume 76 (1968), pp. 169–217.

Hugo Adam Bedau, "Murder, Errors of Justice, and Capital Punishment," in *The Death Penalty in America*, Hugo Adam Bedau, editor (1964); revised as "Miscarriages of Justice and the Death Penalty," in *The Death Penalty in America*, 3rd edition, Hugo Adam Bedau, editor (New York: Oxford University Press, 1982).

Hugo Adam Bedau, *The Death Penalty in America: Current Controversies* (New York: Oxford University Press, 1997).

Hugo Adam Bedau and Michael L. Radelet, "Miscarriages of Justice in Potentially Capital Cases," *Stanford Law Review*, Volume 40, Number 1 (November 1987), pp. 21–179.

Naftali Bendavid, "Neglected Computers Hamper FBI: Ancient Systems Slow Investigations *Chicago Tribune* (Aug 6, 2001), p. 1.

Jeremy Bentham, *An Introduction to the Principles of Morals and Legislation* (London: Payne, 1789).

Jeremy Bentham, *The Rationale of Punishment* (London: Heward, 1830).

Alan Berlow, "The Wrong Man," *The Atlantic Monthly* (November 1999), pp. 66–91.

Alan Berlow, "A Jury of Your Peers? Only If You're Clueless," *Washington Post* (August 11, 2002), pp. B1–B2.

Donald Black, *Manners and Customs of the Police* (New York: Academic Press, 1980).

William Blackstone, *Commentaries on the Laws of England* (1765).

Peter B. Bloch and James Bell, *Managing Investigations: The Rochester System* (Washington, DC: Police Foundation, 1976).

Alfred Blumstein, "Prisons," Chapter 16 in *Crime: Public Policies for Crime Control*, 2nd edition, James Q. Wilson and Joan Petersilia, editors (San Francisco: ICS Press, 2002), pp. 451–82.

Alfred Blumstein, Jacqueline Cohen, Susan E. Martin, and Michael H. Tonry, editors, *Research on Sentencing: The Search for Reform* (Washington, DC: National Academy Press, 1983).

Alfred Blumstein, Jacqueline Cohen, and Daniel Nagin, editors, *Deterrence and Incapacitation: Estimating the Effects of Criminal Sanctions on Crime Rates,* (Washington, DC: National Academy Press, 1978).

Alfred Blumstein, Jacqueline Cohen, Jeffrey A. Roth, and Christy A. Visher, editors, *Criminal Careers and "Career Criminals,"* Volume I (Washington, DC: National Academy Press, 1986).

Barbara Boland and Brian Forst, "Prosecutors Don't Always Aim to Pleas," *Federal Probation*, Volume 49 (June 1985), pp. 10–15.

Barbara Boland, Paul Mahanna, and Ronald Sones, *The Prosecution of Felony Arrests, 1988* (Washington, DC: Bureau of Justice Statistics, 1992).

Barbara Boland and Ronald Sones, *Prosecution of Felony Arrests* (Washington, DC: Bureau of Justice Statistics, 1981).

Barbara Boland and Ronald Sones, *Prosecution of Felony Arrests* (Washington, DC: Bureau of Justice Statistics, 1986).

Edwin M. Borchard, *Convicting the Innocent* (New Haven, CT: Yale University Press, 1932).

David A. Boyum and Mark A. R. Kleiman, "Substance Abuse Policy from a Crime Control Perspective," in *Crime: Public Policies for Crime*

Control, 2nd edition, James Q. Wilson and Joan Petersilia, editors (San Francisco: ICS Press, 2002), pp. 331–82.

Tim Brennan, "An Academic's Guide to the Way Washington Really Works," *The Chronicle of Higher Education* (January 12, 2001), p. B11.

Ethan Bronner, "Posner v. Dershowitz," *The New York Times*, Books Section (July 15, 2001).

Kathleen Brosi, *A Cross-City Comparison of Felony Case Processing* (Washington, DC: Institute for Law and Social Research, 1979).

Jodi M. Brown, Patrick A. Langan, and David J. Levin, *Felony Sentences in State Courts, 1996* (Washington, DC: Bureau of Justice Statistics, 1999).

Robert Buckhout, Steve Weg, Vincent Reilly, and Robinsue Frohboese, "Jury Verdicts: Comparison of 6- vs. 12-person Juries and Unanimous vs. Majority Decision Rule in a Murder Trial," *Bulletin of the Psychonomic Society*, Volume 10 (1977), pp. 175–8.

David Canter, "Offender Profiling and Criminal Differentiation," *Journal of Legal and Criminological Psychology*, Volume 5 (2000), pp. 23–46.

Paul G. Cassell, "Protecting the Innocent from False Confessions and Lost Confessions – and from Miranda," *Journal of Criminal Law and Criminology*, Volume 88 (1998), pp. 497–556.

Paul G. Cassell, "We're Not Executing the Innocent," *Wall Street Journal* (June 16, 2000), p. A14.

Paul G. Cassell and Richard Fowles, "Handcuffing the Cops? A Thirty-Year Perspective on *Miranda's* Harmful Effects on Law Enforcement," *Stanford Law Review*, Volume 50 (1998), pp. 1055–172.

Paul G. Cassell and Stephen J. Markman, "Protecting the Innocent: A Response to the Bedau-Radelet Study," *Stanford Law Review*, Volume 41 (1988), pp. 121–33.

Jan M. Chaiken and Marcia Chaiken, *Varieties of Criminal Behavior* (Santa Monica, CA: Rand, 1982).

Ronald V. Clarke, *Situational Crime Prevention: Successful Case Studies*, 2nd edition (Albany, NY: Harrow and Heston, 1997).

Brian R. Clifford and Jane Scott, "Individual and Situational Factors in Eyewitness Testimony," *Journal of Applied Psychology*, Volume 63 (1978), pp. 352–9.

John Cloud, "What's Race Got To Do With It?" *Time Magazine* (July 30, 2001), pp. 42–7.

Jacqueline Cohen, "The Incapacitative Effect of Imprisonment: A Critical Review of the Literature," in *Deterrence and Incapacitation: Estimating the Effects of Criminal Sanctions on Crime Rates*, Alfred Blumstein, Jacqueline Cohen, and Daniel Nagin, editors (Washington, DC: National Academy Press, 1978), pp. 187–243.

Mark A. Cohen, "Measuring the Costs and Benefits of Crime and Justice," in *Criminal Justice 2000*, Volume 4 (Washington, DC: National Institute of Justice, 2000).

Catherine M. Coles, George M. Kelling, Mark H. Moore, *Prosecution in the Community: A Study of Emergent Strategies – A Cross Site Analysis* (Cambridge, MA: Harvard, 1998) and NCJ 187105 (Washington, DC: National Institute of Justice).

Edward Connors, Thomas Lundregan, Neal Miller, and Tom McEwen, *Convicted by Juries, Exonerated by Science: Case Studies in the Use of DNA Evidence to Establish Innocence after Trial* (Washington, DC: National Institute of Justice, 1996).

Philip J. Cook, "Costs of Crime," in *Encyclopedia of Crime and Justice*, edited by Sanford H. Kadish (New York: Free Press, 1983).

Gary Copson, *Coals to Newcastle? Police Use of Offender Profiling* (London: Home Office, 1995).

C. J. Costello, R. M. Adams, and S. Polasky, "The Value of El Nino Forecasts in the Management of Salmon: A Stochastic Dynamic Assessment," *American Journal of Agricultural Economics*, Volume 80 (1998), pp. 765–77.

David A. Crocker, "Can There Be Healing through Justice?" *The Responsive Community*, Volume 11 (Spring 2001), pp. 32–42.

Francis T. Cullen, "Rehabilitation and Treatment Programs," in *Crime: Public Policies for Crime Control*, 2nd edition, James Q. Wilson and Joan Petersilia, editors (San Francisco: ICS Press, 2002), pp. 253–90.

William C. Cunningham and Todd H. Taylor, *The Hallcrest Report: Private Security and Police in America* (Portland, OR: Chancellor, 1985).

Thomas Davies, "A Hard Look at What We Know (and Still Need to Learn) about the 'Costs' of the Exclusionary Rule: The NIJ Study and Other Studies of 'Lost' Arrests," *American Bar Foundation Research Journal* (1983), pp. 611–90.

J. H. Davis, N. L. Kerr, R. S. Atkin, R. Holt, and D. Meek, "The Decision Processes of 6- and 12-Person Mock Juries Assigned Unanimous and Two-Thirds Majority Rules, *Journal of Personality and Social Psychology*, Volume 32 (1975), pp. 1–14.

Ann Davis, Joseph Pereira, and William M. Bulkeley, "Security Concerns Bring New Focus on Body Language," *Wall Street Journal* (August 15, 2002), pp. A1, A6.

Robert C. Davis and Pedro Mateu-Gelabert, *Respectful and Effective Policing: Two Examples in the South Bronx* (New York: Vera, 1999).

Death Penalty Information Center, "Cases of Innocence: 1973 - Present," DPIC website (2002) <http://www.deathpenaltyinfo.org/innocases.html>.

Carol J. DeFrances and Greg W. Steadman, *Prosecutors in State Courts, 1996* (Washington, DC: Bureau of Justice Statistics, 1998).

John Diamond, "Spelling Slows War on Terror: Confusion Over Arab Names Makes it Difficult for U.S. to Track Suspects," *USA Today* (June 30, 2002), p. 6A.

Shari S. Diamond and Hans Zeisel, "Sentencing Councils: A Study of Sentence Disparity and Its Reduction," *University of Chicago Law Review*, Volume 43 (1975).

John DiIulio, "Three Strikes Was the Right Call," *The American Prospect*, Volume 5, Number 18 (January 18, 1994).

"DNA Testing Turns a Corner as Forensic Tool," (no author) *Law Enforcement News* (October 15, 1995), p. 10.

Robert L. Donigan and Edward C. Fisher, *The Evidence Handbook*, 4th edition (Evanston, IL: Traffic Institute, Northwestern University, 1980).

John Douglas and Mark Olshaker, *Mindhunter* (New York: Simon & Schuster, 1995).

John Douglas and Mark Olshaker, *Obsession* (New York: Simon & Schuster, 1998).

R. A. Duff, "Penal Communications: Recent Work in the Philosophy of Punishment," in *Crime and Justice: A Review of Research*, edited by Michael Tonry (Chicago: University of Chicago Press, 1996).

R. A. Duff, *Punishment, Communication, and Community* (New York: Oxford University Press, 2000).

Detis T. Duhart, "Urban, Suburban, and Rural Victimization, 1993–98," *National Crime Victimization Survey* NCJ 182031 (Washington, DC: Bureau of Justice Statistics, 2000).

Otis Dudley Duncan, *Introduction to Structural Equation Models* (New York: Academic Press, 1975).

Frank H. Easterbrook, "Criminal Procedure as a Market System," *Journal of Legal Studies*, Volume 12 (June 1983), pp. 289–332.

John Eck, *Solving Crimes: The Investigation of Burglary and Robbery* (Washington, DC: Police Executive Research Forum, 1983).

John Eck and William Spelman, *Problem Solving: Problem-Oriented Policing in Newport News* (Washington, DC: Police Executive Research Forum, 1987).

Editorial, "Mr. Hatfill's Complaint," *Washington Post* (August 13, 2002), p. A12.

Albert Eglash, "Beyond Restitution: Creative Restitution," in *Restitution in Criminal Justice: A Critical Assessment of Sanctions*, Joseph Hudson and Burton Galaway, editors (Lexington, MA: Lexington Books, 1977).

Theodore Eisenberg and Martin T. Wells, "Deadly Confusion: Juror Instructions in Capital Cases," *Cornell Law Review*, Volume 79 (1993), pp. 1–17.

J. F. Elliott, "Crime Control Teams: An Alternative to the Conventional Operational Procedure of Investigating Crimes," *Journal of Criminal Justice*, Volume 6, No.1 (Spring 1978).

Robin Shepard Engel, Jennifer M. Calnon, and Thomas J. Bernard, "Theory and Racial Profiling: Shortcomings and Future Directions in Research," *Justice Quarterly*, Volume 19 (June 2002), pp. 249–73.

Amitai Etzioni, "A New American Race?" *The Responsive Community*, Volume 10 (Spring 2000), pp. 10–15.

Amitai Etzioni, *The Monochrome Society* (Princeton, NJ: Princeton University Press: 2001) – example in text cited (p. 80) by Jonathan Marks's review of Etzioni's book in *The Responsive Community*, Volume 11 (Spring 2001), pp. 79–83.

James R. Evans and David Louis Olson, *Introduction to Simulation and Risk Analysis* (Englewood Cliffs, NJ: Prentice Hall, 1998).

Hans J. Eysenck, "Relationship Between Intelligence and Personality," *Perceptual and Motor Skills*, Volume 32 (1971), pp. 637–8.

Hans J. Eysenck and Michael Eysenck, *Mind Watching: Why We Behave the Way We Do* (London: Multimedia Books, 1994).

John S. Farrell, "How Homicide Is Handled in Prince George's," *Washington Post* (June 23, 2001), p. A25.

David P. Farrington and Donald J. West, "The Cambridge Study in Delinquent Development," in *Prospective Longitudinal Research: An Empirical Basis for the Primary Prevention of Psycho-Social Disorders*, Sarnoff A. Mednick and Andre E. Baert, editors (Oxford: Oxford University Press, 1981).

Federal Bureau of Investigation, *Crime in the United States – Uniform Crime Reports* (Washington, DC: U.S. Department of Investigation, 2000).

Malcolm M. Feeley and Mark H. Lazerson, "Police-Prosecutor Relationships: An Interorganizational Perspective," in *Empirical Theories About Courts*, Keith O. Boyum and Lynn Mather, editors (New York: Longman, 1983).

Floyd Feeney, "Police Clearances: A Poor Way to Measure the Impact of Miranda on the Police," *Rutgers Law Journal*, Volume 32 (2000), pp. 1–114.

Floyd Feeney, Forrest Dill, and Adrianne Weir, *Arrests Without Conviction: How Often They Occur and Why* (Washington, DC: National Institute of Justice, 1983).

Glenn A. Fine, testimony before the Hearing of the Committee, "Oversight: Restoring Confidence in the FBI," U.S. Senate Judiciary Committee (June 20, 2001).

Kevin Flynn, "Feeling Scorn on the Beat and Pressure From Above," *The New York Times* (December 26, 2000).

Stephen Flynn, "The Re-Bordering of North America Integration or Exclusion After September 11?", excerpt from the transcript of Panel One, seminar at the Watson Institute for International Studies (February 5, 2002) <http://www.watsoninstitute.org/news_detail.cfm?ID=38>.

Robert M. Fogelson, *Big City Police* (Cambridge, MA: Harvard University Press, 1977).

J. F. Folk, "Municipal Detective Systems – A Quantitative Approach," Technical Paper Number 55 (Cambridge, MA: MIT Operations Research Center, 1971).

David Ford, *Indianapolis Domestic Violence Prosecution Experiment* (Indianapolis: Indiana University, 1993).

Brian Forst, *The Representation of Uncertainty in Expert Systems: An Application in Criminal Investigation* (Ann Arbor, MI: University Microfilms International, 1994).

Brian Forst, "The Privatization and Civilianization of Policing," in *Criminal Justice 2000*, Volume 2 – Boundary Changes in Criminal Justice Organizations (Washington, DC: National Institute of Justice, 2000).

Brian Forst, "Prosecutors Discover the Community," *Judicature*, Volume 84 (November–December 2000), pp. 135–41.

Brian Forst, "Toward an Understanding of the Effect of Changes in Standards of Proof on Errors of Justice," *Jurimetrics*, Volume 41 (Summer 2001).

Brian Forst, "Prosecution," Chapter 18 in *Crime: Public Policies for Crime Control*, 2nd edition, James Q. Wilson and Joan Petersilia, editors (San Francisco: ICS Press, 2002), pp. 509–36.

Brian Forst and Kathleen Brosi, "A Theoretical and Empirical Analysis of the Prosecutor," *Journal of Legal Studies*, Volume 6 (January 1977), pp. 177–91.

Brian Forst, Frank Leahy, Jean Shirhall, Herbert Tyson, Eric Wish, and John Bartolomeo, *Arrest Convictability as a Measure of Police Performance* (Washington, DC: U.S. Department of Justice, 1982).

Brian Forst, Judith Lucianovic, and Sarah Cox, *What Happens After Arrest?* (Washington, DC: Institute for Law and Social Research, 1977).

Brian Forst and James P. Lynch, "The Decomposition and Graphical Analysis of Crime and Sanctions Data: A Cross-National Application," *Journal of Quantitative Criminology*, Volume 13 (Summer 1997), pp. 97–119.

Brian Forst and Peter K. Manning, *The Privatization of Policing: Two Views* (Washington, DC: Georgetown University Press, 1999).

Brian Forst and Michael Planty, "What Is the Probability that the Offender in a New Case Is in the Modus Operandi File?" *International Journal of Police Science and Management,* Volume 3 (Winter 2000), pp. 124–37.

Brian Forst and Charles Wellford, "Punishment and Sentencing: Developing Sentencing Guidelines Empirically from Principles of Punishment," *Rutgers Law Review,* Volume 33 (1981), pp. 799–837.

Lynne ForsterLee, Irwin A. Horowitz, and Martin Bourgeois, "Effects of Notetaking on Verdicts and Evidence Processing in a Civil Trial," *Law and Human Behavior,* Volume 18 (1994), pp. 567–578.

Jerome Frank, *Courts on Trial: Myth and Reality in American Justice* (Princeton, NJ: Princeton University Press, 1973).

Robert H. Frank and Cass R. Sunstein, "Cost-Benefit Analysis and Relative Position," *University of Chicago Law Review,* Volume 68 (Spring 2001).

Richard S. Frase, "Sentencing Principles in Theory and Practice," *Crime and Justice: A Review of Research* (University of Chicago Press, 1997).

Shane Frederick, George Loewenstein, and Ted O'Donoghue, "Time Discounting and Time Preference: A Critical Review," *Journal of Economic Literature,* Volume 40 (June 2002), pp. 351–401.

David Friedman, "Paying for Crime Prevention," *Liberty,* Volume 6 (June 1993) <http://www.best.com/~ddfr/Libertarian/Paying_for_Crime_P.html>.

Milton Friedman, "The Methodology of Positive Economics," in *Essays in Positive Economics* (Chicago: University of Chicago Press, 1953), pp. 3–43.

John Randolph Fuller, "So You Want to Be a Serial-Murderer Profiler . . .," *Chronicle of Higher Education* (December 7, 2001), p. B5.

James J. Fyfe, "The Split-Second Syndrome and Other Determinants of Police Violence," in *Violent Transactions,* Anne Campbell and John Gibbs, editors (New York: Basil Blackwell, 1986).

James J. Fyfe, "Police Observational Research: Demeanor and Substance," *Journal of Research in Crime and Delinquency,* Volume 33 (August 1996), pp. 333–47.

James J. Fyfe, "When Cops Kill, Someone Should Count," *The Washington Post* – Outlook Section (July 8, 2001), pp. B1–B2.

James J. Fyfe, "Missing Cases: Holes in Our Knowledge of Police Use of Force," *Justice Research and Policy,* Volume 4 (Fall 2002), pp. 87–102.

James J. Fyfe, Jack R. Greene, William F. Walsh, O.W. Wilson, and Roy Clinton McLaren, *Police Administration*, 5th edition (New York: McGraw-Hill, 1997).

Stephen P. Garvey, Sheri Lynn Johnson, and Paul Marcus, "Correcting Deadly Confusion: Responding to Jury Inquiries in Capital Cases," *Cornell Law Review*, Volume 85, (2000), pp. 627–55.

William A. Geller, "Deadly Force: What We Know," *Journal of Police Science and Administration*, Volume 10 (1982), pp. 151–77.

Bennett L. Gershman, *Prosecutorial Misconduct*, 2nd edition (St. Paul, MN: West, 1999).

James Gobert, *Justice, Democracy and the Jury* (Brookfield, VT: Ashgate/ Dartmouth Publishing Co., 1997).

Jonah Goldberg, "What Happened to the Angry White Male?" *Wall Street Journal* (October 25, 2002), p. W15.

Michael Gottfredson and Travis Hirschi, "The True Value of Lambda Would Appear to Be Zero: An Essay on Career Criminals, Criminal Careers, Selective Incapacitation, Cohort Studies, and Related Topics," *Criminology*, Volume 24 (1986), pp. 213–34.

Philip Gourevitch, *A Cold Case* (New York: Farrar, Straus and Giroux, 2001).

David Greenberg, "The Incapacitative Effect of Imprisonment: Some Estimates," *Law and Society Review*, Volume 9 (1975), pp. 541–80.

Peter W. Greenwood, *An Analysis of the Apprehension Activities of the New York Police Department* (New York: Rand Institute, 1970).

Peter W. Greenwood, Jan M. Chaiken, Joan Petersilia, and Linda Prusoff, *The Criminal Investigation Process. Volume III: Observations and Analysis* (Santa Monica, CA: Rand, 1975).

Peter W. Greenwood, C. Peter Rydell, Allan F. Abrahamse, Jonathan P. Caulkins, James R. Chiesa, Karyn E. Model, Stephen P. Klein, *Three Strikes and You're Out: Estimated Benefits and Costs of California's New Mandatory-Sentencing Law* (Santa Monica, CA: Rand, 1994).

A. F. Hamlet, D. Huppert, and D. P. Lettenmaier, "Economic Value of Long-Lead Streamflow Forecasts for Columbia River Hydropower," *Journal of Water Resources Planning and Management*, Volume 128 (2002), pp. 91–101.

Valerie P. Hans and Neil Vidmar, *Judging the Jury* (New York: Plenum Press, 1986).

Charles Harper, *Impunity: An Ethical Perspective* (Geneva: World Council of Churches, 1996).

Sidney L. Harring, "Taylorization of Police Work; Prospects for the 1980s," *Insurgent Sociologist*, Volume 10 (1981), pp. 25–32.

David A. Harris, *Profiles in Injustice: Why Racial Profiling Cannot Work* (New York: New Press, 2002).

Thomas Harris, *The Silence of the Lambs* (New York: St. Martin's Press, 1988).

Herbert L. A. Hart, "Prolegomenon to the Principles of Punishment," in *Punishment and Responsibility: Essays in the Philosophy of Law* (Oxford: Oxford University Press, 1968).

Timothy C. Hart and Brian A. Reaves, *Felony Defendants in Large Urban Counties, 1996* (Washington, DC: Bureau of Justice Statistics, 1999).

Henrick J. Harwood, Douglas Fountain, and Gina Livermore. *The Economic Costs of Alcohol and Drug Abuse in the United States, 1992* (Washington, DC: U.S. Department of Health and Human Services, National Institutes of Health, 1998).

Reid Hastie, Steven Penrod, and Nancy Pennington, *Inside the Jury* (Cambridge, MA: Harvard University Press, 1983).

James Heckman, "Varieties of Selection Bias," *American Economic Review*, Volume 80 (May 1990), pp. 313–18.

Georg Wilhelm Friedrich Hegel, *Philosophy of Right* (original 1821; translation by T. M. Knox, London: Oxford University Press, 1945).

Eric Helland and Alexander Tabarrok, "Runaway Judges? Selection Effects and the Jury," *Journal of Law, Economics and Organization*, Volume 16 (2000), pp. 306–33.

Seymour M. Hersh, "Mixed Messages: Why the Government Didn't Know What it Knew," *The New Yorker* (June 3, 2002), pp. 40–8.

Larry Heuer and Steven Penrod, "Trial Complexity: A Field Investigation of Its Meaning and Effects," *Law and Human Behavior*, Volume 18 (1994), p. 29.

Larry Heuer and Steven Penrod, "Juror Notetaking and Question Asking During Trials," *Law and Human Behavior*, Volume 18 (1994), p. 123.

Philip Heymann and Carol Petrie, editors, *What's Changing in Prosecution? Report of a Workshop* (Washington, DC: National Academy Press, 2001).

Celia Ho, "Death Penalty Under Attack," *Rising Times*, Issue 9 (March/April 2000) <www.aclu-mass.org/youth/risingtimes/9dpunattack/html>.

Thomas Hobbes, *Leviathan: The Matter, Form, and Power of a Commonwealth, Ecclesiastical and Civil* (1651).

John Hogarth, *Sentencing as a Human Process* (Toronto: University of Toronto Press, 1971). James O. Holliday (Senior Judge), *Finding and Recommendation in the Matter of an Investigation of the West Virginia State Police Crime Laboratory, Serology Division*, West Virginia Supreme Court, Matter No. 21973 (1993).

Ronald M. Holmes, "Psychological Profiling Use in Serial Murder Cases," in *Contemporary Perspectives on Serial Murder*, Ronald M. Holmes and Steven T. Holmes, editors (Thousand Oaks, CA: Sage, 1998).

Julie Horney and Ineke Marshall, "Measuring Lambda Through Self-Reports," *Criminology*, Volume 29 (1991), pp. 471–95.

C. Ronald Huff, Arye Rattner, and Edward Sagarin, *Convicted but Innocent: Wrongful Conviction and Public Policy* (Thousand Oaks, CA: Sage, 1996).

David Hume, *A Treatise of Human Nature* (1739).

Earl Ofari Hutchinson, "Black Cops No Antidote To Police Violence," *The Black World Today* (November 7, 2000).

H. H. Isaacs, "A Study of Communications, Crimes and Arrests in a Metropolitan Police Department," in *Task Force Report: Science and Technology*, Appendix B (Washington, DC: President's Commission on Law Enforcement and Administration of Justice, 1967).

Kaoru Ishikawa, *What is Total Quality Control?* (Englewood Cliffs, NJ: Prentice-Hall Inc., 1985).

Glenn Ivey and W. Louis Hennessy, "Safeguards for the Innocent," *Washington Post* (June 24, 2001), p. B8.

Tom Jackman, "Judge Seeks Both Sides' Input on Moussaoui Hearing," *Washington Post* (July 25, 2002), p. A14.

Robert H. Jackson, "The Federal Prosecutor," *Journal of the American Judicial Society*, Volume 24 (1940).

James B. Jacobs and Kimberly Potter, *Hate Crimes: Criminal Law and Identity Politics* (Oxford University Press – Studies in Crime and Public Policy, 1998).

C. R. Jeffrey, *Crime Prevention Through Environmental Design* (Beverly Hills, CA: Sage, 1971).

Carl G. Jung, *Psychological Types* (Collected Works of C.G. Jung, Volume 6), Michael Fordham and R. F. Hull, editors (Princeton, NJ: Princeton University Press, 1971).

Harry Kalven, Jr. and Hans Zeisel, *The American Jury* (New York: Little, Brown, and Co., 1966).

Immanuel Kant, *Philosophy of Law: An Exposition of the Fundamental Principles of Jurisprudence as the Science of Right* (1790).

John F. Kelly and Phillip K. Wearne, *Tainting Evidence: Inside the Scandals at the FBI Crime Lab* (New York: Free Press, 1998).

Anthony M. Kennedy, Opening remarks at the 1997 9th Circuit Judicial Conference, cited in *Legal Times*, Volume 10 (November 16, 1987), p. 14 and <http://www.dsl.psu.edu/library/lrr/guides/supct/kennedy.html>.

Randall Kennedy, *Race, Crime, and the Law* (New York: Random House, 1997).

Randall Kennedy, "Race, the Police, and 'Reasonable Suspicion'," *Perspectives on Crime and Justice: 1997–1998 Lecture Series* (Washington, DC: National Institute of Justice, 1998).

Randall Kennedy, "Racial Profiling May Be Justified, But It's Still Wrong," *The New Republic* (September 13, 1999), pp. 30–35.

Ken I. Kersch, "Juries on Trial," *The Public Interest*, Number 150 (Winter 2003), pp. 121–30.

Ronald Kessler, *The Bureau: The Secret History of the FBI* (New York: St. Martin's Press, 2002).

Michael Kinsley, "Racial Profiling at the Airport: Discrimination We're Afraid to be Against," *Slate Magazine* (September 28, 2001).

Albert R. Kiralfy, "Common Law," in *The New Encyclopædia Britannica – Macropædia*, Volume 4 (Chicago: University of Chicago, 1974), pp. 998–1005.

Mark A. R. Kleiman, "Crime Control Policy in California," in *California Policy Options 2000* (Los Angeles: University of California, 2000).

John Kleinig, *Punishment and Desert* (The Hague/Boston: Martinus Nijhoff, 1974).

William J. Kolarik, *Creating Quality: Concepts, Systems, Strategies, and Tools* (New York: McGraw-Hill, 1999).

K.M.L., "Francis Bacon," in the *New Encyclopædia Britannica – Macropædia*, Volume 2 (Chicago: University of Chicago, 1974), pp. 561–7.

David N. Laband and John P. Sophocleus, "An Estimate of Resource Expenditures on Transfer Activity in the United States," *Quarterly Journal of Economics*, Volume 107 (1992), pp. 959–83.

William M. Landes, "An Economic Analysis of the Courts," *Journal of Law and Economics*, Volume 14 (1971), pp. 61–107.

Charles Lane, "O'Connor Expresses Death Penalty Doubt, Justice Says Innocent May Be Killed" *Washington Post* (July 4, 2001), p. A1.

Nancy G. LaVigne, "Safe Transport: Security by Design on the Washington Metro," in *Preventing Mass Transit Crime*, edited by Ronald V. Clarke (Monsey, NY: Criminal Justice Press, 1997).

Patrick J. Leahy, testimony before the Hearing of the Criminal Justice Subcommittee, "Oversight of the Criminal Division," U.S. Senate Judiciary Committee (July 27, 1999).

Patrick J. Leahy, testimony before the Hearing of the Committee, "Oversight: Restoring Confidence in the FBI," U.S. Senate Judiciary Committee (June 20, 2001).

Lucian L. Leape, "Error in Medicine," *Journal of the American Medical Association*, Volume 272 (1994), pp. 1851–7.

Eli Lehrer, "Profiles in Confusion," *The Weekly Standard* (November 4, 2002), pp. 12–13.

John Leo, "Seeing Through Prisms," *U.S. News and World Report* (November 11, 2002), p. 61.

Richard A. Leo and George C. Thomas III, editors, *The Miranda Debate: Law, Justice and Crime Control* (Boston: Northeastern University Press, 1998).

Steven D. Levitt, "The Economics of Crime and the Criminal Justice System," *National Bureau of Economic Research Reporter* (Fall 1998).

Steven D. Levitt, "Deterrence," in *Crime: Public Policies for Crime Control*, 2nd edition, James Q. Wilson and Joan Petersilia, editors (San Francisco: ICS Press, 2002), pp. 435–50.

Eric Lichtblau and Charles Piller, "War on Terrorism Highlights FBI's Computer Woes," *Los Angeles Times* (July 28, 2002), pp. 1, 26–7.

James S. Liebman, Jeffrey Fagan,Valerie West, and Jonathan Lloyd, "Capital Attrition: Error Rates in Capital Cases, 1973–1995," *Texas Law Review*, Volume 78 (2000), p. 1839.

James S. Liebman, Jeffrey Fagan, Andrew Gelman, Valerie West, Garth Davies, and Alexander Kiss, "A Broken System, Part II: Why There Is So Much Error in Capital Cases, and What Can Be Done About It," unpublished report, Columbia University (2002) <http://www.law.columbia.edu/brokensystem2/>.

R. C. L. Lindsay and Gary L. Wells, "Improving Eyewitness Identifications from Lineups: Simultaneous versus Sequential Lineup Presentation," *Journal of Applied Psychology*, Volume 70 (1985), Number 3, pp. 556–64.

Walter Lippmann, *Public Opinion* (New York: Touchstone, 1997), original edition in 1920.

Dahlia Lithwick, "Three Strikes Golfing: Life in Prison without Parole for Stealing Three Callaway Clubs," *Slate* (November 5, 2002).

John Locke, *Second Treatise of Government* (1690).

Elizabeth F. Loftus and T. E. Burns, "Mental Shock Can Produce Retrograde Amnesia," *Memory and Cognition*, Volume 10 (1982), pp. 318–23.

Charles H. Logan, "Criminal Justice Performance Measures for Prisons," in *Performance Measures for the Criminal Justice System* (Washington, DC: Bureau of Justice Statistics, 1993), pp. 19–60.

Cesare Lombroso, *L'uomo delinquente* (The Criminal Man, 1876).

James P. Lynch and William J. Sabol, "Prison Use and Social Control," in *Policies, Processes, and Decisions of the Criminal Justice System*, Volume 3 of the *Criminal Justice 2000* series (Washington, DC: National Institute of Justice, 2000).

Ross Macmillan, "Adolescent Victimization and Income Deficits in Adulthood: Rethinking the Costs of Criminal Violence from a Life-Course Perspective," *Criminology*, Volume 38 (May 2000), pp. 553–88.

Terence J. Mangan and Michael G. Shanahan, "Public Law Enforcement/Private Security: A New Partnership?" *FBI Law Enforcement Bulletin*, Volume 59 (January 1990), pp. 18–22.

Susan E. Martin and Lawrence W. Sherman, "Selective Apprehension: A Police Strategy for Repeat Offenders," *Criminology*, Volume 24 (1986), pp. 155–73.

Robert Martinson, "What Works? Questions and Answers About Prison Reform," *Public Interest*, Number 35 (1974), pp. 22–54.

Kenneth J. Matulia, *A Balance of Forces*, 2nd edition (Gaithersburg, MD: International Association of Chiefs of Police, 1985).

Fred S. McChesney, 1993. "Boxed in: Economists and the Benefits of Crime," *International Review of Law and Economics*, Volume 13 (1993), pp. 225–31.

William F. McDonald, *Police-Prosecutor Relations in the United States* (Washington, DC: National Institute of Justice, 1982).

George McGovern, "Flying the Unfriendly Skies," *Wall Street Journal* (July 29, 2002), p. A14.

Paul E. Meehl, *Clinical vs. Statistical Prediction* (Minneapolis: University of Minnesota Press, 1954).

Karl Menninger, *The Crime of Punishment* (New York: Viking Press, 1968).

Terance Miethe and Richard McCorkle, *Crime Profiles: The Anatomy of Dangerous Persons, Places, and Situations* (Los Angeles: Roxbury, 2001).

Ted R. Miller, Mark A. Cohen, and Brian Wiersema, *Victim Costs and Consequences: A New Look*, Research Report NCJ 155282 (Washington, DC: U.S. Department of Justice, National Institute of Justice, 1996).

Jessica Mitford, *Kind and Usual Punishment* (New York: Alfred Knopf, 1971).

John Monahan, *Predicting Violent Behavior: An Assessment of Clinical Techniques* (Beverly Hills, CA: Sage, 1981).

Mark Moore, "The Legitimation of Criminal Justice Policies and Practices," in *Perspectives on Crime and Justice: 1996–1997 Lecture Series* (Washington, DC: National Institute of Justice, 1997), pp. 47–74.

J. Brian Morgan, *The Police Function and the Investigation of Crime* (Aldershot, England: Avebury, 1990).

Norval Morris, *The Future of Imprisonment* (Chicago: University of Chicago Press, 1974).

Norval Morris, "The Honest Politician's Guide to Sentencing Reform," in *The Socio-Economics of Crime and Justice*, Brian Forst, editor (Armonk, NY: M. E. Sharpe, 1993), pp. 303–10.

Norval Morris and Michael Tonry, *Between Prison and Probation: Intermediate Punishments in a Rational Sentencing System* (New York: Oxford University Press, 1990).

Blake Morrison, "Airport Security Failures Persist: Screeners Miss Even Obvious Items," *USA Today* (July 1, 2002), pp. 1A, 4A.

Jenny Mouzos and Damon Muller, *Solvability Factors of Homicide in Australia: An Exploratory Analysis* (Canberra: Australian Institute of Criminology, 2001).

Damon A. Muller, "Criminal Profiling: Real Science or Just Wishful Thinking?" *Homicide Studies,* Volume 4 (2000), pp. 234–64.

Daniel S. Nagin, "Criminal Deterrence Research at the Outset of the Twenty-First Century," in *Crime and Justice: A Review of Research,* edited by Michael Tonry (University of Chicago Press, 1998), pp. 1–42.

Oscar Newman, *Defensible Space* (New York: Macmillan, 1972).

Oscar Newman, "Defensible Space," *National Housing Institute Shelterforce Online* (May/June 1997) <http://www.nhi.org/online/issues/93/defense.html>.

Robert D. Novak, "The FBI Problem," *Washington Post* (August 29, 2002), p. A31.

Sandra Day O'Connor, Address to the Minnesota Women Lawyers Association, July 2, 2001, reported by Brian Bakst, Associated Press (July 3, 2001).

Office of the Inspector General, *The FBI Laboratory: An Investigation into Laboratory Practices and Alleged Misconduct in Explosives-Related and Other Cases,* Special Report (Washington, DC: U.S. Department of Justice, 1997).

Office of Management and Budget, *Race and Ethnic Standards for Federal Statistics and Administrative Reporting,* Directive 15 (May 1997).

Helen O'Neill, "The Perfect Witness," *Washington Post* (March 4, 2001), pp. F1, F4.

Herbert Packer, *The Limits of the Criminal Sanction* (Palo Alto, CA: Stanford University Press, 1968).

Raymond Paternoster, Robert Brame, Ronet Bachman, and Lawrence W. Sherman, "Do Fair Procedures Matter? The Effect of Procedural Justice on Spouse Assault," *Law and Society Review,* Volume 31 (1997), pp. 163–204.

John Allen Paulos, *A Mathematician Reads the Newspaper* (New York: Basic Books, 1995).

Steven D. Penrod and Brian L. Cutler, "Assessing the Competency of Juries," in *The Handbook of Forensic Psychology,* Irving Weiner and Allen K. Hess, editors (New York: Wiley, 1987).

Joan Petersilia, "Measuring the Performance of Community Corrections," in *Performance Measures for the Criminal Justice System* (Washington, DC: Bureau of Justice Statistics, 1993), pp. 61–86.

Joan Petersilia, "A Decade of Experimenting with Intermediate Sanctions: What Have We Learned?" *Justice Research and Policy*, Volume 11 (1999), pp. 9–24.

Joan Petersilia, "Community Corrections," in *Crime: Public Policies for Crime Control*, 2nd edition, James Q. Wilson and Joan Petersilia, editors (San Francisco: ICS Press, 2002), pp. 483–508.

Mark A. Peterson and Harriet B. Braiker, *Doing Crime: A Survey of California Prison Inmates* (Santa Monica, CA: Rand Corporation, 1980).

Wayne Petherick, "Criminal Profiling: How It Got Started and How It Is Used," *Crime Library*, <http://www.crimelibrary.com/criminal_mind/profiling/profiling2/1.html>.

Anne Morrison Piehl, Bert Useem, and John J. DiIulio, Jr., "Right-Sizing Justice: A Cost-Benefit Analysis of Imprisonment in Three States," Civic Report Number 8 of the Manhattan Institute for Policy Research (September 1999) <http://www.manhattan-institute.org/html/cr_8.htm>.

Karl Popper, *Logic of Scientific Discovery* (London: Routledge, 2002 reissue) (original 1934).

Richard A. Posner, *The Economics of Justice* (Cambridge, MA: Harvard University Press, 1981).

Richard A. Posner, "Security Versus Civil Liberties," *The Atlantic Monthly*, Volume 288 (December 2001), pp. 46–7.

Lucas A. Powe, *The Warren Court and American Politics* (Cambridge, MA: Harvard University Press, 2000).

John Proffatt, *Trial by Jury* (1877).

Michael L. Radelet, Hugo Adam Bedau, and Constance E. Putnam, *In Spite of Innocence: Erroneous Convictions in Capital Cases* (Boston: Northeastern University Press, 1992).

Gerard Rainville, *Differing Incentives of Appointed and Elected Prosecutors and the Relationship between Prosecutor Policy and Votes in Local Elections*, doctoral dissertation (Washington, DC: American University, School of Public Affairs, 2002).

John Rawls, *A Theory of Justice* (Cambridge, MA: Harvard University Press, 1971).

Albert J. Reiss, Jr., *The Police and the Public* (New Haven, CT: Yale University Press, 1971).

Report of the Rampart Independent Review Panel (November 16, 2000) <www.ci.la.ca.us/oig/rirprpt.pdf>.

William Rhodes, Bernadette Pelissier, Gerald Gaes, William Saylor, Scott Camp, and Susan Wallace, "Alternative Solutions to the Problem of Selection Bias in an Analysis of Federal Residential Drug Treatment Programs," *Evaluation Research*, Volume 25 (2000), pp. 331–69.

Jeffrey Rosen, "In Lieu of Manners," *New York Times Magazine* (February 4, 2001).

D. Kim Rossmo, "Geographic Profiling," Chapter 9 in *Offender Profiling: Theory, Research and Practice*, Janet L. Jackson and Debra Bekerian, editors (New York: John Wiley and Sons, 1997).

D. Kim Rossmo, *Geographic Profiling* (Boca Raton, FL: CRC Press, 1999).

Carl T. Rowan, Jr., "Who's Policing DC Cops?" *Washington Post* (October 8, 1995).

George H. Ryan, Press Release (January 31, 2000) <http://www.state.il.us/gov/press/00/Jan/morat.htm>.

George H. Ryan, "In Ryan's Words: 'I Must Act'," *New York Times* (January 11, 2003) <http://www.nytimes.com/2003/01/11/national/11CND-RTEX.html?pagewanted=printandposition=bottom>.

Michael J. Saks, *Jury Verdicts: The Role of Group Size and Social Decision Rule* (Lexington, MA: D. C. Heath and Co., 1977).

Michael J. Saks, "The Smaller the Jury, The Greater the Unpredictability," *Judicature*, Volume 79 (1996), pp. 263–5.

Susan Saulny, "Convictions and Charges Voided in '89 Central Park Jogger Attack," *New York Times* (December 20, 2002).

Barry Scheck, Peter Neufeld, and Jim Dwyer, *Actual Innocence: When Justice Goes Wrong and How to Make it Right* (New York: Penguin Putnam, 2001).

Peter H. Schuck, "A Case for Profiling," *The American Lawyer* (January 2002).

Alfred I. Schwartz and Sumner N. Clarren, *The Cincinnati Team Policing Experiment: A Summary Report* (Washington, DC: Police Foundation, 1977).

Lee Sechrest, Susan O. White, and Elizabeth D. Brown, editors, *The Rehabilitation of Criminal Offenders: Problems and Prospects* (Washington, DC: National Academy of Sciences, 1979).

Thorsten Sellin and Marvin E. Wolfgang, *The Measurement of Delinquency* (New York: John Wiley and Sons, 1964).

Barry Serafin, "Guns Slip Through the Cracks: Gaps in Fingerprints and Background Checks May Have Aided Snipers," *ABCNews.com* (November 1, 2002).

Clifford D. Shearing and Philip Stenning, "Modern Private Security: Its Growth and Implications," in *Crime and Justice: An Annual Review of*

Research, Volume 3, Norval Morris and Michael Tonry, editors (University of Chicago Press, 1981).

Lawrence W. Sherman, *Policing Domestic Violence: Experiments and Dilemmas* (New York: Free Press, 1992).

Lawrence W. Sherman, "Fair and Effective Policing," in *Crime: Public Policies for Crime Control*, James Q. Wilson and Joan Petersilia, editors (San Francisco: ICS Press, 2002).

Lawrence W. Sherman, Denise Gottfredson, Doris MacKenzie, John Eck, Peter Reuter, and Shawn Bushway *Preventing Crime: What Works, What Doesn't, What's Promising* (Washington, DC: National Institute of Justice, 1999).

Eli Silverman, *NYPD Battles Crime: Innovative Strategies in Policing* (Boston: Northeastern University Press, 1999).

Rita James Simon, *The Jury and the Defense of Insanity* (New Brunswick, NJ: Transaction, 1999).

Peter Skerry, *Counting on the Census? Race, Group Identity, and the Evasion of Politics* (Washington, DC: Brookings, 2000).

Wesley G. Skogan, *Disorder and Decline: Crime and the Spiral of Decay in American Neighborhoods* (New York: Free Press, 1990).

Wesley G. Skogan and George E. Antunes, "Information, Apprehension, and Deterrence: Exploring the Limits of Police Productivity," *Journal of Criminal Justice*, Volume 7, No. 3 (1979), pp. 217–41.

Wesley Skogan and Kathleen Frydl, editors, *The Evidence on Policing: Fairness and Effectiveness in U.S. Law Enforcement* (Washington, DC: National Academy of Sciences, 2003).

Jerome H. Skolnick, "Wild Pitch: 'Three Strikes, You're Out' and Other Bad Calls on Crime," *American Prospect*, Volume 5, Issue 17 (March 21, 1994) <http://www.prospect.org/print/V5/17/skolnick-j.html>.

Jerome H. Skolnick and James J. Fyfe, *Above the Law: Police and the Excessive Use of Force* (New York: Free Press, 1993).

Jerome H. Skolnick and Richard A. Leo, "The Ethics of Deceptive Interrogation," *Criminal Justice Ethics*, Volume 11 (Winter/Spring 1992), pp. 3–12.

Douglas Smith and Christy Visher, "Street-Level Justice: Situational Determinants of Police Arrest Decisions," *Social Problems*, Volume 29 (1981), pp. 167–78.

Sourcebook of Criminal Justice Statistics (Washington, DC: Bureau of Justice Statistics, 2000).

Henry J. Steadman and Joseph Cocozza, "Psychiatry, Dangerousness and the Repetitively Violent Offender," *Journal of Criminal Law and Criminology*, Volume 69 (1978), pp. 226–31.

Kate Stith and Jose A. Cabranes, *Fear of Judging: Sentencing Guidelines in the Federal Courts* (Chicago: University of Chicago Press, 1998).

Cass R. Sunstein, editor, *Punitive Damages: How Juries Decide* (Chicago: University of Chicago Press, 2002).

John A. Swets, Robyn M. Dawes, and John Monahan, "Psychological Science Can Improve Diagnostic Decisions," *Psychological Science in the Public Interest*, Volume 1 (May 2000), pp. 1–24.

Genichi Taguchi, *The Mahalanobis-Taguchi Strategy: A Pattern Technology System* (New York: John Wiley & Sons, 2002).

Edward A. Tamm, "The Five-Man Civil Jury: A Proposed Constitutional Amendment," *Georgetown Law Journal*, Volume 51 (1962), p. 120.

Ralph B. Taylor, *Breaking Away from Broken Windows* (Boulder, CO: Westview Press, 2001).

Alexis de Tocqueville, *Democracy in America* (1835).

Michael Tonry, *Sentencing Matters* (New York: Oxford University Press, 1996).

William N. Trumbull, "Who Has Standing in Cost-Benefit Analysis?" *Journal of Policy Analysis and Management*, Volume 9 (1990), pp. 201–18.

Scott Turow, "To Kill or Not to Kill," *The New Yorker* (January 6, 2003), pp. 40–7.

Brent E. Turvey, *Criminal Profiling: An Introduction to Behavioral Evidence Analysis*, 2nd edition (San Diego, CA: Academic Press, 2001).

Tom Tyler, *Why People Obey the Law* (New Haven, CT: Yale University Press, 1990).

U.S. Department of Justice, *Justice Litigation Management* (Washington, DC: U.S. Government Printing Office, 1977).

H. Richard Uviller, *Virtual Justice: The Flawed Prosecution of Crime in America* (New Haven, CT: Yale University Press, 1996).

Daniel Van Ness and Karen Heetderks Strong, *Restoring Justice* (Cincinnati, OH: Anderson, 1997).

Neil J. Vidmar, "Is the Jury Competent?" *Law and Contemporary Problems*, Volume 52 (Autumn 1989).

Eugene Volokh, "Traffic Enforcement Cameras," *Wall Street Journal* (March 26, 2002), p. A22.

Voltaire, *Zadig (Book of Fate)* (1749; originally published as *Memnon* in 1747).

Andrew von Hirsch, *Doing Justice: The Choice of Punishments* (New York: Hill and Wang, 1976).

Andrew von Hirsch, "Doing Justice: The Principle of Commensurate Deserts," in *Sentencing*, edited by Hyman Gross and Andrew von Hirsch (New York: Oxford University Press, 1981).

Andrew von Hirsch, "Proportionality in the Philosophy of Punishment," in *Crime and Justice: A Review of Research*, edited by Michael Tonry (University of Chicago Press, 1992), pp. 55–98.

David Vose, *Risk Analysis: A Quantitative Guide* (New York: John Wiley & Sons, 2000).

Richard H. Ward, *The Investigative Function: Criminal Investigation in the United States*, Unpublished Ph.D. Dissertation (Berkeley, CA: University of California at Berkeley, 1971).

Robert Weber, cartoon in *The New Yorker* (June 3, 2002), p. 35.

Charles Wellford and James Cronin, "Clearing Up Homicide Clearance Rates," *National Institute of Justice Journal*, Number 243 (April 2000), pp. 3–7. Summary of longer report, *An Analysis of Variables Affecting the Clearance of Homicides: A Multistate Study* (Washington, DC: Justice Research and Statistics Association, 1999), is available at <http://www.jrsa.org/pubs/reports/Clearance_of_Homicide.html>.

Craig Whitlock and David S. Fallis, "County Officers Kill More Often Than Any in U.S.," *Washington Post* (July 1, 2001), pp. A1, A8–9.

John R. Wilke, "How Outdated Files Hamper FBI Effort to Fight Terrorism," *Wall Street Journal* (July 9, 2002), pp. A1, A8.

Kristen M. Williams, *The Scope and Prediction of Recidivism* (Washington, DC: Institute for Law and Social Research, 1979).

James Q. Wilson, *Thinking About Crime* (New York: Basic Books, 1975).

James Q. Wilson, "What Mistakes in Death Penalty Cases?" *New York Times* (July 10, 2000), p. A19.

Orlando W. Wilson, *Police Records – Their Installation and Use*, 4th edition (Public Administration Service, 1951).

Benjamin Wittes, *Starr: A Reassessment* (New Haven, CT: Yale University Press, 2002).

Marvin E. Wolfgang, Robert Figlio, and Thorsten Sellin, *Delinquency in a Birth Cohort* (Chicago: University of Chicago Press, 1972).

Marvin E. Wolfgang, Terence P. Thornberry, and Robert M. Figlio, *From Boy to Man – From Delinquency to Crime* (Philadelphia: University of Pennsylvania, 1985).

Ronald Wright and Marc Miller, "The Screening/Bargaining Tradeoff," *Stanford Law Review*, Volume 55 (October 2002), pp. 29–118.

Fareed Zakaria, "Freedom vs. Security – Delicate Balance: The case for 'Smart Profiling' as a Weapon in the War on Terror" Newsweek, Volume 140 (July 8, 2002), pp. 26–31.

Hans Zeisel, "And Then There Were None: The Diminution of the Federal Jury," *University of Chicago Law Review*, Volume 38 (1971), pp. 710–24.

Hans Zeisel and Shari Seidman Diamond, "'Convincing Empirical Evidence' on the Six Member Jury," *University of Chicago Law Review*, Volume 41 (1974), pp. 281–95.

Hans Zeisel and Shari Seidman Diamond, "The Effect of Peremptory Challenges on Jury and Verdict: An Experiment in a Federal District Court," *Stanford Law Review*, Volume 30 (1978), pp. 491–503.

Franklin Zimring, *Perspectives on Deterrence* (Washington, DC: National Institute of Mental Health, 1971).

Franklin Zimring, "The New Politics of Criminal Justice: Of 'Three Strikes,' Truth-in-Sentencing, and Megan's Laws," in *Perspectives on Crime and Justice: 1999–2000 Lecture Series* (Washington, DC: National Institute of Justice, 2001), pp. 1–22.

Index

Other Books in the Series (*continued from page iii*)

Criminality and Violence among the Mentally Disordered, by Sheilagh Hodgins and Carl-Gunnar Janson

Corporate Crime, Law, and Social Control, by Sally S. Simpson

Companions in Crime: The Social Aspects of Criminal Conduct, by Mark Warr

The Criminal Career: The Danish Longitudinal Study, by Britta Kyvsgaard

Violent Crime: Assessing Race and Ethnic Differences, edited by Darnell Hawkins

Gangs and Delinquency in Developmental Perspective, by Terence P. Thornberry, Marvin D. Krohn, Alan J. Lizotte, Carolyn A. Smith, and Kimberly Tobin